Annals of Sandy Spring

or

Twenty Years History of a Rural Community in Maryland

William Henry Farquhar

HERITAGE BOOKS
2010

HERITAGE BOOKS
AN IMPRINT OF HERITAGE BOOKS, INC.

Books, CDs, and more—Worldwide

For our listing of thousands of titles see our website
at
www.HeritageBooks.com

A Facsimile Reprint
Published 2010 by
HERITAGE BOOKS, INC.
Publishing Division
100 Railroad Ave. #104
Westminster, Maryland 21157

Originally published
Baltimore:
Cushings & Bailey
1884

International Standard Book Numbers
Paperbound: 978-0-7884-1409-1
Clothbound: 978-0-7884-8395-0

PREFACE.

The object of writing prefaces to books must consist chiefly in the desire to place the reader, to some extent, in harmony with the subject before him. Preliminary remarks may thus aid in accomplishing the purpose held in view by the writer. There should be a reason for all things; and certainly a *good reason* is required when people resort to print.

In the present case, the writer feels that peculiar justification is needed, which it is his duty to explain at the beginning. He had not the most remote idea, on commencing to write the following records, that they would ever be presented to the public; such a thought was not in his mind, nor was the suggestion then made by another.

A number of persons, engaged chiefly in rural pursuits, desirous of improving their minds while cultivating their farms, united twenty-five years ago in the erection of a comfortable building, to which they gave the name of The Lyceum. Finding much satisfaction in the interesting proceedings that attended their various meetings, a company was formed, and regularly incorporated under the title "The Sandy Spring Lyceum Company." Although the lectures were generally well attended, it was found difficult to get a quorum together at the annual meetings for the election of officers. Francis Miller suggested that if these meetings could be made interesting the people would attend; he proposed that a historian and statistician should be appointed, to give at each Annual Meeting a sketch of events during the year. The idea was cordially seconded, and William Henry Farquhar was elected Historian. The appreciative audiences since have demonstrated the wisdom of the plan; and from it sprang the following "Annals." After listening for twenty years to the reading of these records, it was resolved by a unanimous vote in the session of '83, that they should be published in the form of a book.

The persons of whom the company was composed were chiefly, though by no means exclusively, members of the "Society of Friends," settled over the southeastern part of Montgomery County, Maryland. These primitive settlers of Sandy Spring neighborhood were confined within no precisely defined limits, but were linked together by the ties of similarity in birth, education, and manner of living; without which, the attempt to condense the interests and incidents of ordinary life into one chronicle must be fruitless.

The writer has formed decided and possibly peculiar views in regard to the practicability of considering the people of a whole neighborhood as an entity in itself, one united being, and thus claiming the right to give their Annals the more dignified name of History. Of this it is for the reader to judge. He will find a variety of topics; and, though no abundance of rare or exciting incidents, yet a fair portion of those simple, homely traits in human life and character which are never without natural interest. The book is *new*, and it is *true*. It tells the story of country life as it passes through successive periods, at long intervals. Agriculture is the chief subject and concern of the work; a subject requiring no excuse for intruding upon the people of America. We who are specially connected with it, as the principal business of our lives, cannot fail sometimes to observe that our position in the world is not properly appreciated, nor even fully understood. Believing this to be the case, we would fain supply the rest of the world with some important facts to them unknown. The works written upon agriculture are naturally addressed chiefly to farmers; but it is surely not amiss to promote a closer union of interests and ideas between the *two halves* into which the people of the United States are nearly equally divided, viz. the farmers and those *not* farmers.

The present book is not, as appears at sight, merely a transient local concern, describing the incidents which occur every year to a limited number of ordinary farmers residing in the interior of Maryland. Were that all, it would require some assurance on the part of "The Sandy Spring Lyceum Company" to publish the book to the world. But there is an impression in the minds of many persons *outside* of that company, and confirmed from time to time by visitors impartial and qualified to judge, that Sandy Spring is not quite an ordinary country neighborhood. In defence of this seeming pretension we invite our readers to commence with examining Chapter VII of this book, and the book itself.

If there is any truth in the flattering opinions expressed in the pages referred to (in which we all acknowledge a degree of exaggeration), it must be of some interest to other farmers to trace the course that has led to such results. In reviewing the various chapters it will be observed that one central idea of unlimited association has been the leading influence.

The book will contain an Appendix, which we believe will add to its interest and value. Meteorological Phenomena, carefully observed by Henry C. Hallowell and Allan Farquhar, for many years, exhibit the weather of this region—and all take an interest in the *weather*.

I could not close this preface without acknowledging the benefit which the Annals have received from the assistance of two Friends, Hadassah J. Moore and Mary B. Thomas.

WM. H. FARQUHAR.

CONTENTS.

INTRODUCTION.

CHAPTER I.

1863–1864.

CHAPTER II.

1864–1865.

CHAPTER III.

1865-1866.

CHAPTER IV.

1866-1867.

CHAPTER V.

1867-1868.

CHAPTER VI.

1868-1869.

CHAPTER VII.

1869-1870.

CHAPTER VIII.

1870-1871.

CHAPTER IX.

1871-1872.

CHAPTER X.

1872-1873.

CHAPTER XI.

1873–1874.

CHAPTER XII.

1874–1875.

CHAPTER XIII.

1875–1876.

CHAPTER XIV.

1876-1877.

CHAPTER XV.

1877-1878.

CHAPTER XVI.

1878-1879.

CHAPTER XVII.

1879-1880.

INTRODUCTION.

It must be a natural conclusion of every one who commences to read "The Annals of a People for Twenty Years," that such a people, if worthy of these records, must have possessed something in the character of a *previous history*. In point of fact the (so-called) historian, who first accepted the name, as a mock-title of dignity, had made careful researches into the facts relating to the early history of "Sandy Spring Neighborhood," several years before the Lyceum Company instituted the annual records of which the following chapters consist. In the year 1860 a lecture was delivered by him at the Lyceum, as the result of those researches; many of the historical incidents being obtained from aged persons then alive, as well from all the books in his reach relating to the subject. What follows now will be

The Early History of Sandy Spring.

In order that its position may be rightly understood it is necessary to remind the present reader that it was addressed to the same Lyceum Company which listened to the various chapters that follow.

At the commencement of this history it is proper to fix some definite ideas in regard to the region of the country which is included under the name "Sandy Spring." The most distinguished writers tell us there have always been certain "centres of settlement" for all the principal nations. Humboldt speaks of "the central radiant points" as being of the highest importance first to understand.

Now where is our Central Radiant Point? In order to begin at the fountain-head, both literally and figuratively, I made a pilgrimage to the Spring from which our neighborhood receives its name. A fraction of a mile south of the Lyceum and of our Meeting House, the waters flow out of the earth. I cannot say of them what Whittier tells us in describing the sources of the Saco river, among the White Hills of New Hampshire, that

"There, in wild and virgin freshness, its waters foam and flow,
As when Snowden first beheld them, near two hundred years ago."

Indeed, the place is very much changed since then. No longer does the water bubble up through the white *sand* that gave the spring its name, so famous once that the neighbors sent to it, some distance round, on account of its peculiar scouring and polishing excellence. Where the red Indian stopped to drink, unfastening the wild beast's skin from his swarthy neck; where the white man chasing the deer, the wolf and the bear, first parted the tangled wildwood that clustered thick over the clear, refreshing fountain, we now see only the plain, ordinary spring of our common fields. Wagon loads of stone, together with alluvial deposits of other soil, have almost covered the large original basin, and the white sand of the original Sandy Spring exists only in history.

It is a singular fact that the name of our neighborhood, thus derived, has caused among strangers a double deception. On first hearing it they imagine (giving the latter part of the name a plural termination) that we have here a regular watering place,—an honor to which we by no means aspire. On the other hand, the agricultural traveller expects to find a *light, sandy soil*—the very *opposite* of that which the condition of our winter roads soon makes apparent.

Those who discovered and named our spring had no such quizzical intentions; and it is the sincere, earnest and special desire of the inhabitants that the letters addressed to our postoffice shall omit the final S, so often improperly used.

It is a circumstance much to be regretted that the name of the first discoverer of this particular region has not been found with any degree of certainty.

It appears from the earliest Land Records, that the first settlements were made soon after the beginning of the last century. The tract taken up under the name of "Snowden's Manor," which is now in possession of our friends, the Thomases and Stablers, was dated in 1715; "Beall's Manor," adjoining it on the south, five years later. The "Charles and Benjamin," a tract of land beginning at a point not far from Hawlings river, and extending in a very meandering direction, nearly through the heart of the neighborhood (as was unfortunately too much the old fashion of taking up fresh land), bears the date 1718. In and among and around several of these tracts, an independent grant of near 2000 acres was made to Major John Bradford, the 10th day of August, 1716, and called "Charley Forrest," which must certainly be regarded as one of the chief "centres of settlement."

From this evidence we find very nearly the exact period when the wild lands of this region were conveyed by the Lord Proprietor of Maryland to the first regular settlers. No doubt the roving hunter, always pioneer in exploring new countries, had impressed "the white man's tread" as early as the latter half of the 17th century, or full 200 years ago. What did he find here, and what was the spectacle that met his eye? An unbroken forest covered the whole region, except in a few spots where the wigwams of the native Indian showed around them little patches of corn and tobacco, so few and far between as scarce to break the face of the primeval wilderness. A fact showing that the forest of these days was not, like ours, filled with shrubby undergrowth, was brought to my knowledge in riding with John M. Sandidge, himself a pioneer settler of the forests in the Southwest. He ventured to assure me that any of the old-time settlers would confirm the statement. Going on to "Brooke Grove" we proposed to the venerable Roger Brooke (then past 80 years of age), the opinion expressed by Mr. Sandidge. The old gentleman said at once that he was right, and related an incident that happened at a very early period. "A horse had got loose some miles up in the country and made his way down through the dense forest. His owner was able to follow his course by the distinct tracks left where the horse's feet were placed. This could not be readily done now."

It appears quite certain that the Indians could never have existed here in any considerable numbers, from the circumstance that no burial place containing their remains, so far as I am able to learn, has been discovered hereabout. And this is one of the monuments which perishing mortality is sure to leave behind it, where has been even a moderate population. The absence of graves, and scarcity of other remains, go to redeem our forefathers from any large share in the extermination of that doomed people. Arrow-heads, with a few rude attempts at the manufacture of culinary utensils, are occasionally picked up still in our fields.

Next we come to the wild animals that abode in these forests. The bear, the panther, the wolf, the deer, and some others long extinct, shared the woods with the human inhabitants scarce less wild than they. Evidences of their existence are found in the names given to the tracts of land taken up by the first settlers of our country. Such designations contained in the original patents as "Bear Den," "Bear Garden," "Deer Park," "Wolf Den," and others of similar signification are quite numerous; while "Bear Bacon," one of the very ancient patents, lying on the Laurel road, about Spencerville, serves as a plain indication of the *use* often made of these wild tenants of the forest.

Into this waste and wilderness, bearing scarce any impress but from Nature's hand, rolled slowly and gradually, from the southeast, the tide of immigration. The region of our State lying toward the mouth of the Potomac received its first European settlers in the year 1634. The companions of Cecilius Calvert, a brother of Lord Baltimore, came over in two small vessels, bearing the auspicious names of "The Ark" and "The Dove": Ark of refuge—Dove of peace. The liberal policy of those Catholic founders of Maryland, securing to all who came that rare boon in those benighted ages—religious toleration to all sects—attracted a mingled crowd of emigrants from many lands. The lower counties were first partially occupied; and it required about three-fourths of a century for the tide of immigration, passing successively through, and instituting first St. Mary's, then Charles, then Prince George's, at length reaching our borders. In 1748 what is now Montgomery was made part of Frederick county, continuing so till 1776. The route can be traced by the dates of the Land Patents along the line of the Laurel Road. The tract of "Bear Bacon," before mentioned, at or near Spencerville, is of 1703, while those lying farther east were still earlier. Snowden's Manor, on this side, is only twelve years younger, which shows how slowly the settlement progressed westward. It appears that emigration taking this direction was determined by an old Indian trail, used now as the bed of the road; and the coincidence is not uninteresting, as the same road which formed the avenue of approach for the earliest settlement of this neighborhood, after lying many years almost unused, has become in these times the way by which we communicate daily with the rest of the world. Our best conveyance is still by stage; but great hopes are entertained of seeing the car moving with lively speed along that same road, albeit the "narrow gauge" be the means.

It is time now to show that the true fathers of "Sandy Spring Neighborhood" were not the first settlers. Neither Major Bradford, nor the Richardsons, nor Charles Beall, nor Benjamin Berry, had much to do with laying the foundation. It was left to another band, immediately following, to form the institutions, to impress the character and affix the name. Drawn to Maryland by the religious toleration denied them in the old world, "the Friends," or "People called Quakers," appeared in this colony in considerable numbers at quite an early period. In 1672 George Fox himself came over; and (borrowing now from the work of Lackland Davis) "proceeded on his mission. Being a true reformer, a man of rude but powerful eloquence, his fame had preceded him. Travelling with an energy almost incredible over various parts of the continent, through forests and thickets, through deep marshes and dangerous bogs—crossing rivers and bays in canoes and sleeping in the open woods; preaching at the cliffs of the Patuxent and upon the banks of the Severn, upon the Choptank and elsewhere to Indians and crowds of colonists; speaking before aboriginal kings and leading emigrants from the Old World; giving utterance to the Spirit in words of fire, and with all the power of an Apostle—no wonder he promoted the growth of a denomination which soon absorbed a number of the most distinguished families of the Province." And so it is that George Fox, though never here in person, was the founder of Sandy Spring!

The Friends, who had been fortified by the harsh, but strengthening hand of persecution in the Old World, and fitted to bear the hardships of the New, appeared at this place in sufficient numbers to organize a meeting a while before the middle of the last century. In the minutes of an ancient monthly meeting held at the Cliffs and Herring Creek is contained the first mention that I have seen of the "Meeting at Sandy Spring," presenting its report to the former meeting on "the 27th of the 7th month, 1753." The first members composing the meeting appear to have belonged to the families of the Brookes, the Thomases and Snowdens. It was in 1742 that Richard Snowden conveyed 500 acres, part of his Manor, to Philip Thomas. It is stated on the Genealogical Tree of the Brooke family—a complete and beautiful picture recently produced by the delicate labors of Mary C. Brooke of Avon—that James Brooke settled at "Charley Forrest" in 1728, and founded in our county the well-known family of that name. He was a descendant of one Robert Brooke, who had emigrated from England in 1650 to St. Mary's county, bringing with him a large family and a numerous band of retainers. The Brooke family, like the Calverts, were originally Catholics; but ancestor James had left the ancient faith for the simple tenets of the Quaker; being induced thereto (as is believed) by that influence which converted so many heathen kings to Christianity—namely, the gentle power of woman's faith and love. He married Deborah, daughter of Richard Snowden, in the year 1725, and "went to housekeeping" soon afterward; as stands recorded in his own handwriting in a little ancient book belonging to the Brooke family. Thus settled comfortably at "Charley Forrest," James Brooke continued making large acquisitions of land property, securing near 20,000 acres in one tract, which he called "Addition to Brooke Grove." This patent reaches from the beginning, a high stone still standing in Samuel Elliott's lane, to Seneca Creek, distant some ten or twelve miles.

The Friends Meeting being thus organized principally by the Brooke and Thomas families, to which were joined other sympathizing friends, these energetic colonists proceeded with the serious business of subduing the wilderness. They cleared the forest, planted corn and tobacco, and built comfortable dwellings. It was said by William Darby, the highest geographical authority ever domiciled among us, that when the house still standing on "Charley Forrest" (though considerably altered now) was first erected, it was the only framed building between here and Canada, on this meridian. Another legend (perhaps as doubtful) relates to the brick house of Philip Thomas—now the dwelling of William John Thomas—which is declared to have had the bricks brought from England. It is certain that the building of the largest number of that substantial sort of houses within Sandy Spring is due to the Thomas family.

Among these pioneers a more exciting occupation was

found in hunting the wild beasts; and many a severe conflict was required before their farms were cleared of these fierce enemies. The wolf and the bear ate their young swine and lambs; and the panther made the lonely paths through the woods perilous to them and their children.* The story was told me of an animated conflict which took place between old James Brooke and a panther, that has still a lively interest. A war was then prevailing (it must have been the French War of 1755), which had produced a scarcity of ammunition among the settlers. The oft-mentioned J. B. was out hunting with six dogs, when he came, in the deep recesses of a forest, upon a huge specimen of this North American tiger. The ferocious beast attacked the dogs, and in the twinkling of an eye they were laid out, with his enormous paws, sprawling on every side. At this juncture the old man came up and fired, but ineffectually, on the enraged animal, which now turned upon him. He endeavored rapidly to reload, but found he had shot away his last bullet. The situation was a serious one, but the men of those days were trained for all such emergencies. Cutting off one of the metal buttons of his coat, he dropped it down the capacious mouth of his old musket and blazed away at the panther, striking him right between those cruel eyes and putting an end to the beast. (I fancy there was no scolding at home that evening from his Deborah on account of the *missing button!*) How different is a nocturnal walk

* The curious reader who had examined Scharf's "History of Western Maryland" might be struck with the coincidence between columns of that work, page 773–6, and the above recitals and others that follow. The latter was collected by me, and furnished by request to Mr. Scharf's agent; this was all right—but, perhaps, it would have been as well to acknowledge the source. W. H. F.

through our woods now, from what it was in those days! Many stories are related, some quite humorous and others very frightful, of adventures with wolves, bears, and panthers. The following may be depended upon, coming down as it does through such channels. A carpenter, who had been at work through the day at the first attempt to build a house in the village of Brookeville, was making his way to his own hut in a dark night though the dense forest. Suddenly he was startled at the sight of two *shining eyes* in the path before him. He had no gun, but the axe was in his hand; lifting it he flung it with all his force at the horrid object, and then ran with all his might. On the following morning the axe was found stuck fast in the cloven skull of a young panther.

Tracks in the snow were inspected in those days with painful interest by the children; thus learning the value of an art now too much neglected—the grand art of observation.

Then, the most valuable of all animals, without exception, was the sagacious and faithful dog. Without his efficient services it would have been almost impossible to subdue and settle the wilderness. No wonder he is still held in such esteem, especially by the descendants of the old pioneers, if only for the good he has done. Yet it does seem, in the progress of civilization, that some of the very things most essential at the beginning became wholly unnecessary, and to be regarded as—an *ornament* or—a nuisance. Strange, but true! Well, they say "every dog has his day." May not the same be said of the gun, at least of the *pistol?*—an instrument invented in evil ingenuity, used only in barbarism, and now in wickedness—properly to be banished from the face of the earth.

At length the wild beasts disappeared before the hunter

with his dog and gun. The last bear shot in this neighborhood was brought down from the forks of a chestnut tree, a little way north of "Sharon"; this was in 1780. The wolf and deer were exterminated a short time afterward.

Their first severe hardship past, the early settlers, whom I have partially described, began evidently to prosper in their agricultural pursuits, chiefly by the culture of the great staple, tobacco. So profitable was the cultivation of their precious weed, that in the fear of seeing more essential crops neglected, the Legislative Assembly interposed with a law requiring every planter to put in two acres of corn for each member of the family engaged in working tobacco. The fact is mentioned that Richard Snowden had 24 tobacco houses standing in a row on one tract of land.

Although prosperous in their affairs, the forefathers of our neighborhood maintained great simplicity in manners, food and costume; having great contempt at the introduction of what they regarded as luxuries, of which some are now considered necessaries of life. An instance of this simplicity is shown in the fact, that there was for a time, indeed for quite a number of years, *only one pair of boots* in the settlement. This rare article was in possession of the head of the Thomas family; and was *loaned* out, in the true spirit of the olden time, to any of the neighbors about to undertake the serious enterprise of a journey to Annapolis! It is also well established that a single great-coat served the purposes of the community on similar occasions. Another incident, coming from an authentic source, gives a strong impression of the toughness and hardihood of body possessed by these old patriarchs. For a number of years they had no fire in the Meeting House: it is to be supposed that zeal kept them warm even in winter. At length some efficient members prevailed in getting a stove placed in the centre of the house. Great opposition had been manifested; and one of the hardy elders, determined to show his indifference, on entering the meeting pulled off his coat at the door and flung it on the stove. It happened to be moderate weather and no fire was kindled on that day, so nothing remarkable occurred; but the next time he came the weather was colder and a fire was kindled in the stove. Determined to set a proper example to the weakly ones, the good man walked firmly up the aisle, and exclaiming "Oh, the dumb idol!" he again threw his coat across the stove, and took his place in the gallery. A slight commotion was roused among the younger members (very slight, for the boys were order itself in those days). Surprised at so extraordinary a manifestation he lifted his eyes and beheld his outer garment enveloped in smoke from its own substance. After this he never mentioned the "dumb idol" again. Connecting this incident with the rule in those days relating to bed-covers—to make use of *one blanket* only until Christmas, and never more than two afterwards—we can form an idea of the degree of bodily hardiness possessed by the early settlers—so different from the present customs.

Thus lived and flourished in peace and growing plenty the "rugged forefathers of the hamlet," when that great event occurred which put a new face on the history of the world, extending its influence to the dwellers in the "backwoods" of Sandy Spring. I refer, of course, to the American Revolution. The Friends, by profession and practice, were men of peace. Owing to that love of established order, united to a dread of innovation, which has ever rendered them the most conservative of sects, the

Friends in general took no active part in the great contest. Some exceptions there were. One of the Brooke family joined the army and became a colonel, for which and some other breaches of the peaceful customs of his people he was condemned (according to the superstitions of the times) still to make nightly visits up and down the stairs of the fair mansion on the hill, built by him and claimed as his own. Courage and fortitude of another sort were manifested in those "times that tried men's souls," by Evan Thomas, whose son Philip E. has been called the father of the Baltimore and Ohio Railroad. This excellent man resided in the old brick house near Colesville, and attended regularly the Sandy Spring Meeting, of which he was a solid and faithful minister. Born in this county in 1738, he made numerous friends and acquaintances as he grew up, and entered freely into social circles. When the troubles of the Revolution came on he joined the patriots, and was elected a member of the Convention at Annapolis. Though fully impressed with the truth of Friends' principles, he at first saw nothing inconsistent with them in the bold "Declaration of the Rights of the People" that emanated from the Convention. "The true Quaker," Bancroft says, "is always a brave man, and a true Republican." Evan Thomas was re-elected; but the conviction was soon forced upon his mind that those patriotic resolutions meant war. He turned away from the path into which events were hurrying him, and came back to the strait and narrow path of his convictions of truth. A thorny way it proved to him; for years to come he had to suffer severely in person and goods, for conscience sake. By one of the intolerant laws of the period no person was allowed to preach unless duly allowed by secular authority. But Evan Thomas's warrant to preach came from a higher Power, and he was careful to obey only its behests. Oftentimes he was forcibly dragged from the gallery when he stood up to speak; he was fined and imprisoned; but on the next meeting-day after his release he was there again, pleading for heaven's mercy to his oppressors.

The persecutions ceased with the war. A fair share of worldly success was the reward of his faithfulness to principle; and he was enabled to rear a prosperous family, whose education was duly attended to, and who gained highly respectable positions in life. I have dwelt the longer upon this individual biography because it is of *representative character;* a type of the sort of *moral strength* requisite to carry a community safely over difficulties, and to build up durable individual characters. Many other worthies, as well among the women as the men of Sandy Spring in those early times, might be described as progenitors of the bone and sinew, brain and heart, that aided to give the neighborhood the reputation and influence which it acquired; but now we pass on down the stream of time.

It is here requisite to relate a grand historical event, which has exercised so efficient an influence over the character and fortunes of the people of Sandy Spring that no faithful narrator could fail to give it due place.

A little while before the commencement of the Revolutionary War, about the year 1772, "the Yearly Meeting of Friends in Baltimore," (I quote the words of the ancient minutes) "recommended to the subordinate Quarterly Meetings to keep under the weight of a concern which had arisen in the society some time ago, in regard to members holding slaves." The following year a committee reported that "some appear concerned to discharge their slaves; *divers* are convinced of the injustice of the practice, while too many make excuses," &c. It is evident that great tenderness, patience and deliberation marked every step taken by our society in this weighty matter. Time was afforded to all to examine the subject for themselves. No outside pressure was employed. Appeal was made only to the sense of right in the minds of those immediately concerned. At length the society, impressed by their own convictions, took up "the testimony against slavery," and held it ever since. Under its operation large families of slaves were discharged from compulsory service, who became the progenitors of the useful, and comparatively prosperous "free-colored working people" of the neighborhood. Lives there a man who would deny that a blessing rested on us for this sacrifice made by our forefathers, in compliance with this call of duty?

In the life of neighborhoods, as well as of individuals and nations, there are eras or stages that mark their progress. I note three such periods in the history of our community. The first period includes the settlement of the country, and the formation of the institutions which were to mould and stamp its future condition and character. Without affecting any close precision of dates, that first portion may be said to extend nearly to the close of the third quarter of the last century: this would include a period of about fifty years, bringing us up to the establishment of free labor. To this succeeded a period of comparative quiet, which, toward the latter portion or second era, threatened to become stagnation.

The cultivation of tobacco, which formed the chief wealth of the early settlers, grew to be unprofitable. Our soil, resting as it does on the solid foundation of the primitive rocks, was soon exhausted of some essential constituents upon which that odious weed draws so largely. Agriculture began to languish; old fields, abandoned to broom sedge, became the most striking feature of the rural landscape; and this to an extent that our young farmers can now scarcely realize. Toward the end of this second period, and for the first and last time, a small emigration to the West began to exhibit itself. Yet it does not seem that our people were seriously retrograding. There were at least two enterprises belonging to the quiet period which serve to redeem it from stagnation. One of these enterprises was the building in 1817 of our large brick Meeting House. The erection of so expensive a building (it being, when I took the census in 1850, the largest religious structure in the county), manifested the existence of the old spirit in our people, assisted, however, from abroad. It is told that Philip E. Thomas, son of Evan, as before mentioned, contributed $500 toward the valuable improvement.

The second historical event was the location here of the Fair Hill Boarding School, a year or two after the Meeting House was built. The selection of this neighborhood by the Yearly Meeting of Baltimore as its educational centre, may fairly be regarded an indication of the character for intelligence which Sandy Spring had acquired. Schools have never been neglected by the Society of Friends. From an early period "useful learning" was inscribed on their book of discipline as one of their religious obligations. And so the *cultivation of the mind* was still persevered in, after the time came when the *culture of the soil* yielded meagre results. The price of land, once much inflated, fell off heavily, reaching its lowest point about 1835, when the second era or period of our neighborhood's history may be said to close. A farm in the central part sold for $6, and one at the eastern edge for $2.05, per acre.

It was time for a revival: and it came. The third period then began. A way *must* be found to improve the land. The first experiment was made with lime. In the year '38, nineteen lime kilns could be counted within the sweep of a short radius, the stone being brought from five to ten miles. It is still subject of dispute as to the actual fruits of that lime experiment; but there is no doubt as to the *fruits of the spirit* that dictated it. It showed the *will;* and *that* is bound in all such cases to find the *way.*

The "way" which was found in the next year, '39, to bring about the real improvement which was to come, appears now very strange, almost a *craze.* "Thereby hangs a tale," which had perhaps be better left in oblivion. Yet one of the uses of history is to teach how to avoid the errors of the past; and if mankind ever *did* take warning from the blunders of their predecessors, it might be well to dilate upon Sandy Spring experience with "Morus multicaulis!"

The only thing worth telling about that affair is the very valuable discovery which it led to, in the use of bone dust. A few trials of this article soon showed that we had *found* what we had been *looking* for, viz. a fertilizer that was attainable, and that could be *trusted in.* A few years later, in 1844, that miracle of agriculture—"Guano"—was brought amongst us in appreciable quantities, and—you know the rest.

Radical improvement had begun of the sort sure to go on. Our young people found there was no need now to emigrate to newer, richer soils. Notwithstanding the adhesiveness that has bound them more closely to their birthplace than, perhaps, has been exhibited in any other part of the State, who can believe that one-third of those young men who constitute our junior clubs, and who are now using "Cooley Creamers," "digging Silos," and *such*, would have been content to remain even at Sandy Spring, if bone and guano had never been introduced among us?

It may be said, without using any extravagant expressions, that from the time these powerful fertilizers came into general use, the march of improvement was steadily onward. Energy and industry, thus encouraged by the certainty almost of securing their reward, were not found wanting; and a fair increase of outward prosperity followed. But the discovery and use of bone and guano may be considered as *accidental circumstances.* The question arises, are we sure there was enough of spirit and power within to *control and mould circumstances,* and to make proper use of the opportunities which the more prosperous times afforded? Before enumerating the multitudinous improvements which began to come to light, it is due to a right understanding of these results that we acknowledge the great benefits, along with some drawbacks, which Sandy Spring neighborhood received from the immigration of valuable persons coming from outside its borders. Although these newcomers have been jestingly styled "carpet-baggers" by a few belonging to the original settlers, rather famous for loving a joke, truth requires the statement that these strangers could not have well been spared. "Carpet-baggers" or not, they have mixed with the natives, and continue mixing together beautifully. When we name Hallowells, Farquhars, Moores, Millers, we have made only a beginning of real additions to the worthy folks who happened to come here first. Without the arrival, at a still earlier period, of a certain group entitled "the Stablers," there is good reason to believe that our banks, insurance companies, and other advantages too numerous to mention, might present a less flattering condition.

Belonging to the new era there is another important fact not to be omitted. The rapid increase of the communication between town and country, which commenced in force with the third era, and has gone on with accelerating ratio ever since, has unquestionably exercised considerable influence. Though we may find much fault with the city, and quote the saying that "great cities are great sores," it is undeniable that civilization, with its fruits of refinement and livelier activity, originated there. And it is by the happy action and mutual reaction of town and country that activity of mind is stimulated and brought into the most fruitful operation. Still it is also true that the life and growth of cities are kept up only by fresh importations from the country. Also along with the valuable importations received into the country, there come various customs and fashions which were better left out of the invoice. The city fashion of turning night into day and day into night does not suit country life at all. Self-respect should bar the entrance.

It remains only to set down together the names of the social, literary, and business institutions which have sprung up within a few years, following the beginning of a new era, and proving that such an era had come. The annual records of this book have kept a fair account of these associations, as they were formed within the last 18 or 20 years; and it is proper now only to enumerate some which preceded and formed the basis of a social system which is assuredly the distinguishing feature of Sandy

Spring. In 1842 an encouraging step was taken when Richard T. Bentley (according to my recollection) proposed that Sandy Spring should have a library of its own. The neighboring village of Brookeville has the credit of starting one some years precedent. Thus an excelsior wheel was set in motion the right way. In the beginning of the year 1844 the "Farmers Club" was instituted with general approbation. This book would scarce contain an account of all the beneficial results that followed the successful effort at co-operation by farmers. Four years more were required to put in successful operation that great enterprise, now well known over the whole State, namely, "The Mutual Fire Insurance Company of Montgomery County." Two several attempts had been previously made to organize such an institution by a number of persons, amongst whom the most active were* Dr. Charles Farquhar, Benjamin Hallowell, E. J. Hall, A. B. Davis and Joshua Peirce. A pamphlet was printed; but the plan was not ripe, nor was it satisfactorily adjusted. In 1847-8 Edward Stabler took up the subject; and, after procuring the willing subscriptions of his neighbors, he travelled through his own and the adjoining county of Carroll, where William Shepherd gave him ready support; a company was formed, the charter was obtained, and on the 1st of June, 1848, the greatest public achievement of Sandy Spring went into operation. Several circumstances favored the successful beginning of this institution; but none has been of such importance as was the procuring of an accomplished secretary, Robert R. Moore, who continues to fill the office to the present time.

*Refer to the letter of Hon. A. B. Davis in Appendix, p. 281.

The following statement would exhibit the condition of the Company at the end of the first year:

Total amount of property insured......	$193,695 00
Amount of premium notes in force.............	10,722 95
Amount of expenses from commencement, June 1st, 1848, to date..........................	245 25

ASSETS ON HAND.

Certificate of Baltimore City Stock.........	$205 66	
Cash...	39 93	
		245 59

LIABILITIES.

Due State for tax on policies..................	35 00
	$210 59

WM. H. FARQUHAR,
GEO. E. BROOKE,
RICH'D T. BENTLEY, } *Com. Board Directors.*

Next in dignity and consequence, the "Savings Institution," started just 20 years after the insurance company, occupies a place in which it has been able to diffuse real benefits over a wide extent of country.

In the meantime several other improvements sprung out of the spirit of association, which, being turned into action, is but another name for co-operation. The Lyceum Building, the Sandy Spring turnpikes, were valuable results from the latter.

Equally important, indeed essential to true progress, must be mentioned the co-operation of the ladies, commencing in 1857 with the pure, high-toned "Association for Mutual Improvement," that has set such a healthful example to the sex: multiplying, ramifying, diverging in more ways than can be here described.

Thus it is claimed that under the influences of social co-operation, certain interesting and beneficial results have been obtained in this little section, called Sandy Spring, of which we are willing to transfer some of the benefits to others. Whence did these advantages come? The foundation was laid somewhere and somehow; and genuine good material has been used in carrying on the building. On a previous page I ventured to write that "George Fox founded Sandy Spring." Not in *person*, of course. What I meant was that the Spirit to which he truly assigned all proper moving influences continued to overshadow his people. Without claiming merit to the Quakers for which they are not entitled, no sound and well-informed mind can deny that a power has dwelt with them strong enough to influence nations—Bancroft says "to move the world." Now, if this be so, we have the right to attribute the successful career of our neighborhood to the moral, invisible influences, accompanying fidelity to principle, possessed and partially handed down by our forefathers. Principle it was, and is, and shall be, not *forms*. As regards them, little or no account need be taken now. Old notions of innocent amusements, being contrary to the natural laws, need a complete revision. The same may be said of that narrow view of "building a hedge around our children in order to keep them from contact with the world": it is to be hoped that all such forms are of the past. Only principles are eternal.

The placing duty before pleasure; the giving to intellectual pursuits the preference to all amusements that are in conflict with them; these, with several other solid principles that might be named, belong to those higher sorts of life and conduct from which to depart is certain decline.

A slight, imperfect sketch of the rise and progress of Sandy Spring having now been offered, the thought presents itself, shall it be the work of some future historian —another Gibbon—to describe its decline and fall? Or, may we not hope that its people will hold fast to the *old truths* which experience has proved, while reaching after all the *new* that revolving time will certainly bring; above all, cultivating "the harmony that secures union, in which alone is strength"; seeking and finding the same support which upheld our fathers in the wilderness; and so, speed rejoicing on their way!

Would that some truly magnificent man or woman would rise among our young people and convince them wherein true, lasting pleasure lies! Well, the future of Sandy Spring is in their hands, having entered fairly on a *fourth period* in their history.

ODE READ UPON THE OPENING OF THE SANDY SPRING LYCEUM.

BY SARAH B. STABLER.

We've met at last within these walls,
  And hail the hour with gladsome hearts;
Although we've built no marble halls,
  It matters not to nobler arts.

Here in these woodlands we have reared
  A structure suited to the scene;
And Science' star has now appeared
  Above our vales and walks serene.

By toil we've gained enough to feed
  These bodies, soon to pass away;
Our minds immortal now find need
  Of higher sustenance than they.

In yon log school-house, years ago,
  Our fathers taught, our fathers learned;
In yon old graveyard, lying low,
  The senior forms to dust have turned.

But if their souls look downward now,
  I fain would think they smile to see
The kindling eye, the expanding brow,
  The thirst to know, the joy to be.

A thirst not bounded by the rates
  Attached to gain—on Mammon bent;
A joy that swells above the Fates,
  Above all time and each event.

Let us, my friends, devote our Hall
  To worthy uses of the mind:
If *Science* comprehend them all,
  Then say for Science 'twas designed.

We have our schools for early youth,
  Houses of worship when we will;
But this for scientific truth
  We've built—we'll dedicate—and fill.

Here let Philosophy recount
  Its wondrous secrets to the ear,
And through its aid let students mount
  To knowledge of each rolling sphere;

Dive in the earth for many a gem,
  Not for a sordid, mean abuse,
But that their souls may look through them
  To first beginnings—holiest use.

Here let the Orator profound
  Delve in the deepest mine of thought;
Here lesser lights diffuse around
  The rays with milder beauty fraught.

Here let not Satire plunge its dart
  With poison tipped, to rankle long;
Here Truth still act its honest part,
  By proof of right, to banish wrong.

E'en by this building we have shown
  Our aspirations reach more high
Than aught that we before have known,—
  Excelsior! then be our cry.

Here long may sages lessons teach,
  And here the young their questions bring;
Perchance far higher points we'll reach
  From these old woods of Sandy Spring.
Excelsior!

SANDY SPRING, *2d mo. 16th*, 1859.

ANNALS OF SANDY SPRING.

CHAPTER I.

Object of the book — Nature of history — Movement — Chief duty of the historian — Subscription to a short turnpike — Neighborhood map projected — First invasion by "the Gray" — Sandy Spring Branch of Brookeville turnpike — Establishment of Horticultural Society — The Clubs and Ladies' Association — Literary Society — Reading Circle — School re-established — State Sanitary Fair — Speeches of Judge Bowie, Judge Blair and Gov. Randall — Deaths, births and marriages.

At a meeting of the Sandy Spring Lyceum Company, held April 6th, 1863, an order was passed, appointing a historian for the Company, whose duty it should be to make a record of neighborhood events, and read it at the following annual meeting.

Having been selected to fill this office, after repeated unsuccessful efforts on my part to devolve its duties on another member of the company, I now proceed to discharge the function in the best manner I may. The undertaking appears to be both difficult and interesting. A mere monthly journal of events might readily be kept; but the simplest sketch deserving in the least degree the name of history, while it includes the material of such a journal, implies much beyond. History, in its true sense, is the life of nations, of communities of men. Now we may be informed of all the remarkable incidents in the life of a man (and still more true is this in the life of a woman) and yet know very little about the individual. The biographer worthy of the name must look more deeply, and enable *us* to look more deeply into the subject, than that. History is biography—with the community, instead of the individual, as its subject.

Thus it happens, when I set before my mind the real nature of the work which I have undertaken, that its intrinsic dignity and magnitude inspire a discouraging sense of the responsibility of the performance. One year in the life of a community! Look at it, and reflect! You find it is no light thing. However carelessly we may talk of time as it passes by, however slightly we mark the great current which is sweeping us on—the child to maturity—maturity to old age—sweeping us all, from our starting-point the cradle, to our common landing-place the grave—this eternal, ceaseless, never retrograding *movement* is always the one thing most worthy of profoundest thought. The movement—that is the important matter in the life and history of individuals or of nations: not so much what we *are*, as what we are *becoming;* not so much what *is*, as what is *thence* to be. This affords the proper clue to the complex history of the world: this consideration of the movement, the *progress*, forms the centre round which readily and distinctly group themselves, the else confused, inexplicable mass of the world's events.

Now this neighborhood of ours is also a part of the moving world. But it is a *part* that, in a certain sense, includes the *whole*. It is a microcosm, a little world in itself: the great scheme of earthly existence is all photographed here and now; and thus a true history of our neighborhood for one year is a condensed epitome of universal history.

You will not find fault with me, I trust, for laying the foundations of my work thus broad and deep; making the effort to dig down to the primary rock; even though the immediate structure as now erected should appear of slight proportions. You must have other builders who will raise up successive stories of the never-to-be-completed edifice, as years roll on.

It may be seen from the foregoing remarks that I consider it the chief duty of the historian to note down and to dwell upon those incidents which pertain especially to the permanent interests and progressive movements of the people of our neighborhood.

We commence with the evening of the last annual meeting of the Lyceum. Owing probably to the natural influence of the tremendous struggle in which our country is still engaged, evidences had begun to be apparent that there was a diminution of public spirit, and an abatement of zeal for improvement amongst our people. On that evening, these fears, which perhaps had no actual foundation, were completely dispelled. A proposition being offered to raise a sum of money for the purpose of making a turnpike from the insurance office to the meeting house, a liberal subscription was made up on the spot; the amount was increased by outside efforts, until a sufficient sum was raised, the work was put into able hands, and completed in a highly satisfactory manner to a point beyond the Lyceum. Since this temple of literature and practical science is, as it ought to be, only a station on the way to the house of worship, there is scarcely room for a doubt of the entire completion of the original design.

On the same evening, measures were taken to organize a Union Reading Association. Although this enterprise was ultimately less successful than the turnpike scheme, still the zeal that prompted both alike gave proof that "there is life in the old land yet." But that was not all: a movement was made to take steps for the accomplishment of a beneficial, long-desired improvement, a map of the neighborhood. A committee was named, who agreed to execute the necessary field and office work. Considerable progress has been made in the survey, several members of the committee having completed their share of the duty, and reported the field-notes to the chairman. Some of their colleagues are a little behindhand yet, owing doubtless to busy occupation with other matters.

In the first summer month, the quiet of the neighborhood began to be disturbed by rumors of hostile invasion. The month had nearly passed, and our anxieties on this account were nearly abated, when a serene Sabbath evening, the 28th of June, brought us unexpectedly our unwelcome visitors. A small troop of cavalry, wearing the gray uniform, which we had hitherto only read of, or else had seen under circumstances that rendered its wearer powerless to injure, quitting the large body of 4000, under the famous "Mr. Stewart," actually defiled along the roads leading through the centre of this our own neighborhood. At first we saw them with most incredulous eyes: it was a sight long to be remembered—our first actual contact with the terrible Rebellion. Yet after all (especially to us who lost no horses) it was a mere ripple of the mighty wave. Though no apologist for rebels, your historian feels compelled to record in these annals the fact that Sandy Spring came off wonderfully well from this its first experience of horrid war.

The alarms which disturbed us during the week following that memorable visit were worse, for a number of persons, than the visit itself. The remembrance of these groundless fears may be of value for us to refer to in the days yet to come. Perhaps it is still more advisable not to anticipate future troubles.

The most important enterprise ever undertaken by the combined efforts of our people for effecting material improvements, viz. "The Sandy Spring Branch of the Brookeville and Washington Turnpike," has made fair progress during the year. We were informed in the 5th month last that our road would be received as part of the main stem, so soon as it should be satisfactorily completed. At the same time material aid to the amount of $370 was tendered to us by the other company.

Additional subscriptions were obtained from our own people, amounting to near $600; with this fund the gaps in the road were filled up and various repairs effected. It was unfortunate that the demand for labor in other channels through the summer and early fall seemed to render it impracticable to recommence operations, until the season was so much advanced that the work had to be done under the great disadvantage of short days and inclement weather. The road looked very well, however, in the early winter, and was considered ready to pass inspection, when the breaking up of a frost of unusual depth stirred its foundations of quicksand, and placed it for the time outside the conditions on which it was to be merged in the other road. Still, even in its present state, it is of great value in getting our produce to market. Every one must see that it is by nature an essential part of the main road and must be consolidated therewith. The foregoing details might perhaps be thought to belong more to a report to the stockholders of "The Sandy Spring Branch," than to the stockholders of the Lyceum; but this road, its progress and its prospects are a material item in the neighborhood annals. It has naturally been a subject for criticism and comment; and in the exercise of the former privilege, critics have not always remembered the essential difficulties of the work. Your historian adds, by way of completing the discussion, that the road, though conforming rather to the curve line of beauty than the stiffness of the right line, is not claimed as an ornament, but for its utility, like the houses in which some of us still have to live, and which, beginning with a log hut for a centre, getting a wing added here and there as way opens for improvement, do yet come to be right comfortable dwellings, while possessing no complete apartment. Our turnpike had to be made just so.

We note as an event of the past year, the establishment of a Horticultural Society, certainly a very laudable undertaking. This brief notice must suffice, as your historian, in common with very many other fellow-citizens, has had very little opportunity afforded to become acquainted with its proceedings.

The "Farmers' Club" and the "Club's Wife," (which is so descriptive an epithet as to be not unworthy the dignity of history), the former in its 21st year, the latter just entering her 7th, continue to flourish with unabated vigor and interest. [The proper name of the latter Society is "The Mutual Improvement Association."]

Last fall a Literary Society was organized, designed to combine the idea of a reading circle with other novel and important features. Its success has so far justified the hopes of its projectors; and it will not be difficult so to conduct it as to make it ripen from a pleasing novelty into a settled institution.

It would imply great neglect upon the part of your historian if he were to fail in doing justice to the solid excellence of the Sandy Spring School, re-established just one year ago by Milton Jackson.

It is also a labor of love to refer to the amiable exertions made recently by the ladies of our neighborhood, to contribute worthily to a noble and worthy object, the State Sanitary Fair. The priest and the Levite in the olden time passed with dignified indifference "to the other side," when only *one* wounded man lay before them; now, when 40,000 sick and wounded fellow-creatures implore their aid, the course of the good Samaritan has seemed to our ladies a safe and hallowed path to tread.

The last event in which our neighborhood is specially interested occurred but yesterday; when this hall, "dedicated to the diffusion of truth and knowledge among men," echoed to the eloquent addresses of three distinguished personages, viz. our own Chief Justice R. J. Bowie, Judge Blair, and Gov. Randall. Their theme was Human Liberty; and no more remarkable event has occurred during the past year in this part of Maryland, or any other part, than such a discussion as we then enjoyed.

My imperfect retrospect must presently close. Does it not prove that ours is a "living age," and that our own neighborhood partakes in the new light that illumes the world? The thought will surely stimulate us to press toward higher and still higher modes of life, and produce a grateful sense of the many blessings bestowed upon us. The year just elapsed has brought in its train, not only the cheering evidences of life, but also the mournful visitations of life's dread attendant, Death. On every human record place must be left for him. During the year our neighborhood has had to lament the departure of three valued members of its social circle. On 5th month 12th, 1863, died John Elgar Hallowell. "In the pride and glory of youthful spring," he was called to leave us; and the vacant place is still warm with the life of which he was so lavishly possessed. He was one of the original projectors of this Lyceum, and he continued while he lived to be among its most efficient friends and supporters. 8th month 19th, 1863, Caleb P. Iddings was relieved from his long suffering. Although resident but a few years in our neighborhood, the agreeable impression which he made upon us will be long remembered. 7th month 26th, of the same year, Matilda Gilpin was taken from the amiable band of good Samaritans, with whom she had been an early and zealous co-worker, ever ready to visit and relieve the sick and wounded sufferer.

These were not the only visitations of death during the year. Two little mounds in the neighboring graveyard cover the remains of two precious little beings, transferred for full development to another sphere. "The little feet that never went astray are safe in the Father's dwelling!"

In order to bring my record to a more cheerful close, it is my duty to state, from good authority, that ten children have been born during the year in our social circle. Also there has been one marriage. "How many engagements?" inquires one of my fair friends. These are questions which must be left for answers in the next record.

CHAPTER II.

Ending Fourth Month 3d, 1865.

An eventful year — Election for new constitution — Loss of mail contract to Laurel — Charitable contributions in Baltimore and in Tennessee — Farm crops — Uses of Lyceum Hall — Invasion of Maryland by Gens. Early and Bradley Johnson — The Guerillas — "Battle of Rickett's Run" — Plan of "Home Defence" laid aside — Far more serious losses, by *nine deaths;* their monition to take better care of health.

An eventful year has passed, as well for our whole country, as for that small portion of it whose history we are here to record. The car of the nation's destiny rolls resistlessly onward, carrying us along with it, whether we would or not. But though we may neither stop nor check its course, it is lawful for us in mind to pause and look back on the career we have run since this day a twelvemonth ago. There may be an advantage in withdrawing our thoughts for a time from the whirl of the world's great Babel, in order to contemplate our own special position, to see where we are, and to judge whither we are tending, by measuring the part of the way actually trod. One great lesson will be thus impressed upon us, namely, that of the intimate and inseparable connection of the welfare and interests of each community with those of the whole land. And our young people may learn how important it is to study the duties of citizenship; how mistaken and dangerous to ignore the just claims of the country which protects us.

During this month of last year, our community, in common with the rest of the State, was agitated by the coming, at an unaccustomed period, of an election. We had to choose the members of a Convention whose duty it would be to revise the Constitution of the State and determine some momentous questions affecting its future destiny. Our people took a lively part in the settlement of these questions. Although prevented by the force of superior numbers from having their views represented directly in the choice of delegates to the Convention, yet when the great, decisive struggle came on in the Fall, they turned out in full strength, and gave a nearly unanimous vote in favor of the principles of their forefathers. When the time of trial came, the people of Sandy Spring were not found wanting; unitedly they aided to secure to the rest of their State the blessings of freedom and free labor, to which the neighborhood had so long owed its own prosperity.

Proceeding with the narrative in regular order of time, we note that an event occurred in the month of April from which an injury to the interests of the neighborhood was apprehended. This was the loss of the mail contract by the company which had been running a stage to Laurel for some fifteen or sixteen years, with considerable benefit to our community. The apprehended injury has not so far been realized. Indeed, the result goes to confirm the general principle that individual enterprise is apt to succeed better than corporate companies. Under the management of our accommodating and energetic contractor and driver, that important daily communication with Laurel and the rest of the world has been kept steadily open, while zealous exertions to improve the road by our friend of the Manor, Caleb Stabler, have contributed materially to the satisfaction of travellers.

The same month of April was further distinguished by the successful exertions of our patriotic and benevolent ladies in contributing to the State Sanitary Fair, held in Baltimore. The quality of the articles exhibited and the amount of profits derived from their sale nobly maintained the reputation of the neighborhood. The spirit of practical benevolence was suffered to sleep after the effort of the spring, during a large portion of the year; but was again revived toward its close by another successful effort to excite our interest in behalf of grievous suffering in a distant State. The articles then prepared were sent to a lady in Nashville, who acknowledged their reception nearly in the following words: "Your box was unpacked three days ago, and with it I have made glad the hearts of some of the most destitute and most grateful of human beings." Your historian is so far a believer in the doctrine of imputed righteousness as to hope that these acts of charity will be received as an offset, in part, to manifold shortcomings, much worldliness, and sadly imperfect exercise of continued "love one to another."

The season of growth came on, though somewhat later than usual, yet with full accustomed richness and beauty. The wheat crop was short, but the great harvest of this neighborhood, namely, the hay crop, was very luxuriant, and all manner of fruits unprecedentedly abundant. Interesting exercises were prepared in the month of June for our entertainment. The young men got up an affair at the Lyceum which proved a success; it was their first effort of the kind, and it were a great pity should it prove to be the last. Those who contribute rational and innocent amusement may justly be considered as benefactors of the community.

It may be here remarked how varied and interesting

have been the uses of this Lyceum Hall. When we recall the different purposes to which it has been applied during the past six years since its initiation—lectures, than which none could have been more instructive; public discussions of momentous national questions; meetings of literary and benevolent societies; school exhibitions; draft clubs; defence meetings, &c., &c., may we not all unite in the sentiment lately expressed by a friend: "No building in this neighborhood has ever paid so well"?

But the summer brought other scenes which may indeed be termed historical; scenes which were vastly more exciting at the time than any that I have here recorded, yet leaving effects very slightly proportioned to the deep interest which they inspired while passing. None of the audience will be at a loss to understand the allusion.

In common with the rest of our countrymen, I may venture to say with the whole civilized world, we had watched with intense interest the progress of the great campaign commenced early in May on the banks of the Rappahannock. The main tide of war rolled away from us further to the South; but various alarming intimations received from time to time gave token that we were not to escape its wrath. Early in July it was found that the Rebel invasion of Maryland was going to prove a serious affair. The too well-known sound of cannon in actual battle was heard again. On the 9th of that month occurred the engagement at Monocacy; and the same evening came the news, "the Rebels hold Frederick and the line of the Monocacy." The 10th, which was First day (I now copy notes from my Diary, written at the time), "was a memorable day, probably the precursor of others still more so. Our meeting was large, and the gathering was pleasant and strengthening. Benjamin Hallowell spoke from the gallery with much feeling, and very appropriately to the serious times. Accounts of the progress and near approach of the Rebels crowd upon us throughout the day. In the evening we learn from Charles H. Brooke, who had been for awhile their captive, that they are in or near Laytonville. Men arrive from New Market, fleeing with their horses from the danger. Rumors of the capture of a fort near Washington finished this day.—The 11th. After a sound night's rest, awoke from a dream, uttering the words, 'Is Washington taken?' Went over early to alarm my neighbor, Richard T. Bentley, about his store goods; found him very calm. The next news came, 'the Rebels are at Stanmore,' whence they soon departed, but not empty-handed. Benjamin Hallowell has an adventure with a favorite horse, which he rescues for the time at some risk. Federal cavalry arrive. There is total suspension of business throughout the neighborhood. Washington is certainly invested, and the B. & W. R. R. is cut. Federal cavalry ride by in the night toward Laurel. Thermometer 94°.—The 12th. The excitement has, we hope, reached the highest point to-day. A kind neighbor sent express in the morning that 'more Rebels were at Mechanicsville.' Horses were put under cover. Soon the Graybacks appear, forerunners of Bradley Johnson's large cavalry force of near 2000 men. In passing they take Francis Miller prisoner, and Benjamin Hallowell loses his horse after all, to the shame of the General be it spoken. They rob the Sandy Spring store of a small amount and pass on toward Bladensburg.—The 13th. Heard at Mechanicsville the good news, 'the Rebels have left from before Washington.' Things begin to look much brighter. A beautiful moonlight night for the young and happy.—14th. The excitement is passing away, and reaction coming on."

We may repeat what was said in last year's history, that "only a ripple in the tide of war has swept by Sandy Spring." A few horses were taken, but not so many as in last summer.

It is a well-known experience that the things left behind after a great inundation, the slime and the ugly crawling creatures, are often more to be dreaded than the flood. The after effects and consequences of a disease are sometimes worse than the disease itself. So it happened in our experience of rebel incursions. A robbery committed on one of our friends while riding on the highroad near the middle of the neighborhood, some time near the end of July, was the first unpleasant intimation that person and property were no longer safe from outrage in Sandy Spring. On the night of the 5th of September, Ashton store was robbed of money and goods to a considerable amount, the perpetrators being rebel guerillas, as was proved beyond reasonable doubt. One month later, it being the night of the 6th of October, Sandy Spring was invaded by a band of eleven guerillas, who, after threatening to hang the clerk, broke open the store and helped themselves freely to its contents. So far the outrages committed in the neighborhood, the taking of horses by violence, the pillage of stores and personal robbery, had been suffered quietly and without resistance. I have now to record an occurrence of different character. It is one so anomalous, so outside the long even tenor of life at Sandy Spring, that the recital might be omitted as being an exception; but the truth of history makes an irresistible claim for the statement of facts just as they occur.

After the robbers above referred to had gone their way, the proprietors of the store, without losing much time about it, sent for the Sheriff of the county, whose duty it was to pursue and arrest the perpetrators of the outrage. Under his official sanction, acting as a *posse comitatus*, a number of the neighbors, fifteen, I believe, in all, with the accoutrements required by the nature of the expedition, proceeded in the track of the guerillas. They went to find them, and they did find them. What was the next thing they intended to do this historian knows not; but whatever the intention may have been, the result naturally to be expected actually followed. Somebody was hurt; and, fortunately for us all, it was not one of the pursuing party. The leader of the guerillas, in the act of charging upon our party, with intent unquestionably to kill, was himself killed. The rest fled, it is presumable more through ignorance of the force and character of their pursuers than from any other circumstance. Part of the plunder was recovered; some horses were restored to their rightful owners, and the whole affair passed off as favorably as could be expected under the circumstances. If censure falls anywhere in this transaction when calmly and impartially reviewed, it should be limited to the charge of imprudence. Viewed in the best light, however, it must be owned that there are other things in the annals of Sandy Spring upon which we shall hereafter dwell with higher satisfaction than upon "the battle of Rickett's Run."

These events occurring in connection with the stirring scenes of war in all parts of the country, naturally directed the more fiery spirits among our young men to the subject of "Home Defence." Several meetings were called to examine this question, but after a fair discussion, the counsels of prudence and the influence of early religious impressions prevailed, and the idea of an armed home-guard was laid aside.

This eventful summer was marked by the prevalence of an extreme drought, which, however, proved less hurtful to our interests than was feared. Bounteous fall rains went far to redeem the losses from the dry, hot summer.

Autumn came on. The season had indeed been a trying and eventful one. Rebel raids, highway robberies, pillage of stores, the drought and the draft had inflicted serious injuries. These, the hand of industry, the genial rain and sunshine, and the welcome return of sweet peace, will soon repair. But far more serious losses were now impending, which no human efforts, no rain or sunshine, no gentle peace, can ever mitigate or restore. Only His hand that inflicted the wound can drop the balm.

Our bereavements commenced in the spring. On the 30th of April, Thomas P. Stabler was suddenly taken from among us. No one in the neighborhood was more identified with its history, progress and character, than he. Every house, every farm, every road, and especially every *sick room* knew him; for he was ever ready, by kind action or interesting conversation, to help or to entertain. His clear head and warm heart seemed to grow warmer and brighter to the last. Contrary to general experience, his views of life became more enlarged and liberal as he advanced in years; and he watched with lively interest, aiding by tongue and pen, the cause of social progress. Sound and true were his views of the nature of the great struggle going on in our country; the end of which he predicted, though he did not live to see. The long funeral train that followed the remains of Thomas P.

Stabler to the resting-place he had provided was watched from the window of a neighboring house by a pale, sweet invalid, his little granddaughter. Just a week later, the earthly remains of Evelyn Stabler were laid near those of her grandfather. She was taken in the early morning of life, when only a few had the opportunity to mark the promise of excellence which she gave; but with those few, her traits of solid worth, above all her ripened conscientiousness, will long keep her memory green.

Shortly after midsummer, an infant, Bertha Miller, child of Warwick P. and Mary Miller, struck by a strange, sad decline, fell asleep. A month later, another babe, daughter of Edward and Sophy Peirce, was released from lingering pain.

Thus had death visited the extreme points of the neighborhood, the west, the east and the north. Its next awful visitations were to the south and the centre. It had removed the old man, the budding girl and the tender babe; it was now to cut down youthful and manly prime.

On the 28th of September died Tarleton Brooke, in the 21st year of his age. Of such as he we are told:

> "He, the young and strong, who cherished
> Noble longings for the strife,
> By the wayside fell and perished,
> Weary with the march of life."

If I know myself, no word of eulogy shall ever be traced in these pages which my conscientious convictions do not sanction; but when a youth of noble promise is taken away from the neighborhood, I cannot fail to set it down among the most important, as well as saddest incidents that go to constitute our annals.

November 13th died B. Worthington Waters. Though not exactly included within the local limits of Sandy Spring, the deceased was so near and so intimate with many of our people, it is deemed proper not to pass him by. He died in the prime of years and usefulness; leaving an impressive example of the results that energy can achieve in the boundless field of agricultural pursuits.

November 20th, Alexander J. Brooke, in the 22d year of his age. The best poet of America can best give an impression of his sufferings and his life:

"He, the patient one and weakly,
Who the cross of suffering bore,
Folded his pale hands so meekly,
Spake with us on earth no more."

But life was not all suffering with him. He had high enjoyments too. I have seen his cheeks glow and his fine eyes kindle while exploring with eager faculty the wondrous mechanism of the vegetable and insect world; and in vision I have seen them brighten with unfading lustre, impressed with the wonders of that glorious land which needs no *microscope* to reveal.

November 27th. Another interval of a week, and within six hours of one another, two near neighbors, each a youthful husband and father, are called away from the earthly home to which they were bound by such ties of love. The one, Archibald D. Moore, passed quietly away after an acute illness of just three weeks. His good and gentle life will long be held in tender recollection by his friends,—enemies he had none The other, William Chandlee, was the victim of a sudden and terrible accident. While quietly attending to his own concerns, interfering with none, he was instantly deprived of consciousness, and soon of life, by the bursting of a gun in his own hands.

One more victim of this strange, fatal year! The venerable grandfather, the budding girl and the babe, the promising youth, the energetic man, the long-suffering invalid, the youthful husband and father—these, O Death! were thine! But there is a still tenderer name than these —and thou wilt have the tenderest and best—the young wife and mother—she too must be thine!

November 29th died Mary H. Brooke, daughter of Benjamin and Margaret E. Hallowell, having just completed her 25th year. And now death's hand was stayed.

"What is the use," does any one ask, "of seeking to revive all these sad recollections?" It appears to me there may be much use in it. Here are we sitting where we sat a twelvemonth ago, when all *these* were as full of life as we are now, calling to mind the work of death. Are we not solemnly bound to realize the awful fact, to stand face to face with it, ready to draw the lessons it was designed to teach? We have surely no right to shrink from the contemplation.

It is not for me to point you to the highest, the only efficient consolation; I would in silence share it with you.

But there is another aspect in which to view these afflictions, that I may not pass over. Can you believe it was the design of Providence that these our friends should perish, all (with one exception) so long before reaching full maturity? Is there not good reason to believe that if the conditions which regulate the well-being of our bodily frame received as much attention as so many less important subjects, that the life given us here would generally be prolonged until it could answer the end for which life is given? We possess capacity to know and ability to practice the laws on which health depends. May these solemn monitions serve to confirm the resolve to make knowledge and practice go hand in hand! Remember that "History is philosophy teaching by example," and to be valued only so far as it teaches us.

The clubs and other associations which begin to distinguish our neighborhood are to be regarded as so many wheels in the machinery of social progress; and from the way in which they have been kept running during the past year, we may hope that our progress has been good. The exclusively masculine club, the exclusively feminine association, and the Literary Association which so gracefully mingles the two, have flourished with unabated vigor and interest. The Horticultural *may* become, *if it live* a year or two longer, one of the institutions of the neighborhood.

The Lyceum, at once the focus and crown of our literary and intellectual activity, certainly appears to have lost none of its interest. Fears have been expressed lest the minds of our people should be worked up to a high pitch of excitement by this "dangerous" novelty. No just grounds for such apprehension are perceived by this historian.

Our roads are improving. I had hoped that the Sandy Spring Pike would merit a decided puff; but unfortunately, the recent condition of one section does not admit of such praise; it will have to wait until next year. *Perhaps* the commencement of another sort of road may then be chronicled.

It is altogether in order, I am sure, to mention that marriages have taken place this year in our community to the number of three. The immediate effect has been that we lose one fine woman and gain another, being kept even so far. Also eight have been added to our infantile population, being three boys and five girls.

In conclusion, it seems proper to make the inquiry by weighing our losses and gains,—have we, as a community, or have we not, made progress during the year? A sad weight is thrown into the negative scale by the removal into another sphere of so many valuable members of society. What counterpoise can we place on the opposite side? Even in point of numbers we have lost. Are we entitled to throw into the scale a few acres of land improved, a few investments in stocks, or a multitude of greenbacks? I fear their weight would be insignificant in such a scale.

We can add some show of mental activity—that is well: some works of practical benevolence—that is better. But we are still obliged to confess that the balance sheet is against us, unless we may claim that our grief for the dead has increased our tenderness for the living; unless the wondrous thread of blessings and afflictions woven and mingled together in this past year has served to draw closer the bands of good fellowship and social union.

United we stand—divided we fall.

CHAPTER III.

Ending 4th Month 7th, 1866.

Tame annals, best, of a quiet local character—Unanimity of views—The conservative element prevalent—The peace celebration—Lincoln mourning—Wheat crop declining—Horticultural Exhibition—The Club Junior—Sorghum manufacture—Close of Fair Hill Boarding School—Opening of James S. Hallowell's—New Public School System—Colored School by Mrs. Clarke—Marriages numerous after the war—Six in one year—Contrasted with the deaths, the rate of the latter too large.

"Blessed is the nation that has no history," exclaims one of the most distinguished writers of Europe. I suppose what is true of nations is equally true of neighborhoods.

But the history referred to by that writer was of the sort that usually goes by the name; a record of exciting events, mostly calamities; of wars, with their battles and sieges; of the overthrow of one tyrant, and the climbing to his throne by another, up steps gory with blood. The less of such history the better.

In this sense the neighborhood annals of the past year compared with the preceding, are necessarily tame.

The year had, however, a very animating commencement. On the evening of our last annual meeting, just one year ago, the announcement was made to us from the chair, and received with tumultuous cheering, that the National troops had on that very morning taken quiet possession of the Confederate Capital. Events of most exciting character followed each other in rapid succession for a few brief weeks, and then the great rebellion passed into history; but not into this one. Our affairs are of a local, not a national character. Only as public events affect directly the situation and welfare of this little community, tending to influence its progress, do they become proper material for the present historical sketch. Our connection has been for the past few years of a close kind. We have been both an *active* and a *passive* party, through the late tremendous civil convulsion. In making up a summary of the parts thus performed, it seems proper to acknowledge on the one hand, that our sufferings have been comparatively light and trivial, with a great balance of gratitude due for our preservation; and on the other, we have a right to enjoy the consciousness that our exertions and sacrifices, though insignificant when compared with those of some other communities, were yet mainly on the right side; that we did not stand neutral or lukewarm in a conflict where such transcendent principles were involved, but with a concert of action amounting nearly to unanimity, our whole neighborhood gave its influence by tongue and pen and vote, by hands and purse, to aid the cause approved by our highest convictions of right and truth.

This near approach to unanimity among us on the great question of the age appears to me as a matter of just satisfaction. We have disciples here with widely diverging doctrines. Radicals and conservatives, each with very decided opinions, are to be found among us; although it must be acknowledged that the conservative element has always predominated at Sandy Spring. But in our country's extremity, the conservatives saw that the very foundations of government were assailed, and naturally rallied to the support of law and order; while the radicals beheld in the success of the National cause the triumph of their own cherished principles. Both earnestly desired peace: all came together and joined with enthusiasm in the rejoicings that signalized the close of the contest. On the evening of the 12th of that eventful month of April, this Lyceum building saw another sight than any it had yet witnessed—yes, *saw*, looked out into the night with a hundred burning eyes, while the interior resounded with paeans for union and peace!

When the Nation's birthday returned there was another successful celebration, somewhat unusual in this special locality, but justified by the extraordinary, the transcendent occasion. As our people were *one* with the other loyal people of the land in their joy, so were they *one* in *mourning.* There were few places where the tidings of President Lincoln's assassination produced such chilling horror, such sincere grief.

Equally indifferent to our joy and our loss, the months

moved on. In the fields the season was an unusually early one, and our farmers rejoiced in the bountiful promises of the spring. The summer and autumn fulfilled these promises, with two notable exceptions. The important crop of wheat, which had been declining in our neighborhood for several years, reached what is to be hoped will be the lowest point of production, in an average of eight to ten bushels per acre. The apple, most valuable of fruits, was also a remarkable failure. As to the productiveness of the season in other fruits, in garden vegetables, in corn and grass, some evidence was afforded by a Horticultural Exhibition, or miniature Agricultural Fair, held on the 16th of September, in this building. For a first attempt it was regarded as a decided success, and well worthy of being repeated. If this very creditable affair is to be considered an outgrowth and practical result of the Horticultural Society, whose establishment and progress are noted in our two preceding chapters, the enterprising young institution may aspire to an honorable place among the beneficial associations with which the neighborhood is so highly favored. In this connection, your historian could not think of passing over without respectful notice the birth of a new agricultural society—"The Club Junior," as it is termed in the absence of a distinctive epithet. We anticipate a rich harvest of usefulness from this new enterprise, proportioned to the zeal and energy, and (I hope we shall be able to add) the constancy and perseverance of our younger brethren in agriculture.

Before leaving the subjects that concern us so nearly as farmers, we have to note the establishment of the manufacture of sorghum. About 1500 gallons were made during the year, and growers and manufacturers both seem to regard the enterprise thus far as being a success.

An event occurred during the summer which was of interest to several families. I refer to the final close of Fair Hill Boarding School, and the sale of the property to a private individual, after having been for nearly half a century in charge of the Baltimore Yearly Meeting of Friends. That building has not been without its history. Between seven and eight hundred young persons, principally females, were scholars there. Scattered widely over the two adjoining States, they doubtless retain varied yet vivid recollections of the period passed under the old roof, which would furnish ample materials for many a lively story, destined probably to remain unwritten.

One "boarding school for girls" was closed; another was opened by James S. Hallowell, at Fulford, during the year, under reasonably favorable auspices.

In connection with this subject it is proper to mention that the new system of public schools, inaugurated in our State under the new Constitution, was at once introduced into our neighborhood.

In regard to this important subject, it is well for us to remind ourselves that the grand object and ultimate aim of this vital institution is to level upwards. Therefore, if any community (such as ours for instance) shall consider that it is not much benefited at first, it may be consoled by the self-complacent idea that the high position it occupies has not yet been reached by the swelling tide, perceptible only on *average* elevations. But the tide is swelling, and will reach even them. Let us be patient: the beneficial wave of intellectual light ever rises, and can know no ebb. "For God Himself is Light!"

Another school was organized in the neighborhood during the present year, altogether as successful, and probably quite as useful as the preceding. A school for colored people was no new thing in our neighborhood; and though the attempt to keep it up was often interrupted and the school dispersed by violence under color of law, it served among sundry other causes to attract and retain the more valuable class of operatives. Viewed in a merely material and selfish light, it was a benefit to us all.

These advantages, and many more of a much higher character, have been secured and confirmed by the truly admirable teaching of Mrs. Clarke, the lady who undertook the arduous task of conducting the present colored school, situated in a spot that has borne the name of "Sharp Street." Every person who is willing to visit there, and to give full play to the instincts of reason, justice and humanity, while listening to the exercises, must echo with honest enthusiasm the beautiful couplet they fondly sing—

> "Long may our land be bright
> With freedom's holy light!"

Change we now the theme! "To heavenly themes diviner strains belong." The events now to be recorded demand a pen of rosewood and the juice of roses for ink. Would that I might command language flowery enough to describe the incidents for which this year of grace, judged by the emotions of many of our young friends, was especially made. I keep, however, to the simple facts, and refer you to a certain evening, still fresh in your recollection, when at a meeting of the Literary Society it was found nearly impossible to fix a time for the next meeting, at which somebody or other was not going to be married!

Certainly there was never in our neighborhood such a revival of the matrimonial spirit during any year that I have known it. The parties waited so appropriately for this year of peace and union, thus adding to life's brightest charm its crowning grace.

Six weddings in one year in our small circle show progress indeed. The coming of the most important event in life to at least twelve persons leads naturally to other material improvements. The bird must have its cage, either newly made or enlarged; thus several comfortable additions have been procured to the homes of Sandy Spring.

It seems an abrupt transition, yet one frequently made in this world, to pass from the marriage altar to the tomb; from the commencement of life's serious cares and duties, to the place of never-ending rest. Two sweet stanzas express the peculiar contrast:

"I saw two maids at the kirk,
And both were fair and sweet—
One in her wedding robe,
And one in her winding-sheet.

"One, on the morrow, woke
In a world of sin and pain;
But the other was happier far,
And never woke again."

This page of our record is again filled with many names. On the 24th of August died Elizabeth Briggs. After nearly two years of severe illness she passed very quietly away. In patience, in meekness, and all the mild, unobtrusive virtues that diffuse their light round the domestic hearth, her character was peculiarly blessed. A sportive fancy and playful humor, amusing all and hurting none, were remarked by those who knew her best. Of such as she we do not need to say "peace be with them!" for their lives are wholly peace. A month later, a fine, blooming child was taken away from parents who had already experienced the crushing bereavement. Clarkson Stabler died the 22d of September. Too young to have made a permanent impression outside the circle of his immediate friends, it seems to others a void easily filled, but to the parents that void is deep in proportion to the narrow space which the little life filled. It was a lovely afternoon of the 11th of October, just when the fading graces of autumn flush the dying year, that the sweet, pure spirit of a young girl was rendered back to God who gave it. Isabella Stabler was in her 18th year. To minds concerned only in the things of earth, such a bereavement is utterly overwhelming and irreparable. There was everything about her to give satisfaction to the present and promise for the future. Favored by personal attractions, and in the fairer charms of an amiable disposition, she possessed a mind earnestly drawn to the pursuit of knowledge. All these gifts and graces were reft at one blow. Nay, not wholly reft; they live still in the memory of her friends, who cherish fondly the tender recollection, admonishing them,

> "Though 'tis an awful thing to die,"

('Twas even to her),

> "yet, the dread path once trod,
> Heaven lifts its everlasting portals high,
> And bids the pure in heart behold their God."

Only four days later, Timothy Kirk died at the advanced age of 87. His active years had been spent in another part of the country, but his connection with a valued brother and a beloved sister, both passed away from among us a few years ago, served also to draw him near.

A month later, on the 21st of November, having also reached a very advanced age, Martha Thomas, mother of Edward, William John, and Samuel P. Thomas, closed a quiet and gentle life by a peaceful death. It was remarked by one who looked upon her calm brow, "stamped with everlasting peace," that the transition to another life, often so abrupt, was in her case easy and natural, as if "the gates opened of themselves."

When the new year came, death returned to find his victims among the young. In the early morning of the 18th of March, Edward S. Hallowell yielded up a life most dear and precious. His worth was known and appreciated outside the home circle, in which it was felt with such peculiar regard. He was a good boy: he performed well and faithfully his part while he lived; his short career was speedily accomplished, we shall see him here no more. Cold indeed must become the hearts of our young people, and wholly devoted their minds to gathering the sordid gear or to the perishing pleasures of earth, if they fail to keep green the memories of Isabella Stabler and Edward Hallowell. Another victim still. We are even now just returned from following to their last resting-place the remains of Annie Moore. The little darling of a young widowed mother was soon called to climb to the abode of the other parent, Archibald Moore, whose early removal was chronicled in a preceding page. In gazing on the little face of the dead a few hours ago, we could not but remark that it was the most beautiful one in the whole assembly. How justly may we ask, if death is so beautiful, if the spirit in parting leaves such a celestial impress on the clay, why should we regard the mortal stroke with so much horror?

Turning now from tender sentiment to sober fact, it may be well to remark that in the past three years we have recorded the deaths of 23 persons. "Our neighborhood" is a rather uncertain tract of country, the lines are not determined with such precision as to justify reliable mortuary statistics. But your historian having some experience in that department of business, and being deeply interested in the results which can fairly be drawn from such facts as we can depend upon, will venture to add to this Chapter the following conclusions:

The annual death rate for the three periods must amount to 1 in 45, or thereabout. Now this mortality is far above the rate found to prevail in our whole country. Here is a serious fact which we are called upon to face. Can it be that life in Sandy Spring is really less secure than in the rest of the United States? You do not believe that—neither do I.

We must fall upon more precise statistics if these historical sketches are continued.

CHAPTER IV.

Ending 4th Month 1st, 1867.

Invitation to assist the historian — Farm improvements — Potatoes beginning to be largely grown — Croaking for drought — Wheat almost ceased to be a staple crop, yet the drought was relieved by inundating floods — Life of the clubs, with a spice of rivalry — The Horticultural supported by the ladies' hands excels — The mercantile interest — Sorghum — "Sandy Spring Branch Turnpike" incorporated with the main stem — Tollgate at Ashton — First appearance of railroad engineers — Lyceum porch — Professor of elocution appreciated — The Literary Society less lively — New Debating Society — Newspapers suggested without success — The schools really prosperous — Marriages less so (as to numbers) — Interesting facts relating to some of the deceased — Warning against "the busy tongue."

You are again invited to stop for a few moments the rolling wheel of time, and consider attentively what its last revolution has brought and taken from us.

How many of you, allow me to ask, can at once recall a number of occurrences of the past year which might properly constitute material for neighborhood history? My annual task would be much lightened, as well as rendered more valuable and interesting, if several persons among you would keep a record of such events as each one might consider of the most general interest, suffering me to draw thence the materials thus gathered together.

In the absence of such help, I proceed to transfer from my own brief notes a few leading incidents, accompanying them with such remarks and reflections as they naturally suggest.

As this neighborhood constitutes a community engaged

mainly in agricultural pursuits (although depreciating remarks have occasionally been made to the contrary), we will first take up the farming operations of the year. These commenced last spring in a lively manner. The spirit of improvement was exhibited in the clearing up of grounds and fencing them in, a larger amount being done than usual.

A full spring crop was put in, especially of potatoes; at least 200 bushels being planted by the members of the two Clubs alone. As the season advanced, a drought of unusual severity for the spring of the year set in, and a corresponding amount of the inevitable croaking was an accompaniment. "The grass crop was gone, that was a certainty." Potatoes depend entirely on having sufficient moisture—"our 200 bushels of seed would almost have fed us," and so on. And how did it turn out? Why, just as it generally does. Some crops were unusually good, especially was this the case with corn and potatoes, while others were only moderate. The hay crop was considerably shortened, also the wheat except with a few favored individuals; but wheat has almost ceased to be a staple crop. That drought was succeeded by abundant rains—bountiful rains—almost inundating floods. Probably tons of the most fertile particles of our soil are carried off to feed the fishes. Yet judging from the unusually fine appearance so far of the wheat this spring, there must be a good deal left in the fields still.

As the question is even now being agitated, owing to the quantity of moisture in the ground, resulting from the abundance of fertilizing snows, whether it will be possible to get through with the necessary farm work, it is well for us to be reminded that it has often been *just so before*, only "more so." And that "while the earth endureth, seed time and harvest, and summer and winter, and day and night, shall not cease."

The farming interests of the neighborhood may thus be regarded as having been fully sustained. The Club, and its off-shoot, the Junior Club, which promises to surpass its parent in respect of activity and energy (as indeed it should: we are not jealous of our sons, the more they excel us the prouder we shall be), these institutions and the interest by which they are sustained serve as a gauge whereby to measure the condition of agriculture among us; because they measure the spirit, the life, out of which all real improvement must grow.

In this connection it is a pleasure to acknowledge the Horticultural Society as a very important adjunct to the two Clubs, chiefly because the ladies can join hands and add their direct influence to the great work of making mother earth do her best for us in every way. A second highly successful exhibition of vegetables, fruits and flowers held last fall, ought to be regarded as placing "the Horticultural" among the leading associations of the neighborhood. Is there room for another? Not if it would be compelled to arrogate the title of "Junior"!

Next to the agricultural interest, what comes second in Sandy Spring? Is it the mercantile? This is an interest of considerable magnitude both for buyers and sellers. The business done in this is also one of the gauges to estimate the material prosperity of a community; but being placed rather out of sight, certainly out of the reach of your historian, he is unable to report whether the year's transactions show advance or recession. The manufacturing interest represented in the sorghum mill was apparently prosperous, looking to the amount of sweets produced last fall; but here too I am unable to say whether the bulls or the bears have it.

The social, literary, and other higher interests remain to be looked into. But, first it is necessary to complete the history of one of the important enterprises of the neighborhood, which has been referred to in each previous chapter of our history, and which, it is hoped, may hereafter be dismissed from its pages. The Sandy Spring Branch Turnpike was consolidated with the main stem, and our community thus relieved from its charge. This transfer was attended with a circumstance which at first produced some excitement. One fine morning last summer the peaceful travellers along the road were startled by the apparition of a *toll-gate at Ashton.* It was no shadowy ghost, but a substantial reality, one of the sort which people rarely like to face, that is at first, and until they become accustomed to it. The original managers of our branch road had not achieved a great deal of popularity; they were frequently blamed for being too slow and inefficient: now the complaining parties, viewing this unexpected obstruction, were waked up to find king Stork worse than king Log. However, our people are always willing to pay for any real improvement; and if the road continues to receive the attention which the manager of the main stem has so far given it, there is no doubt we shall soon come to look even upon a toll-gate as one of the ornaments of the neighborhood.

The presence of some railroad engineers in the early part of the winter, and their promise to continue the survey in this vicinity, produced for a time a pleasing excitement. The immediate prospect of getting a railroad seems to be moderately fair. It has been pronounced on high authority "only a question of time" (!) I should like very much to know whether Chapter V, VI, or a still later one of this history, will chronicle the first arrival of the steam-horse over our classic ways; now, alas! one deep gulf of mud.

During the past year, our Lyceum Hall has been improved and ornamented by the addition of a fine commodious porch; which is nearly or quite paid for. This great external improvement would be glory enough for one year, even if there were a slight falling off in the arrangements for affording entertainment and instruction within the hall. The season and the roads have been very unfavorable; but it is believed there is no just ground for complaint in relation to the uses made of this important building. An extraordinary course of readings for the benefit of the library had decided success last summer. It was followed by a more artistic display from a distinguished Professor of elocution, meeting with an admiring and generous support; which showed the appreciative character of the people, as well as their readiness "to go off" into the heroic vein.

The literary society continued its regular meetings. Some indications of a lack of interest gave rise to a fear that the society might be dying out, but at a subsequent meeting the interest flamed up again. It may be considered in a less flourishing condition than at some former periods of its history; but there is no reason for despairing of its life. Perhaps there needs an infusion of fresh blood, perhaps it wants cooking over in some particulars; the meat, the *stuff* is here. A lively impression of the void which would be left by the extinction of these pleasant reunions ought to be sufficient to renovate and preserve them in vigorous health and unfading lustre.

A new Debating Society must be numbered among the improving institutions of the season. It is thought to awaken an interest for argumentative discussion.

A projected undertaking which was not carried into execution, promised at one time to add a very important institution to the number of those which have stirred up our neighborhood. This was nothing less than the scheme of establishing a newspaper. Many favoring opinions and good wishes were expressed for the success of the enterprise; but after due deliberation it was prudently abandoned.

The schools have been for the most part flourishing. In last year's historical sketch, the hope was held out that "the swelling tide of public instruction" might rise sufficiently high to reach the shores of "the Athens of Montgomery County," as some persons have dared to call it. The success of the Sandy Spring School the present year seems to justify that prediction; its numbers, no longer to be contained within former limits, flowed out into a wing attached to the building.

The colored school continues to deserve all that was said of it last year. That people with their prosperous school, their fine new church and certain other prospective privileges, are surely trying for "the third story of Noah's Ark," to use an expression of one of their preachers. The voice of this community is, I am sure, "let 'em up" as high as they have capacity to climb, by the aid of education, religion and eternal justice.

After the extraordinary performances of our young people, the last year, in the matrimonial line, as duly recorded in Chapter III, it is not surprising that one solemnization only of this most interesting event in the life of man should be all that we have to note in this place. Our record of marriages so far stands thus: Chapter I, one marriage; II, three marriages; III, six marriages; IV, one marriage.

Historians find it hard to keep wholly to the past without venturing even a glance to the future:

> "Heaven from all creatures hides the book of fate,
> All but the page prescribed, the present date."

Happy, happy for us that it is so! We know that the revolving wheel of time drops from its circumference each year one person after another, till all that once lived be gone. Who is to go, and who to stay a little longer? But of that we know nothing.

While every inducement that can operate on a sound mind and heart should make us value the friends who are left us a little longer, there is also a powerful motive to cherish the memory of those that have departed. To feel that the neighborhood dead are *ours!* Ours, by the remembrance of every kind act done by them; ours, by thought of every kindness which we might have shown toward them, yet did not; ours, by the hope to meet again.

In the record of deaths the present year we find two little children in one family, Caroline F. and Henry H. Moore, the former on the 13th of April, the latter the 11th of February. In the family of Edward Peirce, another little child, April 27th. The next record is of Mary Brooke, wife of Basil Brooke, on the 2d day of the 11th month, aged 91 years 4 months and 21 days. So far as my acquaintance with the annals of the neighborhood extends, this is the most advanced age to which any of its residents have attained. It would be to me a labor of love to collect some incidents of this long, blameless life. She was not a native of Sandy Spring, but had spent here full threescore years and ten, from the time of her marriage to the day of her death. Born five days before the battle of Bunker Hill, she was twelve years old when the constitution of our country was framed, and she lived through all its vicissitudes, through wars foreign and domestic, to see the assured grandeur of the nation emerge from its last crowning trial. An incident connected with her journey as a bride from Baltimore to her life's home at "Charley Forrest," is noticeable as showing the nature of our republican institutions. The driver of the hack which brought up the wedding party was grandfather of the man (now a prosperous banker of Baltimore) who recently married the niece of a former President of the United States, a lady who had presided as mistress at the White House during his administration, and, as an honored guest, graced the royal banquets of Queen Victoria. If the bride of 1865 leads as blameless a life, and acquires as many sincere friends and as few enemies as the bride of 1795, it cannot fail to be well with her at the last.

November 20th died Julia Miles. The limits of our neighborhood may well be slightly extended to include one who was so frequently a welcome and valued inmate of our homes. Her intelligence and refinement dignified the useful life she led, and won for her warm friends, who sympathized sincerely with her severe sufferings and lamented her early death. February 9th, William Stabler, in the 35th year of his age. Of the persons assembled in this hall at its last annual meeting, whose place seemed less likely to be vacant now than his? Always interested in the concerns of our Lyceum, having contributed his full share of efforts to prosper it from the beginning, it is here in an especial degree we note his loss. In all enterprises likely to promote the general welfare he was ready to do his part, while his industry, honesty, and solid sense distinguished him as one to be relied upon. The loss of such a man in the prime of life, apart from the deep sense of bereavement experienced in the circle immediately around him, is a greater blow to the fabric of a neighborhood's true prosperity than many inundating floods and destructive fires.

Before withdrawing our minds from the contemplation of the places left vacant by departed friends, and while our feelings are softened by the impressions aroused through their memories, it seems a good opportunity for examining whether we have individually anything to *do* that might tend to make our neighborhood the better for our having lived in it, or at least that might preserve it from being any the worse on that account. The appointed work of some is with the hands; of some, with the pen; of others, with the tongue; of all, more or less, with the example of their lives. Perhaps the influence most affecting the *harmony* of the neighborhood (the most important of all) is that which is exerted by the *tongue*. May he who, in future, like the mysterious author of the "Address to a Skeleton in the British Museum," shall undertake to apostrophize ours, may he, unblamed, adopt these impressive lines:

> "Here, in this silent cavern, hung
> The ready, swift and tuneful tongue:
> If falsehood's honey it disdained,
> And, where it could not praise, was chained;
> If bold in virtue's cause it spoke,
> Yet gentle concord never broke,
> That tuneful tongue shall plead for thee
> When death unveils Eternity."

The historian of the decline and fall of nations ever finds himself obliged to trace those melancholy results to the formation of *parties* within the State bitterly hostile to each other. Within the smaller sphere of a neighborhood, there is no question that the tendency to form *cliques* and *parties* is one of the symptoms of decline most to be guarded against. Have ye none of it!

In this historic year eight additions have been made to our neighborhood by the coming amongst us of the "Norwood" family.

Another annual record will complete the 5th year of these annals. It may then be found interesting to concentrate the statistics of births, deaths, and marriages of Sandy Spring, in a more regular form. Thus far emigration and immigration seem to count for nothing.

CHAPTER V.

From 4th Month, 1867, to Fourth Month, 1868.

A changed neighborhood — A fair month following a discouraging one — Profits from the potato — New Road System — The Railroad not progressive — Subdivision of a large farm — Teachers' Association —The New School System — Associations healthful, especially the Ladies' — Literary affairs less promising, perhaps "a little overdone" — Activity of mind kept up — The Post Office mails in 6 months, 10,141 letters — A Savings Institution organized — First Day Readings — Relief to the Southern Section — 4 Marriages, 1 Death — Five years' Statistics.

At its meeting in last month, the Farmers Club of Sandy Spring celebrated its 24th anniversary. Looking back over the long period that had elapsed since its origin, the early members were naturally led to recall the agricultural condition of the neighborhood at that time. The attempt to picture it was not a very easy one; so great is the change which has been effected. If we conceive two photographs taken in the growing season, from a point in space above,—the one representing the condition twenty-four years ago, the other as it is at present, there might be some difficulty in recognizing their identity: the new buildings, and the altered appearance of vegetation, would create the impression of a different country.

Facts of this nature form an important part of the history of a rural community; yet by no means the most important part. They are the result, the outgrowth of causes originating in the character of the people and the circumstances of the times. Manners and customs, feelings, opinions and institutions, change as much as outward facts; and the former have much the greater influence on the happiness of the people, and the present and future condition of the neighborhood in which their lot is cast.

It is natural then to ask, how a life-picture of our community taken some years ago would show by the side of one taken now. In the case of external, material improvements, the changes were so gradual as scarcely to be perceptible from year to year, yet leading to a condition more and more widely different.

Of a nature still more imperceptible, and much less easy to delineate, but assuredly not less actual, are the changes which slowly creep on in the character and institutions of a community; and these, according as they are conformable or non-conformable to the line of progress marked out by the higher powers, will elevate to still greater perfection, or bring down to certain ultimate failure and ruin. In view of this effect, which it requires a considerable period of time to render broadly visible, it would not be difficult for your historian, if permitted to draw material from the whole period of his acquaintance with the events and people of the neighborhood, to show you many an occurrence of thrilling interest. But that is not the purpose of this history, which is confined in each chapter to the incidents of twelve calendar months. It must consider one year at a time. Let us see now what we can make of the last.

It is stated in the preceding chapter, written just a year ago, that the roads were then "one deep gulf of mud," and the question was being agitated, "owing to the quantity of moisture in the ground, whether it is possible to get through in season with the necessary farm work?" Now it is well to commence this record with a reminder of the character of the season which immediately followed. The whole month of April, then just begun, proved to be lovely. Perhaps a more favorable month for farm-work never was. The thermometer did not descend once so low as the freezing point, while fair weather filled the entire month, or nearly so. In making this reference to the weather I am rather encroaching on the province of your meteorologist, who will doubtless favor us with a full report; yet it seemed well, in a moral point of view, to recall a lesson for the benefit of the discontented brethren, which we shall all doubtless remember until the next time the wet or the dry weather shall continue to bother us a little longer than we would desire.

The season continued to be good for the chief farming crops. Rain was perhaps rather in excess, but its injurious influence was less marked than was anticipated. Probably no single production reached the amount per acre occasionally secured in former years. The high prices, however, ought to make up for any deficiencies, so that the profits of the farmer for the past year leave him little to complain of and much to be thankful for. Especially is this the case with the potato-raisers, some of whom realized what would in old times have been considered a small fortune. One of the members of the Junior Club reports an aggregate yield from their club alone of 10,000 bushels of this most valuable of roots, which is becoming one among the two or three most valuable staples of our neighborhood farms.

There has been no lack of energy apparent in the improvements going on in farm-implements, buildings or modes of tillage. The important subject of roads has received the attention it deserves, and the efforts made to procure a better system from the legislature have met with more than usual success. They need to be well followed, as no system will work of itself. Less successful, so far, have been the attempts to get up a railroad. Some new hopes are awakened, but as they are not founded on the absolute certainty which history requires, the subject must be ruled out of this chapter. Before leaving the account of material improvements, at least of considerable changes in such affairs, it is necessary to refer to the sale of a large tract of land near the centre of the neighborhood, and the parcelling of it out into small lots. This circumstance goes to secure the almost certainty that a considerable part of our lands is destined to be cut up into small holdings, owned by the specially operative class. There has been much dispute among political economists who have deigned to discuss the subject, whether this system is conducive to the welfare of an agricultural community. In the course of time we shall doubtless have the opportunity to illustrate the proposition in one way or the other.

Now ascend we from the physical and material department to the intellectual. Such evidences as there may be of progress in this respect, your historian will find his highest gratification in diligently collecting and setting forth.

In the first place may be mentioned the new event of the "Teachers' Association" of Montgomery County, held in this building last summer. Unfortunately the busy season prevented the attendance of many who might have profited by the interesting exercises. The members, of whom many attended from a distance, all testified to the kindness and hospitality with which they were received. Invitations were cordially extended to repeat the visit at a more convenient season of the year. Although, in the opinion of your historian, the State is threatened with serious injury and loss by the change recently made in its public school system, there appears to be no reason why our own neighborhood should suffer. Our citizens have only to take proper advantage of the District-Trustee feature of the new law in order to keep the management of their public school in their own hands. In the meantime the private boarding schools, taking both together in view, may be regarded as decidedly flourishing. And so that essential element of a people's progress, "the School," an element by which Sandy Spring has been distinguished for a full half century, is still preserved to us.

The other improving institutions known as the "Farmers' Club," the "Club Junior," the "Ladies' Association for Mutual Improvement," the "Horticultural Society," were successfully carried on, each in its season, and with its purposes fully provided for. So well has the Ladies' Association fulfilled its mission, gaining honor and interest not only by the subjects which it *selects*, but also by *those* which it *avoids*, that a serious effort is being made (as I am told) to organize another similar one. It has our best wishes, accompanied with the caution that, in choosing a name, there may be no attempt to distinguish the two Associations by any invidious epithet referring to such unimportant matters as a difference of age.

The subject of intellectual progress during the year may now be considered as pretty well exhausted. In former pages of this book, it is true, there were other agencies for mental improvement mentioned; as Lectures, Reading Circles, and such. Perhaps the less that is said on these neglected affairs, the higher will be the degree of our self-satisfaction.

It is only fair to our worthy President to refrain from dwelling upon these omissions, because he is doubtless able to give excellent reasons for practically discontinuing the Lyceum Lectures during the past season. The Literary Society has had its difficulties too; but the design of sustaining it as a settled institution of the neighborhood is by no means abandoned. Vigorous are the attempts which have been made to keep life in its body; and a few weeks will show whether it has only been in a state of suspended animation, or whether those attempts must prove it no better than a galvanized corpse.

We are compelled to own that the experience of the past year indicates a somewhat critical condition for the boasted literary character of Sandy Spring. In the natural course of events we have apparently approached a crisis. The first enthusiasm for the Lyceum has passed away, the charm of novelty being gone. It has now reached the point when it has to contend with that lukewarmness apt to accompany such enterprises as bring no excitement to the senses and no profit to the purse. It has also to meet the depressing influences from the discouraging prophecies of those who declared at the beginning that "they knew how it would be; that it might flourish while it was a new thing, and then would be sure to go the way of such undertakings in other places." Now it may be that the multitude of *societies* amongst us has served to withdraw interest from the Lyceum. It may be, as several of our solid men thought, that "this sort of thing is a little overdone"; causing the just claims of business and industry to be neglected in consequence of too great devotion to literary and social entertainments. However these things be, it is certain that a crisis is upon us; we have to decide a question whose importance cannot easily be overestimated. It is a proposition which I think can be demonstrated: whatsoever other circumstances may have produced an influence in shaping the condition of this neighborhood, *its distinguishing characteristic*,—that which has mainly made it what it has been, and what it is coming to be, *is the mental activity* of the people. I do not claim for them larger *minds* than those possessed by other residents of our State, nor a better or more thorough education; but I do claim, as an unquestionable faculty, a wondrous *activity* of mind. It will be a great mistake then (to use the mildest term) for us to give up such a powerful stimulus to that activity as this Lyceum, with all its appurtenances, affords. I do not believe you will do it. Where men feel a real want they are very apt to appropriate means of supply. But it may be well to remember that it is much easier to keep the flame alive than to restore to life when once suffered to die. An instance of the sort of activity just referred to is exhibited in the following "item" forwarded to me by a member of the committee appointed by my request, at your last Annual Meeting, to assist the Historian by furnishing him with some of their notes of neighborhood transactions. "There were mailed in the last six months from this Sandy Spring Post Office, ten thousand one hundred and forty-one letters." Twenty thousand letters sent from our neighborhood office in one year! I find by inspecting the returns of the British Post Office that about twenty letters for each individual passed through the mails of that country in one year, according to the latest report within my reach; which return apparently includes the letters that pass both ways. The number shown by our office exceeds greatly the English average. This little item (so good and appropriate that we have only to regret there are not more of the same sort from the same source) affords strong statistical evidence much to be relied on in an exhibition of the intellectual life of a people.

Another evidence of life has been recently shown in the effort, zealously and successfully made, to organize and establish a Savings Institution. The general animating interest taken in this enterprise, and the success of its preliminary proceeding, may be set down as the crowning event of the historical year. It will be for future annals to record the full establishment and growing strength of an institution which, we think, is bound to succeed.

In a sketch exhibiting our agricultural, social, literary and business transactions, there should be room made for all subjects of general interest. The higher and purer the motives that lead to any undertaking, the worthier is it of enduring record. In this class of events it is proper to notice the commencement, last summer, of a course of readings in the Lyceum on First day morning. They appeared to be generally well attended throughout, and would perhaps have been more so if held a little later in the morning. In the same class may be mentioned the meeting held in second month last for the revision of the Discipline; wherein the members generally were invited, in accordance with a just interpretation of the requirements of the spirit of the age, to partake in the deliberations of the assembly. Another step forward. On the same high level with these two last events I placed the liberal and unselfish subscription made for "Southern Relief," which was started at the close of a Lyceum lecture, going up with very little effort to the sum of $107. If a man can say truly, "What I kept I lost—what I left behind me is not mine—what I gave away alone remains with me,"—a community may repeat the sentiment with added emphasis.

I now come to the most pleasurable part of my office, in which the degree of satisfaction is proportional to the extent of the record. On this principle the pleasure now is fourfold the amount last year. Four marriages are to be entered here.

Our neighborhood, in common with a large adjacent country, has had abundant cause of thankfulness for the general good health that has prevailed throughout the past year. It has been much the healthiest season since this record commenced. Within the somewhat indefinite circle that comprises our neighborhood I note but one death during the year, but that was of the sort that leaves a wide blank.

Died on the morning of March 15th, Roger Brooke, in the 58th year of his age. On the afternoon following, a large number of neighbors and friends collected at his funeral. A more than usual feeling of solemnity pervaded the assemblage; and many a kind expression evinced the sincere regard felt for one whose warm friendship had been widely shared. His nearest neighbors had the most to say in his praise. One, not a very near neighbor, who had known him from boyhood, was deeply moved in recalling his peculiar manly and honorable traits of character, and loving to dwell on one pleasant incident that had left a deep impression on his memory. It was just thirty years ago, being the spring of 1838, since the writer of this article commenced farming operations where he now resides. The situation was not promising, in fact "it was hard lines" with him. To make it worse, the spring was unusually wet and cold. The month of May was more than half over, and the field designed for corn, on which so much depended, was not half plowed. One morning as "he drove his team afield," not very "jocund" indeed, his poor little team and little old plow—just as the sun was rising—what was his surprise to see the decayed fence taken down at the farther corner, and—enter three fine horses with a big plow and strong, skilful driver; and without so much as saying "by your leave," begin to tear up the ground in a way—well, a way that has done me good ever since. It was Roger's team.

And as I recall the impression which that incident produced at the time, remaining there ever since, it seemed worthy of record here; not merely as a tribute to the departed, but as suggesting that no one perhaps can perform a better act than by lending a little help *just* at the *right time* to a young man struggling under difficulties to make a start in life.

Five years having elapsed since this record was begun, I now sum up, as promised heretofore, the scattered statistics of marriages, births and deaths during the several years of the period; relating to a population, as nearly as I can estimate, approximating three hundred:

For the year from	Marriages.	Births.	Deaths.
1863-4-2 to 4-4-1864	1	10	5
1864-4-4 to 4-3-1865	3	8	9
1865-4-3 to 4-2-1866	6	7	7
1866-4-2 to 4-1-1867	1	8	6
1867-4-1 to 4-6-1868	4	8	1
Total in five years,	15	41	28

An agreeable addition was made to our numbers this last year, by immigration. Two new families have come to reside among us, a rather infrequent but welcome event.

CHAPTER VI.

FROM FOURTH MONTH, 1868, TO FOURTH MONTH, 1869.

What is a neighborhood?—Difficult weather—Disappointment in price—Fruit a failure, also ice—First complaints of poultry—First attempt at a census of the neighborhood—Two large fires and one disastrous flood—Progress of "Savings Institution," and first Directors—More of railroads—Tower of Coast Survey—Porch at Meeting House—Political contest—Science in the Lyceum—Introduction of the piano—Amusements—"Spare the birds!"—"Hard times.".

Before resuming our historical sketch, it seems proper now at the commencement of a second period of five years, the second Lustrum, as the old Romans called it, to make some inquiry into the nature and intent of this sort of record, with a view to satisfaction upon the question whether it is a *real thing*, and not a mere fanciful speculation. Is there such a *fixed fact*, such a real *entity* as a *neighborhood*, possessing such actual existence as might entitle it to be portrayed in a history? Let us endeavor to briefly clear up this subject. It will not be disputed that there is a very general understanding as to what is meant by the claim of country. The events of the past few years have dispelled all confusion of ideas in regard to that matter. We have been taught by stern lessons that we have a country, to which much is due. We have known what it was to sympathize with its distresses, to suffer keen apprehensions in its time of danger, and to feel our own relief at its escape. We have learned to be proud of its good faith, to rejoice in its prosperity, and to mourn over its illustrious dead. To feel, in short, that we are part and parcel of it; that if we were disposed to leave it, it won't let us go.

Now there is a somewhat similar feeling, which may and of right ought to exist in regard to our own neighborhood, the social circle wherein all our immediate interests are closely bound. A natural, healthy and beneficial feeling leads us to take a lively interest in all that concerns its welfare, to be anxious for its improvement, jealous for its reputation, sorrowful for its shortcomings. Perhaps this sentiment is most strongly felt when we are absent for a time. Let any one who has spent a week at the seashore, or in any place where men do congregate, call to mind his emotions when by chance his own neighborhood is mentioned; how lively the interest excited by remarks made upon it; how pleasant to hear favorable comments, how vexatious any sarcastic remark. Under such circumstances we take up for our neighborhood, as if it were our own fireside. Does not this fact show that there *is* such an *entity*, an actual existing thing as a neighborhood? Of course it does. Again, there is another band that draws us still nearer together,—the enclosures of yonder graveyard. We are united into one community by our dead as well as by our living. Who does not feel the force of the hallowed tie? The dead of the past five years are a sad reality; an important, inexorable fact, from which there is no escape. I look over their names set down in the pages of this little book, and think how much we have lost by their removal from the active life of the neighborhood. Names recalling so much of excellence, of promise, of solid worth, that it is not too much to say our whole community would have stood higher at this day if these had been spared to live and labor.

I think then we may justly claim that we place before our minds a reality in the idea brought up by the words "Sandy Spring"; it thus unquestionably possesses a claim to form history. Looking back with varied emotions of pain and pleasure on the past, gathering strength and wisdom from the retrospect, but fixing our eyes and hearts and hopes upon the future, with the steady purpose to sustain the character of our neighborhood, and to raise it to still higher degrees of excellence, let us now give our attention to the special events of the past year.

The weather being a matter of so much importance to an agricultural community, and really interesting to everybody, I am compelled to encroach so far upon the province of your meteorologist as to remark that the spring of last year was a difficult season for farming operations. The frequent rains delayed the sowing of oats so late that it was in poor condition to meet the drought of the last of June and first of July. The result was a crop short in quantity and far worse in quality. The weight per bushel averaged about twenty pounds; not quite so bad as in a recent season, when it scarcely reached above fifteen. The corn planting was also generally delayed to a late period in May, but the season proved more favorable in the end, giving us a full crop of that most important of all agricultural products. Potatoes yielded on the whole a very fair return, both in quality and quantity; but in respect of that other valuable consideration, *price* in the market, there was serious disappointment. It must be confessed that the disappointment was much aggravated, if not, indeed, altogether caused by the high prices of the few latter years, creating anticipations which were not realized. Our enterprising young farmers, as I am informed, are not all discouraged about potatoes, but intend to put in the usual crop this spring.

There was no cause to complain of the wheat crop, in any respect. Hay was abundant, and the price as good as could be expected with such a full crop. The great failure of the year was in fruit. Apples and peaches, the two far exceeding all others in value and excellence, were nearer being a total failure, it is considered, than has ever been the case with us before.

Amongst the failures in important crops of the year just closing, I am compelled to enumerate the ice crop. I know it would have been kind to pass over this deficiency in silence; especially as it might be thought to suggest invidious comparisons. But an impartial historian has no right to indulge any feelings of that sort, nor to slur over an incident of practical importance for the sake of shielding improvident confidence, putting off to January what ought to be done in December. The report of the meteorologist will doubtless show that the average temperature of the first winter month was favorable to procuring ice. On the whole then we find slight reason to complain of the bounty of nature during the past year. With one comparatively unimportant exception, in the case of poultry, there has been a general exemption from disease with man and beast. Some families did appear to have more than their share of affliction; but *not a single death* has taken place amongst the persons included in our special neighborhood.

In order that we might obtain a definite idea of the extent of the circle referred to as comprising the neighborhood of Sandy Spring, I have, with the assistance of a colleague and the suggestions of some other friends, made out a list of families, being a census of the persons who are concerned. Of course it was difficult in some cases to draw the separating line, but our return may be regarded for practical purposes sufficiently correct. The list hereto annexed shows 328 individuals in 66 families.

In this circle there were during the first four years 27 deaths; in the last two years one death only: this seems to be a very remarkable circumstance.

The number of births reported for the present year is seven. Number of marriages, one.

Among the unfortunate contingencies of the year must be noted the unusual circumstance of two destructive fires: the house of Samuel Ellicott, and the barn of Dr. F. Thomas. Also a disastrous flood on the 24th of July, which washed away Thomas Lea's mill. All these losses are already repaired or very nearly so.

The organization of the "Savings Institution of Sandy Spring" was mentioned in the last chapter of this history, with sanguine expectations of its success. These hopes have been thus far fully realized, and indeed exceeded by the actual results. The Institution was opened on the 13th of April, 1868; on the first day of the following March the returns show that in the first ten and a-half months there had been paid in $9545, on which the interest accrued was $240; withdrawn $2665, leaving $7120 on deposit. The considerable number of depositors, 183, shows the extent to which the benefits of the Institution have already reached, and gives reasonable grounds for the hope that its future influence will be widely felt. This success places the new institution in the front rank of our beneficial associations, and entitles its projectors to lasting remembrance.

In each successive chapter of the present record some mention has been made of the railroad, which has been a lively subject of interest and expectation for many years. At length our hopes seem to touch solid ground. The whistle of the locomotive has not yet reached our ears, except from the dim distance of the Laurel Road, but some decided preliminary measures have been taken. On the 15th of June, the engineers so long looked for came to the Manor and commenced operations. They went on to make the necessary surveys, and had fixed definitely upon the line when they were called away. The delays since that period served to confirm the doubts of the skeptical and to temper the ardor of the sanguine; but the latter class having made up their minds for many years that "the railroad was only a question of time," can never be driven from that stand; and the very latest advices confirm the faith of such that the *time* has indeed come, and the coming summer will make it clear to all.

In connection with public proceedings the tower created by the Coast Survey officers must not be forgotten. The constant view of this object ought to inspire a scientific interest, especially when the gentlemen operating from its summit shall have arrived; while the sight from thence is well calculated to widen and correct our knowledge of local points in our neighborhood, as well as to cultivate a taste for natural scenery.

The porch erected at the meeting house is an improvement well deserving of mention; and along with it the whitewashing of the interior, after using it for 51 years without a brush being put on the walls.

Our people took a lively interest in the political contest of last fall. They formed an active club that held its meetings in this building, at which a large amount of speaking, and, on one or two occasions, of real eloquence, was poured forth on the altar of patriotism. They also erected a lofty and handsome pole, unfurling at its top at sundry times a flag, to tell the passers-by where they were to be found politically.

This use of the Lyceum Building was by no means the only way in which it was occupied. After a season of unusual dearth in literary affairs, a course of lectures was revived, commencing with readings and recitations, and sustained by an audience large enough to prove that our people have not lost their interest in intellectual improvement. Their appreciation of the last lecture by Prof. Schaffer, which was highly flavored with real science, affords a gratifying proof of their love of knowledge.

Another course of lectures, on history, which the young persons of the neighborhood have lately started, is receiving more favorable support than was anticipated by the lecturer.

The clubs have been going on in the usual pleasant way. It has appeared to me, perhaps owing to better opportunity of observing, that "the Ladies' Association for Mutual Improvement" has taken on a more vigorous life than ever, as the spirit of the age seems to demand. Its career has been a uniform success. And whether it shall find in the future some more active part to take, or shall continue satisfied with its present quiet sphere of influence, it is certain that entire confidence may be reposed in its perfect discretion.

We cannot but indulge a reasonable expectation that the Junior Farmers Club will attain to some useful results hitherto undiscovered; while the Senior institution may always find enough new subjects to keep up the fresh interest of their meetings.

The social life of the neighborhood has lost none of the agreeable features for which it has always been noted; even though the winter entertainment, in consequence of the total privation of sleighing amusement, has missed a portion of its usual excitement.

An entirely new interest has been added in several families by the introduction of the piano into society. Other amusements have been scarce; the attempt so vigorously made among the boys to get up the base ball game having come to an abrupt termination. Many wise people begin to discover that amusements of an innocent kind are essential to a perfectly healthy development of the youthful mind and body; and it is not unlikely that this natural demand should require some judicious means of supply among us. In the meantime it is not difficult to point to one injudicious sort of amusement, happily not indulged to much extent by those belonging to our immediate circle. When alluding on a former page to the deplorable failure of the fruit crop in the past year, I should have remarked upon a phenomenon that accompanied it, namely, the extreme scarcity of the birds. No accidental coincidence was this. It is universally agreed that insects are the chief enemies of fruit, and that birds are the appointed agents to keep the insect world within proper bounds. It "goes without telling" that our ingenious youth can work out the calculation thus—"I spare that robin—the robin will eat many thousand insects this spring—many apples, peaches, plums, &c., escape deadly injury." It was to be expected that the colored people, so long denied the use of guns, would manifest a disposition to abuse the privileges suddenly granted to them, and I verily believe this is one cause of the recent diminution in the number of the feathered tribe, "enlivening companions of the spring." It is to be hoped that along with their other new acquirements our colored folks will learn so much natural history as will acquaint them with the use and purpose of birds.

Our neighborhood has continued to afford during the year past, ample facilities for the best sort of female education. But for "those not termed girls," there seems to be still a great want only partially supplied. Six youths have been sent away to distant places for the instruction that ought to be provided in some way nearer home.

The subject of least satisfaction to our pride has been left for the last. During the forty years that I have been conversant with the condition of our dear old Sandy Spring, there has never been so much said about "hard times" as in the past year. What is the real meaning of it? The essential comforts of life appear to abound; nobody has been sold out or sent to jail. Merchants are busy; mechanics still have employment, farmers have ample occupation for their own industry and that of the laboring class; but there is—*pressure.* The true nature of this state of things is well worthy of inquiry. Having bestowed considerable reflection upon this subject, and made some calculations in regard to it, I will briefly state the conclusions which have been arrived at.

In order to see how far those persons are correct who trace the difficulties to the heavy drain on our resources required for national expenses, let us look at the figures. The people of our neighborhood as now defined, constitute nearly one one-hundred-thousandth part of the whole population. If we regard ourselves, as I think we may, as forming a fair average between the luxurious livers of the cities and the plain men of the rural districts, we are thus mulcted, directly and indirectly, in the round sum of $3000 annually. This is an average tax of about forty-five dollars to each family; rather heavy certainly, but not enough to break any one down, unless as "the straw that breaks the camel's back." The load must be up to the breaking point before; and that is where the difficulty lies. For several years in recent times, the receipts of our people were considerably greater than they had been previously. By a very natural law, expenses went up in a similar ratio. This was very satisfactory, easy and pleasant. But when potatoes, hay, &c., falling in price or quantity, or both, brought down one side of the balance-sheet, it was not so satisfactory to bring down the other side in the same proportion. Now the accurate adjustment of expenses to receipts is the great financial business of life. It is something that *has* to be done either voluntarily or involuntarily. The wise man does it voluntarily and in advance. In order that this may be accomplished, the practice of keeping accounts, in some simple, correct mode, should be learned by farmers, who as a class greatly need the instruction.

If the inquiry were made of our merchants in regard to the aggregate amount of sales during the past year, as compared with preceding years, it would be found, I am told, that there has been no diminution in that respect, though perhaps rather more delay in collections. Which shows that expenses have not been reduced. Now it is evident, that to make the balance-sheet right it is necessary either to diminish expenses, or to increase receipts—one, or both.

It is well to bear in mind, as the final lesson of the day, that the method of increasing production is much preferable to the other plan. A large, liberal, judicious expenditure (taking due care of the other end of the purse) is the proper accompaniment of national and domestic prosperity.

CHAPTER VII.

From Fourth Month, 1869, to Fourth Month, 4th, 1870.

Descriptions of Sandy Spring by William Darby, Moncure D. Conway, and A. G. Riddle, Esq.—"*Noblesse oblige*"—A dull year—Disappointments about the railroad—Ashton Turnpike—Wheat, oats and corn fairly good, despite the rainless months—Low prices cause reduction of seed—Hay comes to the rescue—On the whole, "a thankful year"—The 16 year interval—The Societies flourish, and a new one, "The Sociable"—"Supper left out"—Lectures by B. Hallowell, A. G. Riddle, T. C. Taylor and Mr. Coleman—The girls ahead of the boys in respect of education—Yet the report is of marriages, None!—Other statistics interesting.

We begin this year's review of neighborhood events by taking a glance at the past. Your historian holds strongly the opinion which he has heretofore frequently expressed, that it is impossible to attain to a right comprehension of the present actual condition of a country, neighborhood, or individual, without referring to the situation in former years and tracing the successive steps of progress. An account has been given in the first part of this book of the early history of Sandy Spring neighborhood, and a sketch of its early experiences. At the present time your attention is invited to three several striking views taken of us at intervals of about twenty years. They are drawn by the hands of three individuals who are perhaps the most remarkable for intellectual endowments of all the visitors or transient dwellers among us, that have been known by me, being men of unique and decided genius.

Nearly forty years ago, William Darby wrote and published in one of the popular magazines of the period a sketch of the neighborhood, as it appeared to him; from which are extracted the following lines:

"Sandy Spring is one of those nooks from which we can see the stir of the great Babel, and not feel the crowd. In all my wanderings over this world of care, and those wanderings were brief neither in time nor space, I have seen no spot where, if my choice was under my own control, I could so willingly spend the evening of my days. The hand that traces these rude lines has been embrowned in the wilds of the West and under the burning sun of Arkansas, Florida and Louisiana; it has been benumbed in the snows of Canada. Under every sky I have visited I have found warm, sincere and noble hearts; but such were in most instances single flowers that bloom alone. In the society of Sandy Spring we find a whole garden. It is a society where useful employment is honor, and where mental improvement goes hand in hand with toil; where no door is shut upon the traveller," &c.

From this delineation drawn by "a diamond in the rough," we pass twenty years onward to a period when there came among us a young man, whose name has since become widely and creditably known, both in this country and in England. In age, in circumstances, education and character, Moncure D. Conway is exceedingly unlike the writer just quoted; yet observe how similar the strain in which he speaks. Writing from London, where he was enjoying familiar social intercourse with Carlyle, Tennyson, Browning, Newman, and other literary magnates, he says:

"My first tottering steps toward the kingdom of heaven were taken at Sandy Spring. And now that old neighborhood, and they who dwell there, have receded into (or gone ahead into) a golden age. Often in the twilight I revisit the old scenes and faces; and sometimes have a vision of myself in old age returning to that spot where I buckled on my armor for a long and weary war. * * * * Ah, how often have I longed for the old woodland walks, the dreams and glories of the days when every bush was a 'burning bush' there in Sandy Spring."

In a book published by Mr. Conway in England, which went through several editions during the war, he describes his first impressions on visiting the neighborhood. "It was quite different," he says, "from any I had ever seen. So beautiful and cheerful was this Quaker neighborhood, with its bright homes and fields filled with happy laborers, the only happy negroes I had anywhere known, that I always experienced an exhilaration in riding there; and have often gone several miles out of my way to go through it to my appointments. I could tell the very line on the ground where the ordinary Maryland ended and the Quaker region began. I found on further acquaintance that I was in a place where mental culture was general, where there was a good circulating library and excellent schools, and the interior life of Sandy Spring more attractive even than the exterior."

Another interval of nearly twenty years passed by, bringing us to very recent times, when an observer arrives in the neighborhood, who is altogether as different in profession, character and style of talents from the two men last named, as they from one another. During his stay in this vicinity, Hon. A. G. Riddle sent to an Ohio newspaper a communication from which the following descriptive remarks are extracted: "I am in the heart of an old-time community of Quakers, who occupy all these lovely slopes and valleys for miles around, with their fine farms and beautifully embowered residences. They are a rich, cultivated and serene, thoughtful, contemplative, cheerful and social people, with many really learned men among them. There are some sixty or seventy families who have occupied this section of Maryland for seventy or eighty years" (he should have said "for a century and a half"). "Eighty or ninety years ago they emancipated their slaves, who, with their descendants, live on small farms around. At Sandy Spring is their store, postoffice, Lyceum, school house, &c., and there too, under the grand old oaks in the margin of a deep wood, is their meeting house. The whole community, southern in type, but northern in political sentiments, is made up of cultivated and refined people. I have seen a good deal of them; and, on the whole, I think they manage to get about as much out of life and the world, in the way of quiet, cheerful happiness, as any people I have ever met."

However rose-colored these descriptions may appear to ourselves, they are unquestionably the sincere expression of sentiments of three truthful and gifted observers—outsiders too, and with no selfish interest whatever in this region of ours. The question now suggested to us is, what can we (who are stated above to have the talent of getting "so much out of life and the world"), how much can we get out of the foregoing portraitures? The poet says, and every wise person has *thought* the same:

"Oh, wad some power the giftie gi'e us
To see ourselves as ithers see us,
It wad frae mony a blunder free us,
And foolish notion!"

There is one notion removed by these descriptions of the past, which I have heard expressed by sensible, but misinformed observers, namely, that the fame of Sandy Spring is entirely of recent origin and due in large part to modern importations; which is not so. I might have gone back more than forty years to a considerably more remote period, and shown that already in those early days the neighborhood had a reputation extending into the adjoining States or provinces, both to the North and the South. Whether deserved or undeserved, the praise goeth back to ancient times; "the people are to the manner born."

It is to be remarked that all those flattering expressions are from outsiders. However graciously they may be received, I have never known the parties immediately concerned to make use of such expressions, except in the way of quotations, contributing to amusement. It is no fault of ours that people will talk so about us; neither is it likely to do us harm. Only weak-minded persons are hurt by this sort of encomiums, which are taken at their real value by the reflecting, who know themselves and their own imperfections better than others can know them. The approval of the judicious is a wholesome encouragement and stimulant, especially to the young. An ancient and animating motto, originating in the times of French chivalry,—"Noblesse oblige,"—admonishes us in that condensed phrase, that nobleness of origin creates an obligation to perform noble actions and live noble lives. If our young people will take this sentiment to heart, and buckle up earnestly to the work that devolves on them, so that some intelligent visitor to Sandy Spring, twenty, forty, sixty years hence shall be able to write and print such flattering descriptions of the neighborhood as those above transcribed, the local historian of the future will doubtless copy them with a satisfaction very similar to mine.

And now it becomes my duty to relate the incidents and the performances of the year. Such a neighborhood so highly spoken of ought to make decided progress every year of its existence. It may be the fault of the historian, but the achievements of the past year do not strike him as having been very exciting. On the contrary, it has been rather a dull year; and that is one reason why he has been induced to borrow some interest by recurring to the long past.

To those who have been for years yearning for a railroad, and who were quite recently excited by strong hopes of an early accomplishment of our desires, it has been a tantalizing year. The arrival of engineers to complete the survey and location of the Laurel Branch was anxiously expected from month to month; but they failed to come. Some relief was experienced in reading the proceedings of Congress, looking to a new line running from Washington City northward: a considerable degree of uncertainty still hangs over that prospect. To aggravate our disappointments, we have been favored within the last week with a long list, published in the principal newspaper of the State, of the various railroads contemplated in Maryland, but not making even the slightest allusion to a route through Sandy Spring. All this succession of disappointments would be enough to damp the ardor of the most sanguine, were it not for a deep-rooted conviction still held by some of the best-informed persons, that the railroad from Point of Rocks through Laurel is a necessity to the B. & O. R. R. and therefore must be made. To those determined believers there are not wanting unmistakable signs of that which is to come to pass: signs that will be visible to others erelong.

In the meantime, without waiting for the railroad, but wisely putting their own shoulders to the wheel, the residents of the eastern section of the neighborhood have made energetic and successful exertions to procure subscriptions for an important turnpike from Ashton to Washington City. The experience of this open winter has confirmed the opinion that roads made of dirt, however ridged and drained, cannot be relied on for the season when transportation is chiefly carried on by farmers. Stone roads are now the great desideratum. The benefit of those previously made in our section is universally acknowledged. In this reference to turnpikes, it is worth while to record the amount of tolls collected at the Ashton gate for the last twelve months, $328.81; in the previous year, $312, varying slightly from being twenty-seven dollars per month for the last three years.

The amount of agricultural produce in the neighborhood the past year may be considered a fair average, notwithstanding a severe drought that prevailed through the middle and latter part of the summer. The yield of wheat, as reported in the Farmers' Club, averaged twenty bushels per acre: probably the quantity sown was not so large as in some years. Oats yielded unusually well and its price made it a profitable crop; the amount sown was not large. The great staple, corn, came up much nearer to the average than was anticipated during the rainless months. Perhaps this favorable yield of a crop considered so dependent on a proper supply of moisture affords a more convincing evidence than any we have lately had of the increased productive capacity which our farms have attained. The other partial staple of the neighborhood, potatoes, also yielded well; not much complaint about the quantity, but a great deal about the price. The falling off in this respect will cause a reduction in the number of acres to be planted in the spring, to little more than one-third of the seed put in the ground the past two or three years.

With wheat and potatoes at half price, the income of our farmers has been seriously affected. One crop, however, came in to the rescue. Fortunately the hay crop was full in quantity, and fairly remunerating in price. Fruit was abundant, as it had not been for a number of years. On the whole one may say, looking fairly into the actual results of the past year, that, although we cannot call it a prosperous one, we may still find much to be thankful for. Especially for this: the farmer's life presents such a variety of resources that it is scarcely possible all should fail. And the most valuable conclusions we can gather from this fact is that we should avail ourselves of it, by increasing the variety of our productions as much as practicable.

There can be no harm in mentioning that the present writer has for several years been anticipating a drought for the year 1870; there being evidence of the remarkable fact that the four dryest seasons of the present century up to date were in 1806, 1822, 1838 and 1854, which show an interval of sixteen years. This would bring the period of regular drought round to the present year. Your historian gives notice that if the drought should not come, he will shelter his prediction under the fact that it came last summer, which was only one year too soon.

The boast of our neighborhood, referring entirely to the declaration of others concerning us, is, that "mental improvement goes hand in hand with toil." What are the triumphs of the year in a social and literary way?

The four settled institutions, clubs and associations, have all gone ahead in their usual interesting and improving course. That outgrowth of the Horticultural Society, the annual fair, held in the ninth month at Lyceum Hall, was highly successful at its last celebration, if we may judge from the opinions freely expressed by outsiders.

It would deserve a more detailed account than the historian can give, he not being present. Another literary association, which has taken the name of the "Sociable," was organized, and has held its first meeting. From the plan and arrangements adopted, there is reason to hope this young institution may be productive of practical advantage and improvement in several ways, if its members "stick." If they do it will be the more creditable to them, because they have left out the *supper*, which has heretofore been found an essential accompaniment of all our permanent associations.

The exercises proper to this building, and for which it was principally erected, have been rather less frequent than usual, yet not altogether neglected. Indeed, the lectures, though not very numerous, were, in respect of quality, quite up to par, if not above it. We had three during the year; one upon Cuba, by Hon. A. G. Riddle, one upon the Indians, by Benjamin Hallowell, and one upon the Yosemite Valley, by T. C. Taylor, which were not behind any of the previous addresses. The lecture upon Ocean Currents, by Mr. Coleman, is also well worthy of special mention. Our next favor in this line depends somewhat on

Mr. Riddle, whose leisure and convenience are questions which our secretary must solve. When the lecture comes we can all warrant its excellent quality.

The schools have well maintained their character. The school at Sandy Spring has been conducted with increased excellence under several professors, male and female. Still there is a want, sensibly felt, of a school for boys of higher grade, if they are to keep up with the girls. Somehow or other it has happened that for many years in the neighborhood, the fair sex have held the reputation of being *ahead* in this business of education, and have no doubt deserved it. Now the question comes in this connection, whether it is owing to this fact of feminine supremacy in culture, that I am obliged to make a record such as was never made before in the seven years which are covered by this narrative, namely, of marriages in the year, *none;* number of births, eight, pretty well distributed round the neighborhood, except in the central parts; number of deaths belonging properly to Sandy Spring, four.

The Savings Institution made better progress during its second year than was expected, even by its sanguine supporters.

	Present Year.	First Year.
Receipts in Bank,	$16,684.24	$9,545
Amount withdrawn,	6,873.82	2,665
Interest accrued,	771.51	240
On deposit,	16,115.75	7,120
No. of depositors,	266	183

Results which may be viewed as encouraging in several respects. Times cannot be so *very hard.*

Before taking final leave of the annals of '69–70, I will ask you to revive with me the recollection of the evening of the 18th January. A literary entertainment had been provided, consisting of readings, recitations, &c., some of them novel in their character. The hall was full to its greatest comfortable capacity, and the attention and interest of the audience were evidently sustained in a lively manner, to the close of the proceedings. The performances were in a general way highly satisfactory, giving assurance that our neighborhood need never want for entertainments of this sort, if only the necessary enterprise is used in getting them up.

But there was a gratification experienced on that occasion, while viewing the room and its occupants, beyond the amusement of the moment, in speculating upon the living material there collected together. Reflecting that the future of Sandy Spring is to be built up mainly of that material, your historian found great satisfaction in observing that it had never appeared to better advantage. The material is still sound at heart; and the building must rise higher and higher from year to year: whether the progress shall be fast or slow will depend entirely on the care taken to develop and employ the intelligence necessary to direct the mode of structure, to discover its proper place for each tie and brace and beam, to dress and shape them rightly, and to do all the work as under the eye of the Master Builder.

Note: Some additional statistics of interest have been prepared by inquiring friends, which, on being carefully verified, are considered worthy of a place in the record.

Number of men over 21 being without wives, 18; number of women over 21 being without husbands, 60; number of widows, 20; number of widowers, 2!

Does this last exhibit indicate (as has been savagely asserted) that the men take ten times as good care of their wives as the wives do of their husbands?

CHAPTER VIII.

FROM 4TH MONTH, 4TH, 1870, TO FOURTH MONTH, 3D, 1871.

Reasons for commencing the Lyceum year with the 4th month — Moralizing — Advance of the seasons — Of the 16 year prophecy — Census of Friends' Monthly Meeting, and of our agriculture — New buildings — On roads, the Norwood Branch — Silence about "Railroad" — "The Home Interests" — The Farmer's Club in reference to the moon — Oyster Shell Lime vs. Phosphates — County Agricultural Fair in place of the Horticultural — The Sociable takes up the subject of amusements — Society and late hours — The "Marriage gale" — Fears for the Lyceum — Visit of Caroline Talbott.

I ask you to join with me in self-congratulation upon the circumstance of our having accidentally fixed this special period as the commencement of our Lyceum year. It is very near about the time which was used by our forefathers for centuries as the beginning of the civil year; and, although some pestilent reformers, just one hundred and twenty years ago, changed the old arrangements, making New Year's Day come near about midwinter (on the same perverse principle by which the *day* begins in the *middle* of the *night*), still it is undeniable that nature has selected this particular period in average seasons for beginning her year. It has also been found in most other neighborhoods with which I am acquainted, to be the best season for business arrangements connected with passing from one year into the next. In the northern counties of this State, and in some of the adjacent States, the first of April, as I am told, is the people's moving day, renting day, hiring day, and general settlement day. It is considered for various good reasons a more *convenient* period than midwinter; and the festive season of Christmas is not *clouded* by thoughts of having to provide the next week for certain pecuniary arrangements which the farmer has not yet had time to meet. My purpose now in bringing these considerations forward is merely to demonstrate that we happened to fall upon the true and natural period for commencing our historical year, with the special purpose of taking a simple, sensible, serious review of the one just closed. It is surely the part of wisdom to do so. I know it has been said "Let the dead past bury its dead!" Very good. We bury the past as we last week buried the seeds of grass, grain and garden, to come up again. "There's the rub," and the good of it: they won't *stay* buried; they will come up. Besides, we know well that if we want clover and oats and sweet corn, we must not scatter garlic and daisy and chickweed.

"Sown in darkness, or sown in light,
Sown in weakness, or sown in might,
Sown in meekness, or sown in wrath,
In the broad world-field or the shadowy path,
Sure will the *harvest* be!"

Your historian is not accustomed to be so *poetical* and moralistic at the commencement of his review. Forgive him! The extraordinary fervor must surely be suggested by the extraordinary progress and early luxuriance of the present season. We have had in many respects an extraordinary year. The most marked feature was an unusual regularity in the advance of the successive seasons. Last spring was not an early one; but when it did fairly commence, it went on with scarcely any of those backsets so common in our climate. No "winter lingering in the lap of May" last year. The summer,—well, the summer went on regularly too, until it attained a high steady temperature, which was of such intensity as probably not to have passed altogether out of your recollection. Then came the autumn, one of the most beautiful that any of us has known: its calm lovely days by no means "the saddest of the year," followed one another in a remarkable succession of gradually reduced temperature overlapping far into December, and putting off the actual advent of winter until all might be supposed ready for his coming. Fresh roses in bloom were plucked from the gardens late into December. At length, winter came just as we like to see it, "short, sharp and decisive"; and withal dry, but especially *short.* From roses in December 26th to hyacinths in March 17th, both in bloom in the open air, was a rapid move. Indeed, March seems to have missed his usual place in the calendar. His absence caused no grief.

We have now made the circuit of the year: yet another matter in regard to the weather remains to be referred to. Your historian undertook, in the review of last year, to make something like a prophecy for the next. How is it as to the fulfilment? Was there, or was there not, a drought in the year 1870? If this question was propounded in many large sections of this country, and also in Europe, there would come a decided answer in the affirmative. I collected various newspaper extracts, which prove the existence of a severe and extensive drought; but it is not necessary to read them. You, farmers, who are so fortunate as to have potatoes to sell, know well enough why the price that you realize is so unexpectedly high. The low waters and dry wells and ice-ponds offered proof of the same fact. There was a considerable drought in the year 1870. But, on the other hand, when we recall the painful recollection of copious and continued rains last June, by which our wheat crop was so greatly injured; added to which that no single crop with us suffered seriously from want of moisture, it must be acknowledged that your historian was justly taunted with having his prediction cast up to him, and is very willing to admit that it would be safer to confine himself hereafter to his proper province of the past. And yet, the practical point which he meant to make was borne out in one important particular, namely, that he who should put in his potato crop in moist land and tend it properly would profit by the predicted drought. I venture to ask you to remember this in 1886.

My reason for dwelling somewhat on the preceding subject will be apparent to you all; and, as many weather predictions are just now coming into vogue, you will excuse the long-drawn specimen of this sort of prophecy: but it is time that we change the theme.

Whatsoever other events of joy or sorrow the year just ended has brought to us, it has taken none of us away. Of the three hundred and twenty-eight persons now included in "our neighborhood," all still live—all of us, with several more added. It has been a year for taking the census in more cases than one. The Friends had it taken of the members of their own Society. The figures show a fair increase during the last ten years. Then, one hundred and eighty-one members of Sandy Spring Monthly Meeting were enumerated; now the number is two hundred and eighteen, an increase of full twenty per cent. The State of Maryland has made an increase of only 13 per cent. in the same period.

The national census furnished some facts in regard to the agricultural productions of our neighborhood which are worth recording here. Your historian having held the office of Census-taker in both the years of 1850 and 1870, is enabled to compare the products of nine farms at those two several periods. The estimate is given in the moneyed value at present prices.

Total value of productions in 1850, $10,365. In 1870, $36,320. Average per farm in 1850, $1151; in 1870, $4035, which shows an increase on the same land over 3½ fold.

This augmented production in the last twenty years will scarcely surprise you: a more important question just now is whether the improvement still goes on in the same ratio from year to year. I think it does. From the best observation that I can make during the present year, there appears to be no falling off in the energetic prosecution of the labors of agriculture among our people. I think that, as an instance of industry well applied, there has been a greater show of large stones taken up in plowed fields than has been usually the case in one year. The plowman who is careful to remove these obstructions is not likely to fail in other measures for ameliorating the soil.

Also there is now going on in the neighborhood a more than usual number of buildings, and these of the best sort for farmers; all this in spite of the alleged "hard times." It may be that the work of improvement is shown more in the number of new *houses* than in new *barns*, which would not be considered a favorable indication in some districts. It is, however, in accordance with the spirit of Sandy Spring, which, though appreciating fine stock at their full value, has always preferred, and it is to be hoped always will prefer, to provide first for the comfort and welfare of human beings.

Next in importance to improvements of the farm, so far

as the substantial material interests of the people are concerned, comes the subject of roads. It was mentioned in the last chapter that vigorous efforts were being made to construct a turnpike from Ashton to the district line, a large subscription, which was a surprise to many, having been obtained. During the year several miles of the work have been done; difficulties remain to be overcome before it is completed, yet none that can stop such men as have undertaken to finish the work.

The year is noted for another enterprise in the line of a turnpike; one to connect Sandy Spring more directly with the main stem from Brookeville to Washington. This enterprise, which may be said almost to have sprung into being full grown, like Minerva from the brain of Jupiter, has also met with drawbacks in the execution, but is now proceeding with steady, deliberate progress. Impelled by an energy "that knows no such word as fail," and backed up by the strong corporation of the main stem, it is sure to be set down in my next record among the finished labors.

After the discussion of turnpikes you will naturally expect some reference to an interesting subject that has had a place in all the preceding annals. But, if it is only for variety I must disappoint you this time, passing on to other topics, scarcely saying the word "railroad." We shall none the less "keep a great *thinking* about it"; and doubtless have a great deal to say next year!

So much for material progress. How is it with things social, intellectual and spiritual?

The incidents of the year, so far as they have been referred to, show no want of life in these respects, but rather the contrary. The various associations which are becoming the chief characteristics of our neighborhood are flourishing and increasing in numbers. A new society was formed during last summer, with the interesting and promising title of "Home Interests." Its peculiar feature appears to be that it is composed exclusively of young married folks. If there is not much known about this society outside its own circle, this is no cause for wonder or blame, since the important and interesting class of which it is composed are always sure to find no lack of subjects within, and concerning themselves alone. This freemasonry will doubtless expand and receive accessions of new members.

The older "Ladies' Association" (using the term only in reference to the date of its formation) pursues the even tenor of its way, neither straying aside on the one hand to urge disturbing political theories, nor on the other to oppose them, but devoting itself to "moral and social improvement"; ready to aid all proper benevolent enterprises in feeding and clothing the destitute at home or in the far West.

The Farmers' Club at one of its meetings last year threw off in a very decided manner any imputation that might be started, of its beginning to feel "the infirmities of age," on the occasion of a suggestion from one of the members that "the time might come" when the *winter* meetings could be dispensed with. The proposition met with no favor. On the contrary, it was agreed by a number of the members to undertake at once a regular series of useful farm experiments, which implies an energy almost youthful in its character. It is not in my power to say whether the younger Farmers' Club is doing its whole duty in that way. If it shrinks from any duty that merely requires a little trouble, the time may come when it will be distinguished from its senior confrere as being the club which meets of moonlight evenings. However, some of its members are engaged in an experiment which I am disposed to regard with great interest: namely, the application of oyster-shell lime. The period has arrived, at least on some of our farms, when concentrated ammoniacal and phosphated fertilizers will no longer suffice to restore to the soil the vast amount of material carried to town in the form of hay.

The Horticultural Society, once deemed exclusive, but really the least so of all, embracing as it does all ages and both sexes, proved its importance last year both by what it did and what it omitted. I refer only to the latter charge. It was concluded, though with reluctance on the part of a portion of the members, to omit the September Fair, and concentrate efforts on the County Fair soon to take place in Rockville. The motive was good, but the result, in its effects, was of doubtful advantage. County Agricultural Fairs, the larger the better, are *good things*, but horse races are *bad things;* and this neighborhood will be untrue, not merely to its religious professions, but to the moral character which its people have certainly claimed, if it fails to distinguish between innocent amusements, and those which, if not essentially immoral, are at least hurtful in immediate or remote influence. Perhaps no question of more importance to the future welfare of the neighborhood has loomed up during the year than that which relates to the subject of amusements.

But I assure you, before going further into this question, that I do not mean to forget that a history is not a sermon. That is to say, not directly such; and yet history were never worth the writing, if it does not indirectly preach the truth to us. It is the saying of some old sage, "Tell me a people's amusements, and I will tell you their character";

and in accordance with this principle they have always been considered within the province of the historian.

In order to perform this part of my task, it is now the proper time to refer to one of the neighborhood associations, hitherto passed by.. If any doubt was expressed in regard to the new institution, called the "Sociable," whether the members were likely to "stick," the customary provision for *feed* being left out of the plan of the society, the experience of the present year has served to banish that doubt. The Sociable has been the most popular thing of the season; its plan seems to have worked well every way. The system of giving attention to elementary principles of education, and calling all the members to bear a part, both with tongue and pen, is calculated to be highly improving. The written essays have possessed real merit, and there are several young writers thus developed by learning their own powers, who, after acquiring by practice the grand attainments of compression and brevity, will be able to sustain and increase the literary reputation of the neighborhood.

Others have *talked* about establishing a paper at Sandy Spring; but these young people of ours have got it up, and very creditably too. Possibly it may be the germ of a larger enterprise of this sort. Were it only as easy to support a paper pecuniarily as to fill its columns with good reading matter, the thing were very practicable here.

The juveniles of the Sociable naturally took up the subject of amusements for discussion. Youth and amusements have a natural connection. They seem to have carried on the discussion with the freedom that belongs to the times, yet with the apparent desire to bring the questions involved to the test of reason and truth. The day has passed when these or any other questions can be settled by tradition or authority. Let the young people freely examine and test for themselves! It has become a very interesting problem at this time, in which the old as well as the young are concerned, and in which the views peculiar to both are entitled to consideration, to determine the nature and limits of rational recreation. Your historian will now only observe, in his effort to impress the lessons of history touching the subject, that all amusements should be brought to these tests: Do they tend to promote health or endanger it? to refine the feelings, or to render them more coarse? to produce respect to what is really worthy of reverence, or to produce the reverse? In a word, does the individual in practicing the sport feel as if he was higher up in the scale of being, or does he feel a little lower down, after it is over? Years hence, the standing of this neighborhood will show the influence of having adopted the one or the other sort of amusement.

We have now discussed the various societies. What shall be said of "Society," technically so called? According to the newspapers, the idea of society at the Capital seems to consist in descriptions of the dresses worn by ladies at parties. Although it must be admitted that the fashion of dress should have a place in history, the present writer feels wholly inadequate to that part of his task. Nor does he receive any help on this point in turning to the valuable information furnished him by the lady who has consented to render some assistance in this portion of the annals. Since she says not a word about changes in the style of attire, from bonnet to slipper, we must continue our sin of omission. It is due, however, to the importance of the subject, to say a word in regard to social usages, for they certainly rise to the dignity of history. In these promiscuous details it may be proper to remark that, according to my observation, there have been fewer parties this past year than in some previous seasons; and this has appeared to be a creditable circumstance, as evincing, in a proper way, the appreciation felt by the lovers of social pleasures, of the rather hard times, and the difficulties experienced by some to fulfil all their obligations with accustomed punctuality.

It is also well deserving of mention, while referring to the subject of social usages, that a *manly* effort was made this year (which scarcely met a womanly seconding) to check the growing evil of "late hours." It is very much to be hoped that an evil so indisputable among country people will resist the influence of city example. There is, in this matter, a positive discordance between the proprieties of town and country. There is conclusive evidence that the "hard times," so often unjustly complained of, is this year not wholly a myth; the operations of the "Sandy Spring Savings Institution" serve to show the correctness of the complaint. The amount received from depositors in the present year is only $9715, being $6300 less than the preceding. The amount now invested is $21,409.94, which must be regarded as a decided indication of a prosperous and useful institution.

Among the most interesting phenomena of the year whose events have passed into history, was one which impressed the country everywhere, so far as our acquaintance extends—a pleasant gale, if we may term it so, which reached our neighborhood in the autumn, and blew for a time with much impetuosity; nor has it ceased yet to agitate the throbbing belles. I refer, of course, to the "marriage gale," whose results (as thus far ascertained) may be summed up in the actual solemnization of three weddings, very near together, so beautiful that none more beautiful have ever been recorded in these pages. The recollection of such events is peculiarly pleasant, even in withered bosoms. Thanksgiving Day of 1870, how inexpressibly bright and sweet and balmy! And yet there was another side to the picture; for the influence of these exciting events served to diminish the interest felt in opening the lecture course of the Lyceum. And being strongly impressed with the conviction that literary culture and the mental activity thereby promoted are immediately connected with keeping up, in a worthy and respectable manner, the exercises for which this hall was built, the least indication of a want of interest in them seems to me a subject for regret. Looking back, however, over the whole winter's course, so far as it has gone, I cannot see anything like failure. The lectures and other literary entertainments have not, in my judgment, fallen below par; in several instances they were considerably above that standard. Thus much can fairly be said of the lecturers. A more important question relates to the audience. Their attendance and deportment, their degree of interest in what is being said, is a far more important matter for the permanent and assured success of such an institution, than the occasional success or failure of a speaker. As was said at the inauguration of the Lyceum twelve years ago, "Furnish us with the right *audience*, and we will insure lecturers fairly satisfactory." Being bound simply to record such facts as he remembers, your historian takes pleasure in referring, in this connection, to the very last lecture, wherein the audience performed *their* part quite as well as the speaker did *his*, and that was highly satisfactory to all.

In the annals of things spiritual, it would be an omission to forget the visit of friend Caroline Talbott during the winter. The thronged attendance on her ministrations proved the depth and earnestness of the interest felt by our people in the high themes of which she discoursed, acceptably to most of her auditors, though not to all.

The number of births in the year was 7, of which 4 were boys and 3 girls.

The marriages, as before stated, were 3, but these are imperfectly alluded to without the names of the parties. That blank is thus filled:

On the 10th day of November, 1870, Philip T. Stabler to Cornelia Nichols.

On the 24th day of November, Walter H. Brooke to Caroline H. Leggett.

On the 1st day of December, James P. Stabler to Alice Brooke.

Deaths—None.

CHAPTER IX.

From Fourth Month, 3d, 1871, to Fourth Month, 1st, 1872.

Influence and variations of weather — More compliments from Mr. Ramsdel — Summer boarders — Combined action — Birth of the various Associations — "Agreeing to differ" — The "Innocents" — Debating Society — The use of "supper" — The turnpikes nearly finished — On toll-gates — Fresh news of railroads — Postoffice reports — The Lyceum fairly active — Horticultural increases in favor — Tile manufacture — The many marriages increase visiting — Origin of the "Farmers' Convention" — First-day school revives.

In commencing this, the ninth Chapter of these Neighborhood Annals, the writer desires to express an intention (if life is spared so long) of making one more addition to the historical sketches of the present volume. Ten years will then stand recorded.

Your meteorologist has frequently and very justly called our attention to the degree of *general similarity* which one season bears to another. At the outset of my present sketch, I am impressed with the fact of the *difference* sometimes observed. I find in looking over last year's record, that a poetical effusion at the beginning was attributed to the genial influence of the balmy atmosphere we were then enjoying. "March," it was said, "seemed to have been left out of the calendar." How about it this year? Was there ever a more genuine March month? You will have no poetry this time inspired by the winds prevailing as I write.

While on the subject of the weather of last year, it may be noted down by way of supplement to the full report you have just had, that the three spring months of '71 were the hottest on record for eighty-two years; average temperature being $57\frac{6}{10}°$. On April 8th the thermometer rose to 88° (in the shade of course). The young people present can remember the alliteration by the repetition of eights. It will probably be long before they have such another experience. Wheat harvest commenced June 10th, ripe oats were cut in the last part of the same month. Rainfall at the Smithsonian for the year now expiring was 32½ inches, to 37 inches for the preceding year; with an average of 40 inches for six years. The dry wells so numerous this season are thus accounted for.

The year just passed away has not been marked by any very extraordinary events. No occurrence of an especially sensational character is now remembered, unless, indeed, it consist in the notoriety which we may have acquired through the appearance of a remarkable description of our neighborhood, published in several newspapers of the county. I have already quoted in former Annals what appeared to me worthy and sincere tributes to the past and present character of the community of Sandy Spring, from men well qualified to form a correct and sober judgment. The sketch to which I now refer is painted in much livelier colors. It came to us half a year ago, in the hot months. Let us take a look at it in these cool days (if we can do so without blushing), and see whether we can recognize our own lineaments.

The writer, after saying some capital things about the fashionable watering-places, gets right up on his high horse and speaks thus:

"Let me tell you of Sandy Spring. It is in Montgomery County, Maryland, 16 or 18 miles north of Washington, on high ground where mosquitoes never come, and where big bills, hotel discomforts, plotting mammas, willing girls, heartless compliments, fashionable languor, gaudy dress and indigestion are never known. Instead, you have a locality where sincerity is the ruling feature, where health is an established law, and where enjoyment seeks incentive in one's own nature. Sandy Spring is a community of Quakers; not the sort that are always theeing and thouing you, always turning down the corners of their mouth and looking grave at the sight of enjoyment, and smiling only in their sleep: but the kind that the love of God has made happy; the kind in whose nature selfishness has given way to fairness; the kind who believe that God has not made men after his own image to groan and weep and lament the wickedness of the world, but rather to read sermons in nature, gratitude in the happiness which every neighbor's family feels, and enjoyment which harmless pleasure brings; where laughter is not a crime, and where music is not regarded as too worldly for the elect. . . . I do not believe there is a place on earth which the love of God and man has so ennobled. Sincerity is the word which expresses their religious quality and describes their dealings with mankind. You may stay among these Quakers for months, subject them to the severest test of constant companionship, and yet you will never hear a hasty, an angry, or an impatient word from their lips, or see a mean action, be it ever so insignificant. They are moral, without seeming to wear upon or about them a look of reproach and warning to others. They are thrifty, without being mean and stingy. They are benevolent without ostentation. They are intelligent, refined and wise, without being didactic; they are careful, judicious and thoughtful, without being suspicious. The location of this newly discovered Eden is perfect." After a good deal more in the same strain, which I have scarce the nerve to quote, bringing as it does the color to the cheek, the writer finishes up with describing the homesteads and the children. Instead of expanding upon the beauty and perfection of the latter, where he *might* have showered praises that would still fail to "come up to the parents' wish," he merely says: "their number I do not contract to calculate, being almost as bad as Ginx," &c., &c. We are informed that the writer of the above sketch (whose name is Ramsdel) expects to become a resident to some extent of the neighborhood so extravagantly eulogized. I hope that he will carry out the scheme; and then we would like so much to hear from him again, say, three or four years hence. In the meantime would it not be nice if we were to become all that his fancy has pictured us? I commenced copying the gentleman's description with the idea of turning it into burlesque, as was probably more than half intended by the writer. But as I proceeded other thoughts came. I remembered a child who was praised for merits that he could but partially claim, and the effect was so decidedly favorable as actually to stimulate him to deserve the commendation. Now there are points in the delineation just read to you which strike me with great force as suggestions for practical improvement. For what else are people made but to improve? "Heartless compliments," "gaudy dress," "gloomy outside religion," "hasty words," "selfish actions," since he acquits us of all these, it may really be that we are so far clear that it would be practicable to become still more so. "Sincerity" is the crowning virtue which he emphatically awards us: let us hope that he had some ground for this tribute (and I honestly think there is a claim for it); on that substantial basis we may build up still more.

An institution of this neighborhood, not referred to in these pages hitherto, is the taking of summer boarders. This practice is one not to be slighted, for its influence has been considerable. It goes back also into old times. According to my impressions, the practice as at present carried on was fairly instituted about forty years ago, beginning at the oldest homestead in this region of country, the original "Charley Forrest." Since that day, how many and what various sorts of people have sought our "classic shades" to rest under "the big trees," and recruit in the heats of summer, sometimes lingering after those heats had passed! The institution now forms an important feature in the arrangements of a number of families. It thus becomes an interesting question for the historian to investigate the influences for good or for evil exerted in this way upon the neighborhood. Having been placed in circumstances favorable for observation, and having also heard the opinions of several old residents, I have been led to speculate considerably on the subject, with the following results: The injurious tendencies brought to my notice might be summed up in the words of caution and reproof (quite familiar to our young people), in regard to the danger of adopting city customs, frivolous fashions and amusements, "heartless compliments," gaudy dress, and the rest of those follies from which we are said to have been hitherto exempt. So far as such adoption extends to the introduction of town ways, which are, from the nature of things, wholly unsuited to rational country life—for example, the turning day into night, and *vice versa*—not to speak of the street-sweeping trains, whose worst effect has been to render walking among the ladies an almost antiquated exercise—so far the influence of summer boarders is, of course, unfavorable. But when we take a wider view of the subject and consider the actual normal relations of town and country toward each other, we shall find many important quickening influences producing decided benefits to the latter. The fault of country people is in being too slow; city folks are sometimes "fast"; at any rate intercourse between the two has the effect to enliven the faculties. The mingling together of opposite qualities is often a mutual advantage. The fact is, town and country are so constituted that each is necessary to the other. In fine, there does not remain a doubt that the advantages which this neighborhood has received from its large and free intercourse with persons from the city during the past forty years greatly preponderate over the evils before mentioned, which are essentially transient and superficial. Our minds have been animated and liberalized, our resources, in a pecuniary point of view, have been increased, and our morals have not probably been impaired.

Assuredly the past year shows no indications of diminished activity, either in a material, mental or social view.

The best criterion of the degree of real civilization and progress in a community has been said, on high authority, to be found in their power of combining together to accomplish beneficial purposes,—the "clubbing faculty," we may term it. Estimated by this test, the year now being recorded compares favorably with any previous one; perhaps it stands in the fore-front.

As these associations are such an important feature of our neighborhood, it is well to make out a list of them, giving the date of their origin and the number of persons composing the body, so far as has been ascertained. They are here put down in the order of their formation, not of their present importance—of course not:

1. The Library Company, organized 1842.
2. The Farmers' Club, composed of 16 members, organized 1844.
3. Ladies' Association for Mutual Improvement, 15 members, organized 1857.
4. Horticultural Society (20 to 30 members), organized 1863.
5. Club Junior (now Enterprise Club), 15 members, organized 1865.
6. The Sociable, 33 members, organized 1869.
7. The Home Interests, 24 members, organized 1870.
8. Montgomery Club (No. 3), 15 members, organized 1872.
9. The Innocents, 14 members, organized 1872.

Total number of members composing the eight associations (omitting the Library Company), is 154. Of these, some are members of more than one association. Probably there are now 125 separate individuals that occupy a place in one or the other society.

The importance of these exhibits, in taking a right view

of the present and future character of our neighborhood, can hardly be overestimated. Man is a weak creature of himself. The interesting partnership with a woman more than doubles his worth and power. The family relation is the germ of all that is of high value in society. Still there is, so far, too much of selfishness in the combining principle. There must be a motive of wider reach to that principle before it can produce its whole effects in elevating society. *Joint action* for a *common* beneficial purpose is the crowning operation of the grand associative principle. Our Mutual Fire Insurance Company (which has not yet received in these Annals the notice to which its importance and success entitle it), and the Savings Institution, are further illustrations of that operating power in our neighborhood. Both are business, not social, institutions; yet the difficulties of originating such would never have been successfully met and overcome by a community which had taken no lessons in the science of combined action. We have now learned some of these first lessons, but I am sure that we do not claim to have attained anything like perfection in the science. We have partly acquired the indispensable qualification to *agree*, but in respect of the more advanced attainment, that of *agreeing to differ*, there is much to learn yet. Joint action is the body, of which harmony of feeling is the *soul*.

It would no doubt be gratifying to give some further particulars in regard to the operations during the year of these interesting associations; especially of two or three youngest ones, their constitution, objects, &c.; but these points have scarcely developed as yet. Taking the very youngest, they (as I am informed) *have no* special purpose, ignoring those prosy subjects of potato culture, pickles and preserves, moral and mental culture, guano, peonies, begonias, and such like; in short, meeting "to have a good time" (don't we old folks envy them!) yet guaranteed by their very name, the "Innocents," from aught unworthy the character of the neighborhood of which they constitute an interesting part. The Club, designated as No. 3, though it has had more names than is the case with "anybody's darling" that I am acquainted with, has started out with some new features which give the promise of usefulness and permanence desired by all.

The Sociable was organized this year with the interesting addition of a Debating Society. The younger portion of this community who feel a desire to sustain and elevate its character, really ought not to suffer this institution to languish and die away. There is surely enough capacity here to maintain respectably these mingled social and literary reunions, which afford, just so long as the spirit is kept up, and no longer, a pleasant means of improvement. The form in which the Association appears this winter is a variation of the old-time Reading Circle; and will go on, I trust, to receive from year to year, new adaptations to the spirit of the times as suggested by the inventive geniuses constantly bursting into bloom. But "the Sociable" cannot be let go without referring to a compliment paid them in these pages two years since, on account of their "dispensing with all entertainments not of an intellectual kind": again in last year it was conceded that they had still stuck to their resolution. Now I am informed they have ceased to *stick;* having yielded to the essential conditions for success and permanence in all institutions gotten up at Sandy Spring. This grave historical fact, showing our weakness on a minor point, received another illustration this winter, in the meetings held at the Lyceum for the benevolent purpose of making garments to clothe the red brethren in or near the Rocky Mountains. Forty-two garments were made at the last meeting! The question was started whether this handsome report could have been rendered without the ingenious addition of a *supper*. It is no use to struggle against nature: it is better, by complying, to march on to new triumphs of association! The Insurance Directors have their feed, and are very punctual in attending to their duties. The bank only has failed to come into it yet; perhaps the sight and touch of tempting morsels may prove too strong for their ascetic self-denial.

In the department of material improvements we note first, in regard to the two turnpikes, that the hopeful predictions made a year ago are precisely fulfilled. The "Norwood Branch" is at least so nearly completed that a very few days of the open weather, for which it has been so long waiting, will add the last smoothing touch. The Ashton road has been pushed through its most difficult points by those "not-to-be-appalled men," heretofore spoken of.

The traveller at this end has of late experienced a similar impression to that felt by the shipwrecked voyager told us by Dean Swift, who, being cast ashore on an unknown island, and coming upon a gallows with a man hanging to it, "thanked God for this evidence that he had got into a civilized country"! A new tollgate is at first regarded as a similar evidence of civilization. I am not aware that it has really inconvenienced any parties, unless it was some of the youths having a nocturnal call in that direction, who found themselves scarce of pennies. Looking round the whole situation it would appear that the said tollgate is judiciously located. Your historian now feels the reward for his abstaining from allusions to the subject of railroads. For, just at the present time a fresh interest is awakened on that subject, and very fresh news is handed round to raise our hopes to the highest pitch. The charter for a new road to run from Washington City on the meridian line, as far as it can get, having been obtained, steps are now being taken to organize, "and commence taking in the money." But this is not the *exciting* news. Most probably there will be plenty of time to tell of the progress of "the Washington and Pennsylvania Line" railroad in our future annals; the other—the long-talked-of "Laurel Cut-off"—is to be spoken of only once more in next year's sketch, and then as being a finished work. The steam-whistle is to be the shrill accompaniment to the president's address at the next annual meeting, and perhaps scare your horses as they come and return. I relate this *very* fresh news as it was told me. It was further confidently asserted that "the road will be in running order by next Christmas"; but I would not like to be held strictly responsible for the entire accuracy of the reports. My faith however is great, being exceeded only by that of a lady friend.

That index of advancing civilization, the postoffice, reports 21,450 letters sent from Sandy Spring in 1871, and eighty different publications taken, with 244 subscribers.

The Savings Institution shows a fair amount of work for the year, a total of $26,774 being saved away (but, says the merchant, withdrawn from active circulation here)—the gain for the year in deposits $5364—with 388 depositors.

The central literary institution, the Lyceum, without accomplishing anything remarkably brilliant this past season, has been sustained fairly well. There has been no falling off in the attendance, nor any apparent lack of interest. The audience has been decidedly respectable and *respectful.* At the annual election a year ago it was urged by one of the old standard members that the Board of Directors should be filled chiefly with *young men.* The president bears testimony that every member of the board constituted in accordance with this idea was in attendance at the called meetings—a thing believed to be hitherto unprecedented, at least for some years back. The success of this effort at infusing young blood indicates the propriety of carrying it further in the choice of officers. Why not try the infusion of another congenial element? It need scarcely be said what is referred to among such admirers of the sex.

(Your president of the past two years takes this opportunity to make his last farewell bow with many thanks for your attention and frequent expressions of satisfaction with the Annals.)

The fair held in last 9th month, under the auspices of the Horticultural Society, assisted by the two Farmers' Clubs, was considered a complete success, attracting many strangers, whose presence added much to the interest of the affair. A new feature was introduced by the exhibition of stock; some disposition being manifested to look forward to a time when an Agricultural Fair based on sound principles may spring out of this flourishing beginning.

One of our citizens having added to his brickmaking establishment preparatory machines for manufacturing drain-tiles, it would seem now to be a worthy subject to call the attention of our Farmers' Clubs to the project. The enterprise is in its infancy, and the same may be said of draining in our neighborhood—in old, rather raw, though somewhat conceited infancy, at present stands our unscientific art of draining.

Now we turn with pleasure from these material worldly concerns to a more interesting portion of the year's proceedings. It was mentioned, "in our last," that a marriage gale was blowing over the land with more than usual intensity. Neither did it stop with the year by any means, but rather continued to prevail with increasing force. The history must do itself the honor of a more particular record than usual, being indebted for this to the lady historienne. Married in the year 1871: 4th month 6th, Arthur Stabler and Annie McFarland; 9th month 12th, Alban G. Thomas and Susan H. Leggett; 9th month 14th, Roger Brooke and Louisa Thomas; 10th month 26th, William S. Brooke and Mary P. Coffin. And then came a lull in the gale; probably temporary.

There will be more of this sort of interesting performances, and what is to be done about it? A puzzling question arose in my mind, on the evening of a day which I had spent very pleasantly in visiting certain of the happy homes, called into existence by the life-partnerships formed within the past two years. The question took this shape: How ever are the good folks of our neighborhood to go the rounds of visiting each other's houses if they keep on multiplying (the houses, I mean) at this rate? It can't be done in the way and manner of the last hundred years; with all the good social feeling in the world, there are limits to its exercise. Note this fact: *our* young people don't *emigrate*, the *tracks* all point *toward*, not *from* Sandy Spring! Must our people then resolve into separate circles—the associations visiting only among themselves? This would be bad—cliques the probable result.

Yet there is a way by which the unity of the neighborhood can be preserved; let some one having "a genius for society," devise a scheme by which everybody shall come to see everybody in a social, hospitable way, at one or more central points—this Lyceum for one. I can only throw out a hint now, leaving it to be developed in the future. As an example, the three Farmers' Clubs might (and ought to) have a system for combining their *wisdom*, and for co-operating in making important experiments. They should hold a general meeting at least once in every year.*

Our friend, Hadassah Moore, who has kindly consented to render valuable assistance in furnishing information of the statistical sort, sends the record of births—five during the year. I am not minded to give *names* in this case, as in the marriages. For while no one ever objects to having the year of her wedding placed on a public record, it might some years hereafter be different in the other case. The Family Bible sometimes tells its tales with inconvenient precision. Delay it as we may, that other solemn record cannot be omitted or concealed. No well-trained mind, with right feelings, can desire to leave that part blank in the simple annals of a united neighborhood. No other part is so suggestive of holy emotions.

"The flowers of love and hope we gather here
Shall yet bloom for us in the realm of God;
They shed not their last fragrance on our bier,
They lie not withered on the cold grave sod."

Death came early into our midst.

Fourth month, 7th, '71, Rachel G. Gilpin died, after a lingering illness, leaving several children, all of whom

*Out of the preceding Quixotic scheme for holding social meetings grew up the very popular "Farmers' Convention," which collects some time in January of each year an agricultural band of one or two hundred men.

were married and settled, except one. Although well advanced in years, she never seemed at all like an *old* person. She was one of a lovely class, who are fully appreciated only by those who have lived in the house with them. Having enjoyed that experience, it is with a mournful satisfaction I join in a tribute of love and praise to her memory.

Fifth month, 30th, again, "in the unfolding of human events, death was to read our people another impressive lesson; to come again into our midst and take from us a bright and loved young friend." William Thomas died in Philadelphia, where he had gone for the benefit of his health. His remains were interred here, followed to their last resting-place by a very large and solemn train. It has been my solemn duty several times in these pages, to express the common sorrow over the loss to the neighborhood, of young men and women who had given promise of future usefulness. I have never felt a stronger sense of such loss than in the present case.

To the clearest and brightest intellect, our loved Willie joined a high moral principle, a conscience almost too sensitive—if such can be. These high qualities gave promise of a career which not even his great modesty could have prevented from being a very shining one. His Creator had decided to call him thus early, and we can only be reconciled.

Ninth month, 17th, at the home of her childhood, Mary Ellen Stone died, after an illness of several months; hastened, if not produced, by her indefatigable energy in the worthy pursuit of teaching school, in which she had already, though so young, gained the approbation of many judicious friends. So young! My eyes often turn to her childhood's home across the way, but where is she?

Second month, 10th, '72, Catharine Chandlee, one of the oldest members of our meeting, departed this life. She had long been frail in appearance, and rather delicate in health for several years. Not very often seen away from home, her kind and hospitable feelings were familiar to all who went to see her there.

Thus there have been this year four marriages, five births, four deaths, amongst us; a remarkable approach to equality in these three great events of human life.

We close this chapter in noting one more incident, the revival of the First-day school. An interesting group of scholars and teachers devote a portion of the afternoon, with perseverance, to education in its best sense, not limited to scholastic attainments. We know that our children are endowed with *emotional* as well as *intellectual* faculties; with a heart and soul, as well as a mind. Thus may their way be opened to right and true culture!

CHAPTER X.

FROM FOURTH MONTH, 1st, 1872, TO FOURTH MONTH, 7th, 1873.

Progress of the History — The "Dry Season" attended with some good crops — The "Epizootic" — "How does farming pay?" Cautions to young farmers — The Labor Question — Quotations of value — On "polish" — On *wild* "tame beasts" — Severe remarks on railroads — Extent of the "Association Principle" — Diminished interest toward the Lyceum — Dramatic entertainments — Summary of ten years' statistics — The Historian's Farewell.

It is stated on the first page of this book that "at a meeting of the Lyceum Company, held the 6th of the 4th month, 1863, an order was passed appointing a Historian, whose duty it should be to make a record of neighborhood events, and read it at the following annual meeting." This duty having fallen upon me, it has appeared to be the proper thing to keep up the custom for a full decade; and now, for various reasons, it is my desire to be released from a duty which has been hitherto a pleasure, because of the tokens of apparent interest and expressions of kindly approval which my efforts have received from you. I am very sensible of the imperfection of these sketches, considered as a record of events, and am conscious whatever merits they possess in this respect must be divided with the Lady Historiennes, who have furnished reports of remarkable accuracy. My own contributions appear to consist largely of moral reflections, and effusion of sentiments "wise and otherwise"; but you always listened patiently, so as to leave the impression on my mind that, in these annual assemblages, we were having rather a good time in looking at ourselves and pretending we are thus to appear in History. I must venture to trespass on that patience still further this evening, and indeed put it to a harder proof than it has yet sustained. The pictures of the neighborhood presented in the previous pages, drawn by the hands of talented and disinterested parties though they were, are a little rose-colored, are they not? Mainly just and true, perhaps; certainly very comfortable and encouraging, yet rather one-sided; the *lights* being employed in the picture more conspicuously than the *shades*. Now we know very well that all true pictures of things earthly must have their shades too.

It is not necessary, and, as I think, not beneficial, to dwell on the dark side; but after reading over several of the preceding chapters, I am impressed with the conviction that variety (not to mention any other motive) requires a sort of description somewhat different from the eulogies which filled several pages; in short, neither praise nor dispraise, but simple Arcadian truth. Your historian, as he has been called from the beginning, is not going to shoot a Parthian arrow, firing and then running away, but will try to avoid an excess of sentiment, and bear in mind that we are all a set of plain, simple farmers, making no claims to any other title than this.

It is altogether natural that an agricultural community, in reviewing the year just past, should first direct their attention to that great fact upon which so much of their prosperity depends, namely, the weather. This subject is generally considered commonplace, and yet a very popular one amongst people of all classes. When we rightly examine it, we find abundant reason for the general interest, in the infinite variety therein perceived. No two years of the past ten have resembled each other, and the last is especially distinct. While the chief facts belonging to the weather are duly reported to us from the proper quarter, there are always other and more general considerations connected with the influences of the seasons, that also claim a place here. In the year now closing, the dry, the hot, the cold, and (throughout last month) the windy, have all been distinguishing characteristics. The dry influence prevailed in the spring and early summer, in a degree really alarming. When a dry April was followed by a dryer May, with very little improvement in June, it was all up with the grass crop. Hay was put down in the estimate at one-fourth to a third of the average yield. The springs, the wells and streams failed in corresponding degree. My own spring, which had kept up a fair flow for the previous 34 years, ceased running for some days; the Patuxent had but one-fourth its usual summer current (as Thomas Lea informed me), and some of the oldest inhabitants said it would require to go back at least half a century, indeed even to 1806, to find a year when the streams were so low. The greatest inconvenience was sustained from the failure of the wells. Then was the digging of wells and the lengthening of pumps the liveliest business going on. It was during the first half of June that the word "famine" came to be frequently mentioned.

Now, mark what followed. Our farmers were surprised to find on harvesting and threshing their wheat, that the amount of grain bore an extraordinary disproportion to the meagre straw; in fact, that it was a superior crop. The great corn crop was still better, being generally above the average. Fruit was abundant, and of better quality than usual. In short, the apprehended famine did not come. It is well to recall these unrealized fears, and with the recollection confirm our faith, that "while the earth remaineth, seed-time and harvest, and summer and winter, and day and night shall not cease."

The deficiency in the two other important productions, hay and potatoes, not fully compensated by their increased price, still left the season, pecuniarily speaking, with a balance on the wrong side. Then in the fall there fell upon us, as it was were from the clouds—well, we don't know how it did come, certainly in a mysterious, unprecedented way—that calamity of the horse influenza, or Epizootic, with its other unpronounceable names. We heard rumors of the pestilence through October, as first appearing in Canada, then crossing the border (without regard to the tariff), swooping down upon town and country, disturbing trade more than farming, and at last reaching us at the close of the month. Wherever there was a horse, a mule, or a donkey, *there* was the disease. There were comparatively few fatal cases, but the suspension of work was almost total. Then did some folks recover an accomplishment little used since they were infants, finding they could actually *walk* miles. On one meeting day (First-day, too), there were in the stalls so few horses (only two or three), we would scarcely have known that any were there if it had not been for the cough. A lady was drawn in her carriage a couple of miles to church, by man, or rather, boy-power. Fortunately the disease came at the most favorable season for the farmer. It still remains to be proved whether its consequences have yet entirely disappeared.

A pretty hard year, on the whole, for the agricultural interest. The worst of it is, that our young people show increasing signs of restlessness under the condition of things, and fresh doubts are being started on the important question, whether farming at Sandy Spring is a profitable business. Grave and settled men are discussing the question, "How does farming pay?" A big question, involving many considerations, going deep into political economy, and still deeper into *other economies*, not to be settled without reference to the highest principles. In order to start from the solid basis of statistics, I have taken some pains to estimate the amount of land possessed by the 65 or 70 families who constitute "our neighborhood," as included in these annals. I find between 10,000 and 10,500 acres, which gives an average of full 150 acres to each family—a very fair farm.

Now let us consider there are different systems of farming. There was (and it still exists) the old Maryland system. I need not take up space here to describe it, being too well known to need description. Without using harsh language, it may be justly claimed that that system has no proper place now in judicious agriculture, but belongs to a state of things gone by, as we hope, forever. A new era has come; new men, new ideas require a new system, and whether we like it or not, we have got to conform to it, or be dropped out of the agricultural circle. What is the course going on in Sandy Spring? Let us refer to statistics. One of the principles insisted upon by many, though not by all, is that farming operations require to be concentrated upon fewer acres. Our average of 150 acres to a farm would be regarded, according to the notions of olden times, as quite too moderate; but a different conclusion will be formed when we take into view the changed circumstances in regard to the *market* for farm products, the labor by which they are produced, and, I venture to add, the probable future means of conveyance to market. There is surely room for a greater concentration yet. When this fact comes to be properly realized, the talk about the necessity of our Sandy Spring youth having to swarm and leave the native hive—where honey does so abound, and prevented from cloying by the stings always inseparable—that sort of talk will be regarded as absurd. Plenty of room for a century yet! What is required in order to make a place for every figure in the multiplication table, and to put plenty on the *table* for every figure that comes, is a simple conformity to facts. Our two great and growing cities want all that we can produce; but *we* cannot produce profitably all the sorts of things which they want. We must be smart enough to find out what articles it will pay us best to direct our attention to.

The stern logic of facts may require something else than knowing what to *sell*. We must see and judge calmly and intelligently, what we ought, and what we ought not, to *buy*. There is one very plain fact which some persons find it difficult to learn, namely, never to buy what you cannot pay for. As we are dealing with facts (which are the special province of history), there is another one, not unconnected with political and domestic economy, which may be put into the following aphorism: "If young people insist on *beginning* where their parents left off, they may have to leave off where their parents began." Very good, but perhaps not wholly original.

Leaving the suggestions pertaining to economy, which is the least popular, and perhaps least lovable of all the greater virtues in proportion to its real value, it is not amiss to refer to another fact, which the whirligig of time has made conspicuous, and is yearly making more so in all places, and even at Sandy Spring. The desire to get rich, always too strong, is continually growing stronger; and the worst part about it is, people want to get rich without working for it. They want the results without the labor by which alone it can be legitimately obtained. It is a horrible confession, but too true: we *want* something without giving its equivalent. Is this honest? If not, then we all know that it can never really and truly succeed. And as we are all honest in intention at least, there must be some awful blunder made in the lessons we learn regarding the true purposes of life. If education means what the best authorities in unison with common sense declare that it does mean, namely, the fitting of boys and girls to fulfil the duties of a useful, noble life, when they become men and women, then it must be very far from having attained as yet to anything like a perfect system. Most true is it that one effect of the great work called education is to diminish taste for labor; I mean for hard work.

But this is a repulsive subject. We leave it with

expressing the hope and expectation, as you know I am a devout believer in progress, that the grand improvements in machinery will ultimately render hard work on a farm unnecessary. In the meantime it is not the worst thing we have to do.

I have dwelt so long upon this branch of my annual sketch, that there is but little room left for remarks upon a subject that has become of vital concern—the labor question. Yet would the annals of the year be very imperfect if our experience in relation to this matter were wholly left out. Taken altogether, the experience is less satisfactory this year than usual; especially is this the case in the female department, wherein the troubles seem to portend, if they have not reached, a crisis. The difficulties with respect to *field* labor appear to find a reasonable explanation in the extraordinary demand for workmen created by the magnificent enterprises going on within the District of Columbia. The high wages offered there would necessarily tend to draw away our regular hands; but this inconvenience is probably only temporary. Our neighborhood had been favored, owing to the operation of *moral* causes, beyond the adjacent communities, good labor being generally abundant. It is reasonable to anticipate that the men will return. But this explanation does not promise relief from the difficulties connected with a scarcity of female help, which shows no very hopeful signs of improvement. However, we may indulge the expectation that affairs being in a transition state, are likely to settle down in some agreeable way. They almost always do.

Efforts are being made in neighboring communities of our county and state, to introduce foreign labor to cure the prevalent evils. The proceeding demands our serious attention. After looking all around its probable influences, we may come to the conclusion that "it is better to bear the ills we have (trying to cure them) than fly to others that we know not of." Having lately met with the best article I ever saw on this subject, I transcribe a small portion, which clearly points out the high ground that can alone be successfully maintained.

"It seems that civilized society is on the verge of very grave experiences in what is called the 'question of labor.' The relations between employers and employed, between rich and poor, are everywhere coming up for readjustment. In what direction and how far the changes will go, how profoundly they will affect the whole status of civilized life, are questions which thoughtful men are beginning to ponder very seriously. We must not be deceived by general phrases and big words into supposing that the 'Labor Question' is something vague and far off; something for the editors and writers and politicians to settle, as being a matter which *we*, the common people, cannot understand, and in which, therefore, we have no duty. Of all subjects, it *belongs to us*—to us, the whole people of the land, to our everyday lives, our business, our families. The great danger and difficulty of the whole matter lies in one word—selfishness. The way, and the only way, to a just, peaceful and happy issue lies through each man's caring for others as well as for himself. There is great talk about Human Rights, but rights without duties mean sheer failure and wretchedness. So long as every one is intent solely on his own rights, or exacting from others what he believes his due, the world is simply a great battlefield of selfish passions. When I pay my hands for their work, does that end my obligation to them? No! they are your fellow-beings as well as your workmen. There are thousands of women who live under the same roof with their servants for months and years and never exchange a word with them, except about work. We must come to the simple doctrine, 'Do unto others as ye would that others should do unto you.' Without that there is no solution of the 'labor problem'; with it, there can be no failure." Such is the whole simple truth, and all adverse doctrines of business interests or political economy are the feeblest outcome of a science which excludes the most important data of the case.

From "female help" to summer boarders is quite a natural transition. That institution, now so much increased in numbers and magnitude, may be regarded as a success. Some apprehensions in respect to the influence on the social tone of the rural neighborhood produced by so large an influx from the city, are still occasionally expressed; but, "whether for good, or whether for ill," summer boarders are an institution fixed and likely to go on, at least while it continues to pour the vitalizing stream of a thousand dollars a week into the current of neighborhood business. And then you know it gives such a *polish* to rustic youth! You may say, "Polish is a thing merely on the surface"; but I have always noticed that a mineral must have a good grain all through to be susceptible of fine polish; you can not.polish *chalk*, but you may marble and the precious metals. May our young men be firm as marble! Our young women are sure to be precious!

It is a fact not to be called in question that our summer guests are often as solid and as little frivolous as ourselves; men and women whose friendship is a real and lasting acquisition. And sometimes they undergo barbarous treatment amongst us when fierce animals endanger life and limb. A brief entry on my notes is headed "Bulls on the rampage!" which recalls two cases that excited so lively an interest in the neighborhood last summer, as to claim a space among the annals of the season. Those wild beasts threw mad dogs quite into the shade. It would not cause regret to some persons if mad dogs and those bulls could be thrown into the same inclosure, provided a strong, high wall shut them in.

The only "unfinished business" which I find coming up from last year relates to the Ashton turnpike. The energetic and practical gentlemen who first stirred up the interest to undertake the work have the honor of completing it, in a way that cannot fail to be satisfactory after the two finishing essentials for these roads, time and travel, shall have done their duty.

Another piece of "unfinished business" came near being forgotten—such is the frailty of human memory! That railroad, our standing excitement, now in danger of becoming a *standing joke*, was "to be in running order by Christmas." It may be recollected that the Christmas of what year was not stated. Indeed, some proceedings occurred which were calculated to cast a doubt upon the desirability of having any railroad at all. When it was seen that, in the near future, "the sacred soil of Sandy Spring" was about to be profaned by the invasion, then rose the spirit of the Old Dominion, and like a lion prepared to bar the way. It seemed dreadful that a farm must be bisected, that the old arrangements of fields must be altered; the loss of time by the field-hands looking up every hour or two from their work at the passing trains began to be estimated; and more serious results inseparable from those rapid, rushing railways loomed up in the future distance. What influence upon the early construction of the road may be produced by these expressions of adverse feelings it is impossible to say; but rating the effect at the lowest point, there remains this fact, which (as having had some experience in railroad works) I consider unquestionable; that, as railroads are planned and constructed by *men*, a kindly and liberal course pursued toward those who administer them is sure to have a favorable influence in securing important advantages.

If it were not that a historian is essentially an impersonal being, I should feel some delicacy in throwing out these remarks; but, as Carlyle says, "history is a looking before and after"; and I should be very neglectful of that latter outlook if I failed to suggest that for those who come after us, the objections as to "the new arrangement of fences," "the cutting off of corners of fields," and such changes as a railroad would now require, will seem to *them* of very much less importance than they do to us now; and, if securing the greatest of material advantages shall have been put in jeopardy by us for objections no stronger than these, there will be small thanks awarded by our posterity.

Looking down upon our neighborhood as if it were spread before our mental eyes, the most prominent feature that it now presents is, the extent to which the principle (and practice) of association has extended among us. It is very rare to meet an individual who has not been drawn in. Close and near together come the meetings of clubs, of societies with various objects, and some with none at all, except present gratification. This is certainly an interesting and important fact in the progressive career of the community. In this very book, line upon line has been written, claiming the highest utility for these social and business gatherings. Among them all, none has been more successful than the attempt to get up a meeting of the meetings, a club of the clubs, an Annual Convention of the Farmers. Widening out the objects of the growing agricultural clubs, this Convention held a preliminary meeting in November, and assembling about the middle of January in large numbers, laid the foundations for an organization which holds out the prospect of extensive future usefulness. Its projectors may do well to remember there is always some danger that a band which binds beautifully a limited number of homogeneous threads, may possibly break if stretched too far; but when strengthened by the golden thread of unselfish motive and true desire for improvement, there is nothing to fear.

That other large enterprise, the Horticultural Fair, has proved that an association may be conducted so as to deal successfully with a number of heterogeneous elements. Each Fair seems better than the last, even despite inclement weather.

Seeing the rapid spread of these societies, the cautious observer of frail human nature must put the serious question, whether they may not be carried to extremes and so "run into the ground." Experience shows there may be too much of a good thing. Let us pause a moment and regard the several associations, simply on rational grounds. The Farmers' Clubs are not mere pleasure gatherings; to carry them out rightly includes considerable labor. When you have to work there is not much danger of going too far in one direction.

Of the Ladies' Association, I must say, though extremely averse to flattery, that mischief and such as *they* cannot possibly go together; their gatherings are unmixed good.

I doubt not the same, or very nearly the same, may be said of "the Home Interests," when their members shall have passed beyond the giddy verge of youth. The Horticultural comes next, and now we begin to *mix things;* perhaps all the better for that; the members are certainly nice, mingling both sexes and all ages, from 10 to 70 years. The interesting and able Debating Society more than sustains its credit. The Sociable is surely endowed with the faculty of perpetual existence, from its name and nature.

We have summoned to the bar of History a number of our Associations, and find them not guilty of "going to extremes."

It was stated that another, with the sweet title of the "Innocents," had organized, with no special object save to enjoy themselves and "have a good time." Neither is any charge laid against these, so far as your historian has heard. All seem to keep within the limits wherein alone pleasure has any real existence.

A friend to true enjoyment says,

> "Oh watch ye well in pleasure! for pleasure oft betrays."

And another and nobler bard, with deep pathos, exclaims:

> "Lives there the man who has not tried
> How mirth can into folly glide,
> And folly into sin?"

While I should be the last person to disparage the beneficial influences exerted in so many directions by the multitudinous associations that have started up vigorously amongst us, I must be excused for expressing regrets at the diminished interest shown toward the Lyceum and its peculiar exercises. I think this circumstance, in part, attributable to the recent multiplication of social engagements; but the fact is evident, whatsoever the cause. The

Annual Course of Lectures designed for the past winter, has not been well sustained. I know it may be said that the officers of the Lyceum have not furnished as many opportunities to attend lectures as usual; but *there* is not where the difficulty lies. In the first address ever delivered in this building, some fourteen years ago, the promise was confidently made, that if audiences were properly kept up, lecturers would not be wanting. And it was so, and always will be so. Now, how has it been this winter? The directors proposed a course of literary and scientific lectures which cannot be said to have succeeded; though there is no place in the country (I say it deliberately) where just such lectures are more wanted than at Sandy Spring,—thorough information, such as the times and our reputation demand, in regard to the fundamental principles on which depends all correct practice in the mechanical and agricultural arts, in finance, in true economy, and in the best way of living.

Passing over the neglected lectures, one of which at least deserved a better fate, your historian is bound to refer slightly to a circumstance which a number of our most interested auditors, our most concerned members, were pained to observe, namely, a gradual deterioration of that quiet and attentive deportment that marked our early meetings. Lecturers of that day spoke admiringly of the good order of the audience. Some of the best in recent times have received quite a different impression. It might be a mitigation of the complaint if we could lay the fault upon the youthful pupils of the schools, who often helped out our numbers; but not justly could we "lay that flattering unction to our souls."

Every one must see that the Lyceum proper cannot be kept up without the observance of good order. The old charge, "a word to the wise," is all that is needed at Sandy Spring!

It is true that Sandy Spring got along a good while without a Lyceum; it might, doubtless, continue to exist were the hall to become a ruin. But would there not be left a void which few of us in this stirring age might like to see?

Since the above lines were written, a meeting was held at the Lyceum, the third in the regular course, which was very numerously attended. No falling off in numbers or diminution of interest could be complained of on that occasion. And yet your historian, although much gratified at this evidence of life among us, does not see reason for taking back any of the remarks previously made. The entertainment spoken of being *dramatic* in its character, was so different from the old-fashioned Lyceum exercises that it is not to be judged by the same rules. The introduction of this species of amusement is something new; probably it is the commencement of a gratification which in all ages and quarters of the world has produced the most lively pleasure among the people who have witnessed it. Now, although we all desire that the entertainments at this hall shall continue to be of the highest and best quality, it is very certain that neither sage nor saint can edify people who fail to come and hear. Allow me to propose this compromise: let those who incline to come here chiefly for entertainment, attend and feel interested in the lectures for *instruction;* and let those who consider instruction the main object, not fail to countenance by their presence, restraining within proper limits, those meetings where *innocent* amusement is the attraction. So will all be lovely!

The rest of the chapter must be told in a few words.

My respected colleague has furnished a list of events, which forms part of the record—being preserved along with it. We find by reference to that list, while our "Savings Institution" boasts of an increase of $7000, having now in its vaults a solid round sum of over $33,000, that our neighborhood presents a richer increase of a better sort than in any one of the past ten years—little treasures more precious than silver or gold—being eleven babes! The mention of it draws out our poetry—

"As the cradle rocks in the peasant's cot,
So it rocks in the noble's hall;
And the richest gift of the loftiest lot
Is the boon that is given to all."

(Not quite to *all;* there being not a single babe within a mile of the centre of Sandy Spring.)

Referring to babes, it requires to be stated that they had a rough time of it through the winter with the whooping-cough; which disease was not confined to them, for mothers and even grandmothers were compelled to sympathize personally. Still we have cause to be thankful that no vacant chair at home, no little mound in the churchyard, witnesses the visit of the rude disease.

There were two marriages this year:

1. Llewellyn Massey and Emily Thomas, 8th month 8th, 1872.

2. William Parker and Anna M. Bentley, 11th month 12th, 1872.

The deaths properly belonging to the neighborhood were four:

Wilson Scott, 6th month 4th, 1872, after a suffering illness of several weeks; last of the children of one of our old settlers, the quiet, respected Isaac Scott.

A summer child was born to Charles H. and Anna F.

Brooke; his little life was just like a drop of morning dew, that "just as it touches earth, exhales into heaven."

7th month 11th, 1872, Isaac Bond, of consumption, long latent in his system, but wearing him away rapidly at the last. His case is scarcely one which can strictly be included as belonging to Sandy Spring, as he came but to die. Yet neither can he be wholly separated from the community with which he was always most closely connected and where all his affections were fastened.

1st month 6th, 1873, Ann Wetherald died at the age of 83, having survived her distinguished husband, Thomas Wetherald, for forty years.

3d month 10th, Virginia F. Moore died in Alexandria, where she and her little daughter had gone to spend the winter. This book contains the record of her youthful husband's death in 1864, and of a little darling in 1866, by which mournful events her young life, before as bright as any we have known, was darkened by a shadow never to be lifted on earth.

Much sympathy is felt for the death of W. H. Bukoffski's two only children.

Summary of the marriages, births and deaths of the last ten years:

Marriages, 25; births, 79; deaths, 40,—in a population of about 330.

Several interesting features pertaining to the past year should not be altogether omitted: among these are the flourishing condition of the First-Day School, the close of James S. Hallowell's "Fulford Boarding School," and the establishment of one for boys by Coleman and Marshall.

I have found that considerably more space is now required in order to make out anything like an annual sketch than when the task was first undertaken.

And now the pen, which has recorded the long train of events that have constituted a very imperfect biography of the Sandy Spring neighborhood for the past ten years, drops from the weary hand. Under the decided expectation that the writer has made his last entry in these annals, he asks you to listen to a few closing words—they shall be a prayer: that when the fingers that held the pen are stiff, and the heart that dictated its many utterances is cold in yonder churchyard, may some friendly voice be heard to say of the writer—"He was a sincere wellwisher to his race and a true lover of Sandy Spring."

W. H. F.

CHAPTER XI.

FROM FOURTH MONTH, 7TH, 1873, TO FOURTH MONTH, 6TH, 1874.

Resumption of the History — Influence of the age — "10 years ago!" —The solid basis — Former prices — Increase of travelling — Also of the use of fresh meats — Country stores — Economy and Micawber — Wheat exceeding former products; 42 bushels per acre — Dairy business extending — Railroad located from Hanover through our farms — Rise of the Grange: its character and influence — Good lectures at the Lyceum, by Rev. J. F. W. Ware, Samuel Stabler, of California, and others — The "Black Friday" did not weaken the "Savings Institution"; but the "Mutual Insurance Company" suffered losses by fire of over $40,000—The Rockville and Horticultural Fairs "better than ever before"— The Telegraph established at Olney, and the Metropolitan Railroad by Rockville — No marriage this year, but interesting "golden wedding" of Edward and Ann R. Stabler — "Silver wedding" of Warwick P. and Mary M. Miller — And the "golden wedding" of Robert H. and Anna Miller: all of which occurred within our historical year, from 4th Month, 1873, to 4th Month, 1874.

Since it is your expressed desire this history, commenced ten years ago, should not be suffered to drop yet awhile (as was the sincere expectation of the writer), he resumes the pen without making any further explanation of his change of purpose. He would warn you in advance that there is a period in the life of every man, coming at different ages in different persons—some reach it at sixty, some at seventy, others at a still later period—when the individual experiences an honest conviction that he ought to give up responsible business: but if he proceeds beyond that period the conviction leaves him; he gets further and further from perceiving or acknowledging the gathering shadows, and clings with nerveless hand to the sceptre, the pen, the gavel, or whatever may be the instrument of his office. An anticipation of this sort is before the mind of your historian. Started again on the course, you may expect a succession of volumes rivalling Bancroft in numbers, or simulating even the Chinese historians. Being now supported by two lady assistants (for he is gratified to announce that Mrs. Mary B. Thomas has consented to join the editorial corps), he is quite unable to promise when the undertaking will come to a final close.

In entering upon the second decade it seems entirely consistent with the nature and objects of history to take a retrospective glance at our situation when the last decade commenced. The doctrine so frequently uttered that "history is philosophy teaching by example," renders it highly proper to take such view.

Ten years used to seem a long while to me. To some of the audience it doubtless so appears now: (I know; because about forty years ago a young lady sent me a copy of verses—I have them yet—entitled "When we were young, ten years ago!") The period seems quite brief now. Yet when we think how much has occurred, if we only refer to the changes which this book records—the marriages, births, deaths—ah! it scarcely seems the same world!

But in making the comparison of then and now, we must guard against the mistake of regarding as changes in the object, what are in fact only changes in ourselves. We old people are quite liable to this error; which is simply unavoidable, if the subject is viewed as colored by our own feelings. The only way to avoid it is by sticking to facts. Here statistics, figures, come in, to strip the subject of illusions, and render our conclusions of some value and interest. Your historian has been brought to see, partly against his will, certainly in opposition to all his imaginative and poetic instincts, that the prosperity of a community must rest, like all other things, on a solid material basis. It would be disagreeable, and only partially true, to say, that in this, as in other material things, money is the measure of value. Poor indeed, wretchedly poor, is the man or the neighborhood that is not distinguished for something better than money; which is of the earth, earthy; like the foundation-stones of a building to be kept out of sight—*low down*, where it belongs; not to be compared to the beautiful pillars, walls, bay-windows, mantels, &c.; and yet, where are all those valuable and beautiful things when the foundation gives way? These are facts which it is well to face. I return to the *figures*, with which I shall not detain you, but only present a very meagre specimen to illustrate the point. I find in a record of nine or ten years back, that agricultural productions stood at prices far beyond the present time: Hay brought $30 a ton, oats were 97 cents a bushel, pork 18 cents a pound. Compare those figures with the corresponding prices for the last two or three years. Flush times were those, for money came in faster even than it went out. Is this the case now?

Let us turn away from the grovelling thought, to read a lively passage from the contribution of my new lady assistant. She says: "Our people seem to have done more travelling this year than ever before; persons from Sandy Spring have visited Boston, New York, Philadelphia, Mauch Chunk, Gettysburg, Watkins Glen, Niagara, Ohio, Indiana, Valley of Virginia, Rehoboth Beach, Cape May, St. Louis, Chicago, Quincy, Omaha, St. Paul's, Utah, Colorado, San Francisco, Mammoth Cave, Chattanooga, &c." Not to be behind the times, various "American citizens of African descent" took advantage of a cheap excursion to Richmond, Virginia. There were also forty-five individuals from this place present at Baltimore Yearly Meeting in the fall. Now *here* is a go for certain! You couldn't find anything like that ten years ago, or indeed ever before. The most snarling critic cannot deny that travelling has a great effect in expanding the mind, conducing to progress. But when one has a leading subject weighing on his mind, he is apt to find a connection between it and some other things that appear quite different. That our people should have done so much travelling is a thing to be proud of, but indeed it does cost!

In this connection too let us state another very different fact, but ending in the same result as to pecuniary gains.

Thomas J. Lea reports a great increase in the consumption of fresh beef.

Add to this our other supplies of fresh meats, and there is an amazing total. Of course the summer boarders are responsible for part of this large consumption, though only for a small part.

This is really and truly a sign of progress. It shows

that we are changing our meat diet from the pork and bacon that served as the staple for our forefathers, to the more wholesome mutton and beef. I think it is probably worth all it costs, but (like the travelling business) it does cost. The money in this case stays in the neighborhood too, which is a good thing. It is also a favorable circumstance that the money spent in our stores, or at least a fair fraction of it, remains among our own people.

The mercantile statistics of the neighborhood, so far as relates to our dealings with the stores, would form an important item of the general prosperity, especially if the review were extended over the period of the past fifteen or sixteen years. I speak only of the collective operations, not of the dealings of particular individual storekeepers. Such review would, I think, refute the remark made recently by one of our prosperous citizens, to the effect that "these stores were the greatest evil of the times"; which was of course a hasty exaggeration. When we reflect on the fact that the three or four stores at which our people mostly deal, receive in cash or promises to pay an amount equivalent to the interest of a million dollars, there is some difficulty in understanding how the amount is made up from the producing capacity of the surrounding estates in addition to other large necessary expenditures. No one can be so unfair as to attach blame for this condition of things to the persons who keep the stores; who are all too well known and too highly esteemed to need any sort of excuse or explanation. It is probable these gentlemen could enlighten us better than any one else as to the point where the real mischief lies; not so much in the amount of goods bought, as in the amount not paid for.

These are times when, throughout the length and

breadth of our land, a deeper concern than I have ever known before is felt by all reflecting citizens at the heavy debt which is piling up everywhere by individuals and communities. Our national law-makers are now in the act of relieving the pressure of the debt by *increasing* its *amount*. Probably some individuals would like to pursue the same course with their private obligations; a road to ruin which does not very much concern Sandy Spring; at least we will hope so. Still, inasmuch as human nature is much the same everywhere, and as nature allows no exceptions to her laws, it is, perhaps, not a superfluous caution at this time, to direct your attention to that practical principle in the right conduct of life which is nowhere better illustrated than in the words of Micawber: "Income, £20; expenses, £19 19s. 6d.; result, peace and happiness. Income, £20; expenses, £20 10s.; result, misery and ruin!"

Examine the figures, young people; the magic numerals that comprise such momentous issues! It is a solemn fact requiring no prophetic insight to discern, that all the culture which this neighborhood has attained, all its social advantages, its respect abroad and comfort at home, will be unavailing to prevent a catastrophe, if the groundwork of human prosperity fails: industry directed by intelligence, prudence, and the resolve never to incur a debt without rational assurance of being able to pay. (Congratulate me on being through with this portion of this year's history!)

Tokens of energy and improvement during the year are by no means wanting. Agriculture, the foundation-rock on which our chief prosperity must be built, can show some considerable successes, while it can scarcely be called a very brilliant year. The wheat crop may be boasted of.

One of our farmers (whose initials are S. P. T.) raised 420 bushels on ten acres, a production probably never exceeded in this part of the country. Such a return might be considered exceptional; but I have to add that the Farmers' Club, consisting of a corps that might be excused for showing some falling off, if such a privilege may be claimed for any cause, raised 7000 bushels of wheat last summer. There is no report as yet from the younger clubs; but if the men whose average years are now just 55½ have done thus much, what may we not suppose of the vigorous youth whose age is just about one-half their fathers? Sandy Spring farming is going on all right. When one crop fails there is sure to be success in another. For example, the peach crop this year was one of the worst, but there were some favored exceptions. In connection with the dairy business, as yet only begun, a notice of "a most superior milk wagon" was put up; but, unfortunately, the vehicle was forwarded to Philadelphia. Still, it shows the enterprise of an Ashton manufacturer. This is probably a slight forerunner of the new direction which our dairy business will take as soon as *that railroad* is finished.

We come now to one of the two great incidents that distinguish the year. One day last spring the railroad engineers entered the neighborhood. Fire and flame heralded their approach. The mode pursued of getting rid of timber on some 25 acres exhibited the quality of dispatch for which railroads are distinguished; though the owner of the land thus despoiled probably failed to see the beauty of the operation. No more did some of the landowners through whose farms the location was made, see much beauty in leveled line and curve. The new location, however, proceeded, greatly to the satisfaction of the engineers on one side, and certain gentlemen of the neighborhood, "whose ox was not gored" this time, on the other. The straight line was located from Hanover to Gaithersburg, the engineers resting from their labors when summer came, since which the railroad has also rested.

Your historian, reviewing the remarks made a year ago on the subject of railroad incursions and land damages, sees no reason, from the threatened personal injuries of the past year, to recall the sentiments there expressed. A railroad is the great want of our neighborhood. Let her come, even if some nervous individuals have to get out of her thundering track. Will Sandy Spring ever have one? That is the question.

It is scarcely necessary to inform you that the other illustrious incident of the year is the institution amongst us of the new order of the *Grange*. It comes among us, not like a railroad, bringing public benefit with private injury, sacrificing the comfort and sometimes the very home and hearth of the individual to the greater benefit of the community; but with designed injury to none, and kindness and good-will to all. The idea of the Grange is simply an expansion of the principle which underlies all the pleasant and improving associations that distinguish our neighborhood; it may almost be termed a peculiarly Sandy Spring idea; hence the degree of acceptance it has met, sufficient to counterbalance the obstructions with which it had naturally to contend. It was unavoidable that a people trained as ours should shrink somewhat from entering a strange "Secret Order." We are, among ourselves, a united people—more so than most communities; united, and yet isolated. It might be predicted that the Grange would be slow in overcoming these natural obstructions. Yet we find that already a considerable number, knowing themselves to be farmers, could not refuse their countenance to the first grand combination formed to benefit the farmers; having experienced the pleasure and profit of associating together in so many ways, they readily received the idea, so congenial with their own experience, of trying the principle on a larger scale; being nurtured and trained in faith in the equality of woman, they were naturally attracted to the first national business association that acknowledged her equality, and the essential requirement of her presence, her assistance and counsel. Having been continually reminded by their own excellent ritual that social love and kindness are the true fruits of religion, they found it an easy step from the doctrine "becoming their own Christian profession," to the doctrine that these qualities are also most becoming, without distinction of profession, to all.

The Grange proposes for itself all these things. Three orders have been established amongst us, comprising about 150 members. Their permanence will depend on the continued zeal in carrying out the cardinal principles of the Order. I confess to considerable curiosity, not free from some uncertainty, in regard to this part of next year's record. But, in the meantime, whether our friends stand clear or join, there is not the slightest ground for unpleasant divisions; *he* must be a false Granger who desires to throw a stone at any one outside. The question has arisen, whether the new association will interfere with the good old ones. No indications of that sort are apparent yet. The Farmers' Clubs are natural auxiliaries to the Grange; the various associations in which our ladies take either the entire arrangement, or divide the work with their brothers, find a congenial spirit among the Patrons of Husbandry, so that it will be only a question of distinct or of combined action in the same direction. Each association has at present a beneficial purpose; all may find it true economy, both of time and power, to concentrate.

The literary interests of the neighborhood, as finding expression in the transactions of the Lyceum, have not been neglected; the lectures not very numerous, but good. Mr. Ware favored us again in the fifth month, but the weather again refused to favor his kind effort for our benefit. We may reasonably hope, since the weather is fully as capricious in its frowns as in its smiles, that when he comes as he has promised to do next month, the bright May season will be on its best behavior. Mr. Ware comes a long distance—all the way from Boston—to entertain and instruct us; but we (just among ourselves, would not have it get out you know!) can understand how naturally a man should revolve first on one and then on the other "hub of the universe!" For the present Lyceum season, science was declared in order, and a very successful exhibition of its brilliant and recondite mysteries was had.

Another lecture on a branch of science less brilliant, but not less important nor less interesting, is promised. It is sure to supply deep and needed instruction about common things; always the most valuable. Among the lectures delivered here last season we must not omit the mention of a life-like picture of California, drawn by Samuel Stabler, one of our Sandy Spring boys, who wandered off to that distant region; one of the few worth keeping whom we have lost in that way.

The lectures spoken of, like the best speeches of all description, have been "fit, though few." Also the condition of Lyceum Hall has been improved. Ventilation, that all-important and much neglected feature in public rooms, is ingeniously provided for. Indeed, it may be admitted that the younger hands into whose charge the Lyceum has passed, have done their duty "passing well." This transition by which young blood was substituted before the old fluid was quite chilled in the veins, appears to have been a master-stroke, accomplishing more objects than one.

Long live the Lyceum! It has done good service, and has more (and better, I trust) yet to do. The true quality of work is not best seen while being done, at least this is the case in work where the *heart* of the doer is the active power.

It would never do to pass the year '73, with three months of '74, without any reference to the "Black Friday" of last September. Our people are becoming more and more interested in the financial condition of the country. Although there must be ground for apprehension in regard to business affairs, it is to be noted that our Savings Institution shows that some people have saved money; its deposits having been increased this year by a full six and and a-half thousand dollars.

The Fire Insurance Company had much the hardest year of its existence, paying for over $40,000 of property destroyed by fire. This rapid agent of destruction was at its work in our very midst: the barn of Wm. H. Stabler, together with a number of vehicles and farm implements, but fortunately no stock, being consumed in the early morning of the 1st of June.

It should have been stated among agricultural matters, that the Second Annual Convention of all the Clubs was held at the appointed time, and numerously attended. In the opinion of our new lady historian, the "Rockville Fair and our Horticultural Exhibition" were, if possible, better than ever before. The telegraph recently established at Olney, and the opening of railroad travel through our county, (but not alas! through Sandy Spring) were glorious improvements.

The statistical account shows of births, five boys and four girls, total nine. Amongst these new arrivals in our happy community, my younger assistant specifies a boy, making a graceful allusion which I cannot forbear to quote. She writes, "July 20th, '73, at Rockland, a child was born, who received the name of one whose memory is yet green and bright in Sandy Spring, J. Elgar Hallowell."

The list of deaths during the past twelve months, of those who can properly be assigned to our neighborhood, is short but deeply impressed, being in number only two.

May 24th, 1873, Walter Bond, son of Samuel and Sarah A. Bond. By this sad event, the band which had joined two interesting twin brothers was parted. The bereavement seems in some way more conspicuous, more constantly brought to mind by the presence of him who was left. They appeared in life to be always so closely united.

October 28th, 1873, died Isaac Briggs. Born at Brookeville in 1803, he had just completed the term of the Psalmist, threescore years and ten. His eventful life was closed at the "Church Home" in Baltimore, among strangers, who ministered to his dying hours with the tenderness of true "Sisters," the name they so well deserve to bear. It is their own statement that they were peculiarly attracted to the expiring man. And over the wide extent of country through which he wandered, in all the various places and situations into which an eccentric genius led him, he made and left behind him everywhere many warm friends. As the friend who assists me writes,

"The kindliest of all human natures,
He joined to courage strong,
And love, that reached to all earth's creatures,
With sturdy hate of wrong."

He was a man that had no use for outward profession; "no tithe took he of mint or anise or cummin"; but in the weightier matters of the law, kindness and justice and truth, there lives no man nor woman who can bear witness against him. Exposed in his wanderings to temptations, which, fortunately, few of us know anything about, he walked clear and pure in the *reality*, while caring too little, indeed, for the *appearance* of wrong. Unhappily for himself, he formed none of the closest ties, the nearest and dearest; yet his death has left a blank with some that will never be filled. After his long wanderings his remains rest in yonder grave, among his kindred.

There is another department in the three divisions of our record of family statistics which must be left vacant this year, for the second time only since the record began. Of marriages (within the year) none.

Happily for us, in the gloom we are not left without some rays of light. The dark cloud, as we may term it, has both a silver and a golden lining. Although weddings are admitted by all the world to be very interesting affairs on the occasion of their first occurrence, it may be seriously claimed that their solemnization, after long years of "truth-tried wedded love," is something still more impressive and interesting. The year 1873 has been thrice honored in this way.

The Golden Wedding of Edward and Ann R. Stabler was celebrated on Christmas Eve, the 50th anniversary of the marriage and the home-bringing of the bride to the house which has been her dwelling ever since. There was but one opinion among the numerous guests in regard to the interest and beauty of the celebration, a full account of which is preserved in the neat little pamphlet dedicated to it. The Silver Wedding of Warwick P. and Mary M. Miller was celebrated the 9th of May. Shining with *milder lustre*, it gave a delightful evening to a large circle of friends. Another deeply interesting affair of a similar kind took place on the 23d of April. Though occurring outside the limits of our neighborhood, the large number of our people so intimately connected with the celebration renders it quite proper to speak of the golden wedding of Robert H. and Anna Miller. The peculiar circumstances attending this celebration will long keep it in the pleasant memories of hundreds of closely interested persons. On the 10th of March following, the husband (father and grandfather) passed from earth.

CHAPTER XII.

FROM FOURTH MONTH, 6TH, 1874, TO FOURTH MONTH, 5TH, 1875.

"The bright side, the true side"—Progress always—Yet named a "dry year"—Sandy Spring less affected by drought—Low price of hay some advantage—The Colorado Bug makes its appearance—Encouraging views—A co-operative laundry suggested—The Horticultural Society furnishes a fine display—The 3d Annual Convention of Farmers' Clubs highly successful—The Grange flourishing—Also all the other Societies—False charges against the Lyceum, where eleven lectures were delivered in the year—The fiery element shows abatement—Deposits increase in the "Savings"—Lines borrowed from the sea—Voyage to Europe—Telegraph withdrawn—Interesting statistics—An "Old Folks Party" at Stanmore.

In casting thoughts backward over the year just transpired, we cannot say that the experience of Sandy Spring contradicts materially the general impressions in other places, that it has not been one of the prosperous years to farmers. Since the bright points are not very numerous or striking, it may require more than the usual effort on the part of your historian to discover and describe what few there be. It is certainly not worth while to dwell upon the opposite sort. It would not pay you in any shape or fashion to come here and listen to a recital of troubles, failures, disappointments and such—Oh, no! let me be excused from that. We do not propose to waste your time and spoil an evening, which has many bright and pleasant reminiscences in the past—now getting to be a *long past.*

It is my serious conviction, formed in early life, and confirmed both by its sad and its happy experiences, that the *bright side* of human life and things is the *true* side; and history means (if it has any sensible meaning at all) the record of human progress along the meandering, but ever on-flowing current of the way. Although there is often a seeming retrogression, it is like the bends of the Mississippi river in going to New Orleans: the great flood in its windings only *seems* to go back; while all the time it is making its resistless way on—on to the great deep which is to swallow it at last. So with the river of Time.

It goes on progressively to its destined end and aim, and nothing can divert its course; evolving perpetually new and higher forms of being. It is only by believing in and actively co-operating with this grand scheme of progress that we can truly obey and really experience the fruits of obedience.

Last summer I visited the "Jardin des Plantes" in Paris, and saw there the most famous sun-dial in the world. Placed on the summit of a high circular mound, it bears the memorable inscription—"Horas non numero, nisi serenas"—or, "I take no account of any but the calm, sunshiny hours." This motto I propose for my history, and stick by it so far as human weakness will allow; not wholly to exclude the serious troubles and misfortunes, that may not be entirely ignored, and which rightly viewed must be essential elements and causes of progress

The reports of my associates, upon which I have greatly relied, are very satisfactory, as far as they go, but are unfortunately rather brief. Especially is this the case with the report of the junior member of the historical firm, who gives us this year only a taste of the valuable material which she is so well qualified and so well situated to accumulate. Her opening sentence is "Nothing of vital importance seems to have transpired." We make this our first note then—a dry year! Our meteorologists will no doubt dilate at proper length upon the weather; they will show, I presume, that it has been in several respects quite remarkable. The temperature at the close of last April was unusually low, destroying the fruit in many places, though not universally. The drought of the summer is an incident too common of late years to be considered remarkable, but its continuance through the autumn, especially the absolute rainlessness of October and part of November, is without precedent in my recollection. The winter of '74–5 has become historical, not so much by extremes of low temperature, as by persistent cold. Happy are we not to live where whole farms are covered many feet thick with blocks of ice, which cannot prove a desirable top-dressing.

We find in regard to the first subject we touch, that the year has had about it something quite "remarkable." As we go on, perhaps we shall find it exhibit other features of characteristic importance and interest. Time is like other things in this: its degree of impressiveness depends very much upon the way we examine it. Only put on the right glasses, and there does not exist an object in nature that fails to offer wonders of structure and beauty. Surely, then, twelve months can never roll around a numerous, active, intelligent, diversified, but united body of men, women and children, without changing, marking, and leaving traces of the mark as they pass by.

Still keeping in view the idea that our paramount concern is with the reviving features of the year, we note that the favoring spring and early summer brought us full crops of grass and wheat; while the other one of the trio of most important productions, Indian corn, endured the drought and came out with us a fuller crop decidedly than was the case in the country generally. I think it is an established fact that we suffer less in seasons of deficient moisture than do most other fertile sections of neighboring counties. The higher price of corn has helped out bravely; though it has scarcely sufficed to compensate for the diminished price of wheat and hay. It is the opinion of some of our judicious farmers, that a price of hay, too low to tempt such large exportations as we have all indulged in of late years, might be no real disadvantage; and that a better return would come of using grass in certain other forms.

The constitutional tendency of which farmers are accused, to croak and grumble, found this year a strong justification for venting itself, in the advent of a most unwelcome visitor, the Colorado bug. This was, indeed, a new experience. It came upon us without preparation. We had heard much about the animal, but there is a great difference between the sympathy felt for a misfortune experienced by our fellow-laborers across the Mississippi, and the shock of its sudden arrival at our own doors. It appeared as if the ugly animal had made a quick jump across the Alleghany Mountains, and lit down on every potato patch throughout the land around us. In this there was a striking resemblance to the epizootic among the horses in a preceding year. I think the bug was first seen by the farmers on the first day of June, '74, keeping on with increasing numbers till about the middle of August.

One of our potato-growers estimated that he caught at least thirty gallons of the bugs in a ten-acre lot, and the vines, though cleared of the pests one day, were found covered with them the following morning. So far as I can gather the results of this first year's experience, it would seem to show that diligent picking with the fingers will effectually prevail against their ravages; but so much labor is required as to render this favorite production in many parts of our neighborhood a doubtful crop to depend upon, while the enemy stays with us. Our club designs to plant forty-nine acres this year against the eighty-nine planted last year. The efficacy of Paris green appears to have been tried successfully; the fears of its infecting the tuber with its poison may be regarded as groundless. In parts of Germany, potatoes are raised in soils containing a far larger quantity of arsenic than is in the Paris green. Well, we shall have something to look forward to: perhaps the freezing of the ground to an unwonted depth last winter may have destroyed the embryo of the nasty little beast. I reckon we had better plant the tubers, if not quite in the usual quantity.

Whatever may be said in regard to the pecuniary results of farming operations in our neighborhood, it cannot be alleged that there has been any falling off in diligent effort. "Our old men have doubtless their usual visions" (of better days long ago) "and our young men dreamed dreams" (of better days to come), but neither dream nor vision has weakened the busy hand nor dulled the active mind. While the spirit survives with fraternal feeling, Sandy Spring is safe, whether money be plenty or "tight"; perhaps all the safer when it *is a little tight.* The apprehension that we cannot make a living here, out of the ground, in some honest way, is simply preposterous. While the earth endureth, and men crowd the cities, grain, hay, roots, meat, butter, cream, fruit, one or the other, all or a few, are sure to be in demand, and to supply all the real wants of the best sort of living.

There has been a considerable manifestation this year of a spirit of inquiry and experiment among the younger farmers, and this is a very good thing. Also some show of an effort to economize expenses. One of the valuable associations, yclept the "Home Interests," has the merit of starting the bold project of a "co-operation laundry," which claims to introduce economy into an important and troublesome department of the household; not only economy of *expenses,* but the saving of the hardest part of woman's work, by making steam and machinery perform it. I believe this is only a *project* as yet, "the sinews of war" not having been fully provided.

Other indications are not wanting to show there is a full measure of interest and spirit connected with things relating to our great business of life. The Horticultural Society was kept up with unflagging zeal through the season; and with the ready assistance of others outside its necessarily restricted membership, presented to the surrounding community in September a highly successful exhibition of vegetables, fruits and flowers. My associate also notes an increased interest in our County Fair, evinced by a creditable display from this vicinity. In the same connection we record the Third Annual Convention of the Farmers' Clubs of Montgomery county, having been so interesting and popular as to merit being considered an established institution. The design was first shadowed in this little book. In the record made three years ago it is remarked: "The Farmers' Clubs might (and *ought* to) have a system for combining their wisdom and for co-operating in making important experiments; they ought to hold a general meeting at least once a year"; and the Lyceum was named as the proper place. Now since the idea thus thrown out has borne such fine fruit, it may be as well to remind you where it originated. People are always willing to own a child after he becomes in any way distinguished!

Next after the sketch of the progress of agriculture among us, generally come remarks upon social institutions and the general condition of the neighborhood. Between these two, and as being closely connected with both, properly comes a notice of the recent institution of the Grange. It is, however, impracticable from the very nature of the Order to give any definite description of operations from which the outside world is of course excluded. As a subject in which many of our people are directly interested, it is proper to note in this Record the erection of a fine building at Olney, for the accommodation of the Order, also affording a spacious lecture room, where several excellent and instructive public addresses have been already delivered. The construction of the building was distinguished by the strict carrying out of the principle of "punctuality in all our dealings," which is so often impressed on our own peculiar people. Indeed, it is no more than fair to claim that the commendable characteristics of Sandy Spring have been impressed in considerable degree upon the new Order, contributing to its solid prosperity.

The Grange not being a special institution of our neighborhood, these local annals do not need to dwell upon the subject: the less so because, unfortunately, there is a difference of sentiment in regard to it, while the satisfaction, the very life of this record depends upon its referring to subjects and events in which all of us can feel a common interest, and which all may recognize as a sort of common property. I pass the subject with this remark — coming from one who knows whereof he speaks—no permanent trouble is to be apprehended where there is no real ground for a difference, because both parties are seeking the same end, and by almost the same means, namely—co-operative action and "unity of the Spirit in the bond of peace."

Other institutions which may be characterized as the Agricultural-Social, Moral-Social, Home-domestic-Social, and the Literary-Social, still live and flourish. What a social people we must be! Although predictions have been made of extinction by absorption of several of these associations, there is a spirit prevailing amongst them that seems to refuse to perish. As this spirit is, within itself, probably the best trait we have to boast of, may it continue to wave! if only it does not quite use up some of the young people who are animated by it beyond reason and moderation at the expense of sound sleep and rest.

In reviewing the operations of the Lyceum proper I discover that it has been slandered by some of us. It was reported as being in a languishing condition—thus, "lectures not well attended"—"the people satiated with them," and other similar accusations of failing interest in this literary centre.

Now we find that there have been eleven lectures delivered in this hall during the present year. When were there ever more? Look at the variety of subjects! "Poetry of the Bible," "Sketch of the Colorado Country," "Afternoon of the 19th Century," "The Dairy," "The Dignity of Labor," "Local Option," "Visit to Aston Rowant," "Spain and Palestine," "Pictures of Rocky Mountain Scenery," "Sinai." Naturally some of these were better attended than others, and no doubt better merited attendance; but all were instructive. Rev. Mr. Ware's lecture combined merit and interest in a high degree; and as he was at last favored with a beautiful evening, the audience was as large as any in Lyceum's best days. Again, the Magic Lantern brought a crowd that showed how the youthful fondness for pictures survives among us all. Appeals to the eye are more attractive than to the ear, which known fact may be explained in this way: When we are children we are apt not to understand the subject clearly, or may be repelled by excess of advice; and when we are grown up our self-love revolts from the idea that "the fellow can teach us anything." Perhaps we are satiated with lectures of quite another sort. We love to look at pictures—they do not offer insults in any way. Popular lectures should always have something to *show*, if practicable. Still, when we come to think seriously, there are not many of us who would hesitate to acknowledge that we might learn a great deal more from sound, rational lectures without adventitious aids. "Were men to live coeval with the sun, the patriarch pupil would be learning still." If those lines could be truly said in the times of Young's "Night Thoughts," how much more forcibly might they be uttered now!

The two solid institutions doing business at the Insurance Building, corner of two neighborhood Turnpikes, present in their recent annual statements a favorable condition of affairs in both companies. The fiery element, so prevalent for several preceding years, showed a decided abatement in '74 (though it makes a lively start in '75). The increase of deposits in the Savings Bank is steady: a trifle less than the increase was last year, making over $45,000 now, and giving promise that the eighth year will show savings to an amount exceeding $50,000 if all goes well. Of the investments there are a little more than $3500 loaned to individuals properly secured; a circumstance which indicates that the bank is widening its sphere of usefulness without any diminution of safety. No security is so safe as land. * * * * Thus we see the ship moves on—ship that holds our common destiny. Watchman, what of the night? Where is she now? Any breakers in sight? How are the engines working? Is there still proper depth? Above all, how is she steering? and whither? All secure, master! plenty of steam from the boiler—breakers wellnigh passed. She is steering calmly on—the only gale to be feared has, it is hoped, subsided. Breezes will of course arise, but only such as disturb the surface; for,

"Though winds are raging o'er the upper ocean,
And billows wild contend with angry roar,
We know, far down beneath the wild commotion,
That peaceful stillness reigneth evermore."

And while the *social depths* are kept sweet and calm and pure by the salt of religious principle, to which this neighborhood owes what it has of most value, there will ever arise from those depths an influence powerful to calm the surface, though ruffled by transient gales.

The foregoing figure of speech savors plainly of the sea; which was for a time during the past year the abode of several of your fellow-citizens of Sandy Spring. There were at least seven who tried the Atlantic waves, although only three of us reached the European shores. Four of the seven made a shorter trip along the American coast; one of whom, Charles F. Brooke, has since tried a more extensive journey to the Far West, and *his* reports of the *land* nearly resemble *mine* of the *sea*. No brother or sister of our neighborhood is likely to be deluded into a passionate love, either of the ocean or of Colorado, by the relation of his experiences or mine. The European party had, on the whole, "a good time"; one of my associates is pleased to write: "September 24th brought the return home of our European party in renewed health, and with a host of pleasant recollections, which they have shared with some of us who were not so fortunate." That party can never forget another composed of fifty friends, who came one bright moonlight evening, the 28th of June, to bid farewell to the travellers; nor the kind greeting that welcomed the return.

I regret to wind up remarks upon the travellers of this year with an observation from the notes of one of my assistants, rather severe, but doubtless just, running thus: "June: numerous husbands off on trips, while their self-denying wives attend to home matters." Who is hit?

Among the losses of the year we have to note the withdrawal of the Olney telegraph. It was a short-lived benefaction, but while it existed a great advantage in several instances; the loss is much to be lamented. The deprivation in this instance does not seem to be chargeable to a want of enterprise on our part, but to circumstances beyond our control. The failure or disappointment is not properly a reflection upon our neighborhood. It is undeniable that, for telegraphs and railroads, we are obliged to depend upon others. The enterprises and performances within our own power, which we accomplish, are the only sort to find proper mention here. As to the question now of some interest, whether the road, when it comes, shall start from Laurel or Hanover, and shall begin in this year or some other future year, that is the concern of John W. Garrett. We can do nothing to hasten or retard. The historian of Sandy Spring regards it as a want of proper dignity to dwell upon this matter any further, particularly as he has no recent information to communicate.

We proceed to a conclusion with a record of affairs which are peculiarly our own; the three most important concerns of human beings, the subjects which arouse the most powerful and deepest emotions of joy and grief.

For the ten years recorded on previous pages there was an average of 2½ marriages amongst us per year (though it may be considered by fair young maidens as almost an outrage to treat weddings as questions of average, and to speak of *half* marriages too!) This year we are favored with three weddings, which is of course "too many by half."

On 9th month, 24th, married, Joseph T. McDowell to Annie Stone. The bride was taken away from the quiet country to the great metropolitan city.

10th month, 6th, Gerard Hopkins and Emily Snowden. Whether we are to lose finally the happy pair in the bay region of Virginia, or to rejoice in their return, time will make manifest.

11th month, 5th, Edward C. Dickinson and Fannie I. Lea. Again the bride is taken away from among us to Northern Pennsylvania. Doubtless in each case our loss is their gain.

It is hoped that in another year *we* shall be making gains at the expense of some other neighborhood, so as not to keep on *losing*. So far as the mere question of population is concerned our gains are nearly triple our losses.

In the blooming month of May, the extreme southwestern verge of our neighborhood, the dwelling of Roger B. Farquhar was gladdened by the arrival of a boy. In the following month, a daughter brightened the opposite extremity; and a boy, her first cousin, was born near midsummer. Autumn afforded another boy. Then in early February a little girl came to keep company with its sister near the well-travelled turnpike. March arrived, and before its close three children, a girl and two boys, joined the procession. My associate, who takes special care of this department, was confessedly unable to keep her record fully up. It stands thus: Eight births this year—five boys and three girls.

Under date 10th month, 30th, my associate writes: "Truly our neighborhood has been blessed with health the past year, which should be a cause of gratitude and thankfulness to the Good Father. There has not been a funeral at our meeting house since this day a year ago, when Isaac Briggs was buried."

Though very healthy still, the neighborhood has not altogether escaped the visits of the king of terrors. 5th month, 22d, the remains of William D. Stabler were brought from Frankford, Penn., and buried in the cemetery. He was a very good young man, with mind exceptionally bright, till overcome by mental disease. The wanderer is freed and at rest.

12th month, 17th, died at the residence of Edward C. Gilpin, Elizabeth Feast. From want of acquaintance, I am not able to add anything to the simple announcement, which indeed suffices for the last page of mortal history for us all. On the same day died Roger Brooke Nesbitt, at Longwood, the residence of his grandparents, E. J. and Mary Hall.

While we have reason to be thankful for the general health of ourselves and our friends, it is proper to note that it has been a year of extraordinary mortality among our colored neighbors; and their losses have been more in quality than in numbers. That energetic, useful and respected citizen (as my assistant justly terms him), William Bellows, would have been a loss in any community; "like Robert Collyer, he kept a book by his anvil and studied as he toiled." Considered as a farmer, old Samuel Pumphrey was an example, and I miss him greatly. Thomas Marriott was one to be singled out amongst his people as an industrious, honest, thriving man. Such men are a serious loss to their employers, and to their own people who need the encouragement of good example.

During the year just past, the anniversary of two Golden Weddings came round, which my senior associate refers to in beautiful terms, mentioning that feeble health prevented their celebration.

The parties were Benjamin and Margaret E. Hallowell and William H. and Eliza Stabler. She further remarks that in the last week of the year '74, "our young friend Charlie Kirk met with a very severe accident from the horns of an Alderney bull, that cast quite a gloom over our neighborhood."

Two social events from two extremes of life will close the present chapter. On New Year's day, a party came off at Stanmore, consisting of twenty guests, whose ages averaged 60 years. Whether called the "Old Folks Party" or "the Centennial," it was enjoyed with a gusto that might compare very favorably with younger gatherings.

Again, a few evenings ago, the very juvenile scholars of a bright little school taught by Elizabeth Bond, gave a series of recitations and tableaux, which excited enthusiastic praises of a numerous audience. In fact our schools are still looking up, all bright at Sandy Spring and Stanmore; a new duty is imposed upon them to follow the fashion now prevailing over the country, and to get up, with proper assistance from this whole audience, the amusing and improving entertainment, "A Spelling Bee."

CHAPTER XIII.

FROM FOURTH MONTH, 5TH, 1875, TO FOURTH MONTH, 3D, 1876.

Cause of grumbling among farmers — Changes going on in Sandy Spring — Connection with "The Centennial" — Proposals to bring out old china, &c. — Past, present and future — "All's well" if the farm is — Abundance better than scarcity, even if low prices seem to equalize them — Paris green is effectual against the potato bug — Use of oyster shell continues — A Dairy Association instituted — A reporter of the *Sun* appears at "The Farmers' Convention" — The wells continue dry — *Pairing* of the societies — Centennial Debating Society — Lectures fruitful, on London and on "Injustice" — Horticultural Fair — A blind performer well supported — Other performers were M. D. Conway, Francis Miller and Dr. J. Wilson Magruder — People more reckless about fires — Sandy Spring Railroad, "a sure thing" — The historian takes to moralizing — The three brothers — The deaths exceed aggregate of births and marriages — Marcus Nutting appears on the scene.

The 13th annual return of the day on which we open this book of history finds the neighborhood "with little to complain of, and much to be thankful for." This is said, notwithstanding the unusual prevalence of influenza and other catarrhal diseases, which have in some cases been quite severe; also without meaning to intimate that our farming community has given up its time-honored privileges (which truly were more honored in the breach than the observance) of complaining and grumbling. Having taken some pains to ascertain the origin of this chronic disposition of our fraternity, otherwise so sensible, I find it is because we are more than any other class of people brought into direct connection with a greater variety of things that will not go just the way which we would have them to go. Our prosperity is dependent at every turn upon an infinite number of variable circumstances; especially on that most conspicuous one, the weather. We can do nothing to change it, and we can not blame ourselves for the injuries that in consequence befall; so we think to take refuge in fretting. Now it is indeed a fact that we are touched in more tender places than other people; we are more dependent and therefore more helpless. At the same time if we would but look at the subject rightly, we might see that the continual contact at every point of our business with nature and her grand laws, ever varied yet ever the same, is the very thing that renders our position the most enviable of all upon earth.

With this merited encomium upon country pursuits and country pleasures, which every passing year more strongly confirms in my mind, I turn to the survey of the one just closed. The general impression left in looking over it is one of life and activity. This quality has been heretofore claimed as one of the leading characteristics of our neighborhood, and I cannot see that it has lost anything in this trait. It seems to me we have been quite active, of course in different degrees, our young people especially, as should always be the case. Another impression of no slight import comes in casting the eye of the mind over the neighborhood, viewed as a whole, is that Sandy Spring is growing less and less homogeneous. "Whether this be for good or whether for ill, it is not mine to say," but I am convinced of this fact: in order that there be reason and propriety in undertaking to sketch the history of a community, it is necessary there should exist a considerable degree of similarity among its people, besides strong common interests, and decided characteristics that distinguish it from other contiguous districts. Such, it is believed, has been the case with our own. General, though not universal agreement in the important particulars of religion, politics and social customs has marked the community, and set it off as possessing that separate individuality which gives a sort of distinct existence, admitting of being made the subject of real history. Now it is the impression of your historian, that even within the period of his official supervision, there can be perceived a notable change in several of these particulars. In the first place, the family groups constituting the community of Sandy Spring have considerably increased in number, and are more widely separated in space. New associations have been formed; new interests developed; in some parts the ties have been drawn more closely, in others they have been loosened; while in a conspicuous degree, the dividing lines that separated our own from contiguous communities are less strongly marked, or even measurably erased; so that it seems not unlikely the time will come, perhaps already is, when "Sandy Spring" shall fail to comprise the community to which we have been accustomed to attach the name. Let the railroad be once made, and the influences tending to change will be so increased that we may scarcely know ourselves to be the same people. Perhaps we may be better—there is still room for that—richer, doubtless, but not quite the same. However, it is going beyond my duty as historian to express an opinion as to the question whether these changes make us better or worse; it suffices to note the fact. While these metamorphoses widen the field of this sketch, they also confuse and dim it; thus removing some of the justification of its continuance.

Our narrative, like almost every other proceeding of

the present year, naturally connects itself with the great Centennial Anniversary, so full of historical associations of the most interesting character. We are drawn to look back to the condition of our neighborhood at the epoch toward which so many views are now strained, and would fain recall the situation one hundred years ago. What would we not give for a true picture of people and things belonging to that period! So gradually do the generations of men melt one into another, as they come successively up the scene, it is only by taking a long retrospect that we can realize the wonderful change. I can think of nothing that would be so interesting as a life-like view of the men and women, the youths and maidens, the boys and girls of '76 presented to us now, unless it were such a view of the future realities of 1976. A suggestion has been made to attempt a celebration at the Lyceum with the aim of restoring the times of '76, in some faint degree, by a collection of old china and other such genuine ancient articles belonging to the period, of which a few fine specimens still remain, chiefly among the Thomas family. By recalling also from such sources as are within our reach, stories of incidents then occurring, with sketches of individuals living in the olden time within our region, not omitting old costumes and all such. So many persons throughout our land are now manifesting an interest in these reminiscences, it must surely be a natural and not unworthy impulse that leads to sympathize with them. On the contrary we may readily believe it is our better nature that is stirred by reviving the memory of old times, especially "the times that tried men's souls," that brought out some of the finest characters in history, and created the nation to which we belong. We ought to feel grateful to those who have interested themselves in this Centennial work, and be willing to take a little trouble to assist. It is all very well to say, "Let the dead past bury its dead,"—"Act, act in the living present," and so on; these ideas are good in their place; but it is also true there is a time for all things. The *present* is not all; it requires past, present and future, all three, to fill the mind and soul of man and satisfy his infinite cravings. They who attend exclusively to either of the three divisions of time, lose at least a fraction of life, *real life*, well worth the living. Let the old revive the memories of days gone by, and of incidents related by their fathers; and let the young listen to the narratives, and extend their scope in reading books that tell of the period; it will not be lost time, but quite the contrary. It is at least safe to say that people can afford to do all this once in a hundred years. Those who live at the Bi-Centennial will thank us for making a permanent record of what we are doing now. Even this history, should it be preserved, may afford some amusement to the antiquarian of those future days, who shall hunt among the rubbish of the long, long ago. How strange are the fancies that cross the mind given up to such meditations!

It may be safely said that the fellow who is supposed in those last lines to have got hold of this 13th Chapter will be puzzled to conjecture the subject to which it forms the preface. I have never thought it necessary to apologize for want of system in the arrangement of these sketches; perhaps the less systematic they are the more like the life they are intended to portray. Country life, however charming, cannot boast of much system; in fact it would not be hurt by a little more. Still it was always designed to start the narrative with an account of what the year has done for the agricultural interest; knowing if a good exhibit can be made of this department, we can adopt the cry "All's well!"

The season was marked with more variety than usual. While the unprecedentedly large corn crop, due to the copious rains of August (8¾ inches), forms a leading feature in the list of productions, the severe drought of May and June cut the grass very short and almost destroyed the young clover. Wheat came out pretty well on an average, taking yield and price both into consideration. If the profits of the potato crop disappointed expectation, neither the season nor the bug can be blamed. Over production is sometimes as bad for pecuniary results as is partial failure. Still abundance is to be preferred to scarcity when we take an intelligent view of their effects. Although 7½ barrels of corn at $4 seems as good as ten barrels at $3, every farmer knows that it is not so. As regards the potato bug, the bugaboo of '74, though it appeared again in June of '75, in large numbers and with undiminished voracity, the free use of Paris green is found to be so effectual that the ugly little monster is viewed comparatively with contempt. It must be due to other causes than fear of the bug that the Farmers' Club diminished the field of planting from forty-nine acres last year and eighty-nine the year before, to thirty acres only the coming season. If the course pursued by those prudent old farmers is assumed as an indication of the action in this respect over the whole country, somebody will make a good thing of potatoes next fall.

Among the bountiful products of the season the great peach crop must not be forgotten. The growers of this most delicious of our fruits suffered from the same disadvantage as the potato planters; the very abundance of production seriously depressed prices; but that was not nearly so bad as a failure of crops. This is about all we have to say on the most important subject in which our community is concerned; except that if our farmers are "carrying" as much wheat (to borrow a phrase from our brothers of the mercantile profession) as of corn and potatoes, at the date we now are, it is even a little *better* with them than merely "*well.*" As one of my associates says, it is pleasant here to notice that two farms in our neighborhood have recently been purchased by gentlemen from Baltimore, who intend to reside with us at least half of each year. This is not only complimentary to our agricultural and social advantages, but also a welcome acquisition to us in respect of the latter feature at least.

The younger class, upon whose shoulders have already fallen "the burden and heat of the day," appear to have sustained their character for enterprise and the spirit of improvement, which is a sure pledge that the agricultural reputation of Sandy Spring neighborhood is in no danger of going backward. The use of oyster shell lime continues. (It is much to be desired that your historian should be able to report the quantity of lime and other fertilizers which have been applied during the past year. There ought to be another assistant, if this history is worthy to be continued.)

A Dairy Association has been recently instituted that indicates the extent to which this important branch of agricultural industry has attained in our community. The object is so worthy as to entitle the new association at once to a distinguished place amongst the neighborhood societies that bloom (and bear fruit) in such abundance.

The Annual Convention of Farmers' Clubs held its fourth annual meeting in January, and was successful as heretofore in drawing a goodly number of the "bone and sinew" class, who manifest a fair degree of interest in its proceedings. A new feature in the scene showed that the interest extended beyond our boundaries. When the President, Henry C. Hallowell, entered the room (and here I feel called upon to mention a name closely connected with this, and that other distinguished institution, the Horticultural Fair), he, the president, was agreeably surprised to find a regular reporter of the Baltimore *Sun*, with paper and pencil, on the spot. We were also again favored with the presence of the editor of the *American Farmer*, which seemed to be a very proper and natural part of the proceedings; but that other evidence of fame was something new. Distinguished characters must pay the penalty of renown. Well, I reckon *we* can stand it—if our admirers can; having had enough of that sort of thing to get used to it.

As my associate observes, the subject of the weather has passed into other hands; still she cannot avoid mentioning as a remarkable fact that no thunderstorm occurred in May. But July made up for the deficiency; on the 10th of that month the lightning struck Ashton store and several trees in the neighborhood, cutting up some very queer antics, as it often does. It is also a circumstance worthy of record here, that while the stress of drought ceased after midsummer, so far as the surface of the ground was concerned, its effects on the streams and wells continued to be felt in places for months afterward. The veins of water that supply some of our wells must have been lower than at any previous period for forty years.

It was observed in last year's record that the Grange holds a place connecting agricultural and social interests. After the experience of another year, I must still view it in that light. As it cannot be considered a special institution of our neighborhood, and as it has the domestic character of reserving its best things for the home circle (like all well-regulated families), it is not necessary here to devote to this subject the wide space it might otherwise justly claim. I am required, however, to state the fact that the Grange at Ashton, which belonged peculiarly to Sandy Spring, withdrew from that location, translating its truly valuable membership to a more ample sphere at Olney. The sentinel at the "outer gate" declares that so far "All's well."

From these friendly borders we come out to dwell with undiminished interest upon the rich and ample field occupied by the various associations with which we are all familiar. It is the remark of a wise man, that when a people are prosperous, all their affairs proceeding in a healthy and satisfactory manner, the history of the country becomes barren for want of subjects. I suppose it must be so with descriptions of our numerous societies; all going on pleasantly, harmoniously, improvingly, with nothing special to record. Yet I do not like to let them off so, forming as they do, the most distinguishing feature of the neighborhood, without counting them over to see if I have them all. For convenience sake, and because it sounds more affectionate, let us pair them thus:

1. Farmers' Club	with	2. Ladies' Association.
3. Enterprise Club	"	4. The Home Interests.
5. Montgomery Club	"	6. The Sociable.
7. The Horticultural	"	8. Dairy Association.

There were the same number of associations recorded in 1872, and with the same titles, except that the Dairy has taken the place of the Innocents. Shall this be regarded as evidence of that progress which we all so earnestly and above all things desire? Let us suppose so. (But a mysterious whisper has reached me, of the rise of still another society; its name and purpose have not fully developed.)

There remains another and a decidedly meritorious association. As we have none to *pair* this with, its members being safely left to attend to that themselves, it is proper to describe further. The name was well chosen—"Centennial Debating Society." It seems to have adopted a judicious plan in selecting as topics for discussion such subjects as have a direct and present interest, instead of old, unpractical, abstract questions. Having had the pleasure of attending their closing meeting for the season, I can readily testify that the debate was more than usually interesting. Only one public meeting was allowed; why not more? Why not give the ladies opportunities to enlighten and improve their minds too?

No one can say that the Lyceum has not been well used this year. Let us recall some of the work done therein. The "Spelling Bee" recommended at the close of last year's sketch came off with success a short time afterward. The prize was carried off by one of our married ladies who happens to reside just now in an adjoining county. About a month later (in May), a lecture was delivered for the benefit of the Horticultural Society, the subject being the "Largest City" and the "Finest Gardens in the World." The contribution thus brought to the funds of the society was rather meagre; although the lecture was by a member who had recently crossed the seas.

The next scene at the Lyceum was of more lively character, being a dramatic entertainment given by the "Sociable." It is a deserved compliment to say that there was real talent developed on that occasion; and the inquiry arises (addressed to the more rigid members of our society), "For what is a faculty given that promotes enjoyment, unless it be used?"

Passing over the summer months, during which this Hall usually has vacation (although the presence of many strangers in the neighborhood would probably secure an audience for any species of lively entertainment that our young folks might devise, as summer boarders don't want anything very solid), we come to the 21st of September, the day of the Horticultural Fair, when the Hall puts on its gayest aspect, and an audience or band of spectators of varied fashion assembles to enjoy and encourage a display of rare interest. Much more might be said of this institution lately grown up among us, which finds its parallel in very few country places, but deserves to be cherished with increasing satisfaction. The effort made by the president to place the Fair on a broader footing was partially successful. So far as related to relieving the financial condition, and enlisting a wider circle of co-operating officials, the plan was excellent; but your historian knows that he has your unanimous voices in favor of a protest, absolute and irrepealable, against making any change in the presiding officer; all of us are "third termers" in this case, which means an extension to three times three.

The regular winter course of lectures began rather later than usual. This was through no omission on the part of the President of the Lyceum, who was unwearied in his efforts to gratify the somewhat jaded literary taste of the Sandy Spring audience, by securing the services of distinguished lecturers from abroad. The course was opened in December, by a discourse of Dr. John Wilson Magruder, who gave a spicy and successful lecture on

"Injustice." There was a good audience, who highly enjoyed his telling hits at the faults of the day, including their own.

On the last evening of the old year and the first of the new, a large crowd collected here to view the wild scenery of California and the Rocky Mountains, exhibited by Jonathan K. Taylor, of Wilmington. People of all ages delight to see pictures, and this display afforded ample gratification.

Two more evening entertainments, also very successful in their results, followed in the 2d month of the year, consisting chiefly of dramatic recitations; the blind performer attracted much sympathy and regard from the neighborhood, which were evidently reciprocated by himself.

February 25th, Moncure D. Conway gave us a lecture on London, which is too fresh in our recollections to require comment. The same may be said of Francis Miller's Centennial Address, closing up the course. When we come to think over all these demonstrations, we must admit the considerable value of the Lyceum.

Now let us look at some business concerns, of a general character of course; private or individual business belongs not to history, but to a special department, sometimes confounded with it, called *gossip*. And what is a better index of the general prosperity than that afforded by the condition of the Savings Institution? Measured by this criterion, we were never more prosperous. The anticipation expressed in last year's sketch of reaching by another year the amount of $50,000 deposits, is more than fulfilled; approaching to $60,000. You will find in the Annual Report some details worth reading; they show a healthy condition. Since it has been unanimously agreed by the Directors to make loans upon the solid security of land, up to one-fourth of our deposits, the objection heretofore made against our mode of operation, as tending to drain all the surplus money away from the country to the city, is no longer justified. The Mutual Fire Insurance Company, whose headquarters are with us, while its operations embrace nearly the whole State, is not adding to its ready money, though the actual capital is continually swelling, the premium notes now in excess of $800,000. Recent experience goes to confirm the unpleasant statement that the general liability to burn, of the houses in this State, is greater than formerly. People are more reckless.

There follows an extract from the Baltimore *American*, giving the last and most authentic news about the never-to-be-omitted "Sandy Spring Railroad": "Mr. Keyser exhibited a map, showing a line from Hanover on the Washington Branch, to the Metropolitan Road, which would relieve the Washington Branch entirely of the through business. That road would have been built before this, but for financial difficulties. It will be about twenty-five miles, and cost about $1,000,000. That road will yet be—must be—built."

I always told you that a railroad through Sandy Spring was a sure thing—as sure as taxes!

My associate mentions that we had a large, good Quarterly Meeting, in Sixth Month last. This item of the year's history recalls another of quite sufficient importance to make it matter of record. A move was made toward dropping the Sandy Spring "Preparative Meeting," as having become rather matter of form than of substance. Difficulties were found to be in the way, which led to a general agreement not to urge the matter, though it can scarcely be said that the convictions of its advocates were changed.

The page which contains a reference to Meeting affairs might be considered a proper place to record delinquencies of our young folks (of course old folks don't have any of the sort referred to); I mean those excesses of the social impulses that lead to turning day into night, or night into day, one or both, and the hurtful loss of sleep, or its transfer from the earlier parts of the night to the earlier parts of the day. If this sketch were a moral discourse, instead of a History, I should feel just like Franklin, when his graceless nephew desired to write a promissory note acknowledging a loan: the wise old man said: "You have the money, but don't waste paper." Your historian is differently situated; he has nothing to do with reforming people—his business is to record facts of sufficient importance; and one of these facts is, that the delinquency aforesaid has increased, is increasing, and ought—but it is not my province to dictate what any person ought to do. Still a historian, while bound to relate facts that may affect the manners and morals of the community which he describes, may indulge himself in an ejaculation such as this: "How soon will our young people discover that their own homes have social claims on their leisure moments, and that 'evenings at home' might often be made as pleasant as in any other place?" Of course they all expect to find it so, with the proper companion. But ah! it seems to require preparation and use to know how rightly to enjoy the home. If the bee did not learn to make honey in the parental hive, before swarming, he would fail in the new one, had he ever so fine a queen; mayhap there would be little honey, but plenty of *stings*.

This last allusion (to the honey, of course) naturally

14

brings us to the record of marriages for the year. This department is brief, but oh, how much can be told in one short line!

Married, 10th Month, 7th, 1875, Annie Miller to Joseph M. Shoemaker, of Philadelphia. When these strangers (be they ever so nice) come and take away our girls, it is some satisfaction to place her name first, as being that with which we are most concerned.

This portion of our record being small the present year, there is some satisfaction in referring to an associated anniversary, always interesting,—the Golden Wedding in August last, of Caleb and Ann Stabler, grandparents of the bride just named. Although at the request of the parties there was no celebration of the event, yet none the less did many an affectionate prayer go up from numerous friends, that their remaining days may be lit up with golden reflections from the memories of their well-spent lives. The last month of the year saw their old homestead broken up, but *not* their *home*.

Close in the same neighborhood another anniversary took place, the Tin Wedding of Asa and Albina Stabler.

Being "short" on this marriage stock, it is proper to make much out of little. Tin Weddings are not much; but while discoursing of the historic subject, it is proper to record the remarkable circumstance that the three brothers Stabler—Edward, Caleb, and Henry—should have passed the 50th anniversary of their marriage within less than two years of each other; making, with Benjamin Hallowell's, four such anniversaries, all in the same neighborhood.

My associate writes, that in order to repair an omission made last year, she desires me to record the marriage of G. W. C. Beall and Mary Palmer.

Births in the neighborhood during the year, 3 boys and 1 girl.

The next and last part of our record for the year shows a result altogether unprecedented in our Annals; the number of deaths exceeding the aggregate of births and marriages. It is with pain I proceed to the narrative; pain softened by the sympathy of many hearts present.

It is proper that I should use the pens of my associates, instead of indulging too far the expression of my own feelings in the delineation of persons so near and dear to myself individually, though better known to none than to me.

At Falling Green, Fourth Month, 18th, 1875, Mary B. Brooke, just two months after a pleasant gathering of near relatives at her residence, to celebrate her seventy-seventh birthday; loved and respected by all who knew her, she possessed a character in which rare intelligence and sweetness were combined.

Two weeks afterwards, at Rockland, Fifth Month, 1st, Margaret E. Hallowell, wife of Benjamin Hallowell (and sister of the writer), closed a long, useful and precious life, wanting a few months of seventy-seven years. She was married in the same year as the preceding cousin: they were close friends in their youth, womanhood and old age; their remains rest side by side in the "old kirkyard."

Fourth Month, 23d, Joseph Scott, an aged uncle of Caroline B. Scott, died at her house, and was buried at the Meeting House. Known, as I believe, to few, no harm was ever said of him.

Eleventh Month, 22d, Samuel Thomas, son of Edward, died after a very long and suffering illness. "He has no doubt entered the beautiful land where the weary are at rest." His custom of friendly salutation with the warm pressure of his hand remains still in my memory.

"An empty cradle," my associate says, "stands for the next record." A page of the last chapter, written a year ago, mentions that "in the blooming month of May, the extreme southwestern verge of our neighborhood was gladdened by the arrival of a boy, to whom was given the name of Robert M. Farquhar." His little frame of more than ordinary beauty was struck within a few months by a strange disease. Being carried in the hope of relief to Lakeside, Baltimore county, he died there on the 20th day of the Tenth Month, and was returned to his parents' home.

My young friend adds these lines from George Herbert:

"It is not growing like a tree
In bulk, doth make man better be;
Or standing long an oak,
Three hundred year,
To fall a log, at last,
Dry, bald, and sere:
The lily of a day
Is fairer far than they;
Although it fall and die that night,
It was the plant and flower of Light."

Second Month, 21st, 1876, Aunt Sally Gilpin died, aged ninety-five years and eight months. This is probably the greatest age ever reached in this neighborhood. While she lived, five generations subsisted at one time among us.

These six deaths are all that properly can be said to belong to our neighborhood. Yet it would seem unnatural to omit the mention of the death of Benjamin P. Moore at Fallston, Harford county, on the 25th, Fourth Month, in his eighty-fourth year, so numerous are his relatives and friends here, who highly esteemed the man that filled the measure of a Christian gentleman.

It is also proper to notice the burial, Fourth Month, 10th, of Mortimer Osborn, whose dying request was fulfilled, that he might be brought to Sandy Spring to be interred.

I close with decidedly the most startling and sensational event of the year. This was the sudden appearance of a person professing to be one Marcus Nutting, well known in the western border of our neighborhood, who left his family twenty-seven years ago, and was universally supposed to be dead; but now returns to claim valuable property, sold by his family years ago in order to provide subsistence, and greatly improved by other hands. He would fain reap where he did not sow. Perhaps it is lawful to hope it will turn out a Tichborne case.

CHAPTER XIV.

FROM FOURTH MONTH, 3D, 1876, TO FOURTH MONTH, 2D, 1877.

Ancient recollections — Questions touching the future — Animated pursuit in agricultural improvements — Various products of the crops — How hay should go to market — Of the potato prediction — Peculiarities of the weather — Improvements of mills — Railroads very slightly referred to — Sandy Spring at the Centennial — The tramps and murderer; how the latter was caught — Discussions of the Presidential election — The beacon lights of true progress — Monkey and hand organ — Defence of the Lyceum — Science invites more attention, as comprising all that is worth knowing, all that there is to know — Triumph of the elder Farmers' Club at Annual Convention — Sleighing and Burns — List of visitors to the Centennial.

I preface the narrative of the present year by reading a historical sketch of our neighborhood, referring to a period considerably further back than any hitherto described in these pages. (See Appendix.)

According to the recollections of this ancient chronicler, it would appear that Sandy Spring had its attractions and its notabilities, even so long ago as the beginning of the present century; that there were men and women here of worth and character, even before we came on the stage of action, and pointing to hopeful grounds for believing that "wisdom will not die with us." In reminiscences such as these, and the prospects they suggest, lie the interest and value of history.

A distinguished living writer, whose profound work on the "Intellectual Development of Europe" has lately been added to our Library, strongly advocates the doctrine that every institution, community and nation, large or small, has, like the individual, its beginning, growth, maturity, decline and extinction. I am not quite satisfied with the evidences which Mr. Draper gives of his theory; but if it is indeed an inexorable law of nature, then shall we also have to contemplate the fate of our neighborhood as something inevitable. We may, however, derive some comfort from the reflection, that the modern scientific prophets are by no means stingy in the length of time they allot to periods past and to come. With a lavish hand they give us years, centuries, aeons, as necessary to bring about the changes that have occurred, as well as those which they predict. The sun himself, scientifically as well as practically speaking, "is but a spark of fire, a transient meteor in the sky"; containing the elements of his own inevitable dissolution, he must pass away into other forms—but not very soon; he will, by the lowest calculation, endure for several millions of years yet. So, as is written in another valuable book, a precious old treasure which is also just added to our Library by its liberal-minded Directresses, so

> "It must come, the day decreed by fates,—
> How my heart trembles while my tongue relates!—
> The day, when thou, imperial land, must bend,
> Must see thy heroes fall, thy glories end!"

Even so, doubtless, will it be with Sandy Spring.

Without giving way to melancholy emotions, it is interesting, and quite pertinent to the present occasion, to ask which of the three possible stages of existence we may have reached: is it growth, maturity, or decline? What answer does the history of the last year give to the momentous query?

Taking a fair retrospect, we find the tokens of more than usual activity and movement, such as might be looked for in the Nation's Centennial Year. It is also undeniable that activity is life; though it is well to remark that in estimating permanent effects, it makes a material difference *what direction the movement takes*, and whether it has been such as to advance the more important, permanent and higher interests.

As before observed, the material interests of this neighborhood are essentially agricultural; and taking the condition of our agriculture as the criterion, I see no reason to doubt that the general result shows *progress*. This is especially visible in certain departments of farming industry; perhaps more in the dairy business than in any other. Whether we consider the Dairy Association as cause or effect of the recent animated pursuit (and it may be justly regarded as both), it has certainly been the means of diffusing information in a wider circle, of the success attained by those among us who have devoted a larger portion of time and labor to this interesting branch of rural industry. So wide is the renown already acquired by this Association, that its proceedings have been noticed in that other "Hub," away in Boston! Of course this is all right. Harmony requires the two hubs to make corresponding progress.

In regard to old staples of the farmer, you may recollect that the returns of crops made at the Annual Convention in the 1st month showed that there was no falling off in aggregate product. The wheat crop rather exceeded the general average, being a little over 20 bushels per acre. Corn was not so good as in the previous year, which was exceptionally bountiful. Some grumbling there was—not without cause—about the low price of hay; yet when we consider the immense amount produced, and that the profits are mainly derived from sales to town horses, and a limited number of town cows, it is not surprising that prices fall below the former exceptional figures. There would be small hope of better times in this respect if farmers could not look to any other uses of their corn and hay. Set before your mind's eye, in one heap, the huge production of corn and hay in this country, and on the other side the chance of selling the whole surplus to feed city cows and horses, and the view is despairing. Fortunately, however, the field is widened materially—in the case of corn, by a foreign demand lately springing up, and in the case of hay, by the well-established fact that for the best present and future profit the hay "should go to market on its own legs," or else in tin-cans and the butter-box; in short, should be made to feed *man* instead of *beast*. He will always pay better for his own personal gratification than that of his animals.

In regard to the once great staple of potatoes, I must

revive your recollection of something that was said on the subject in the sketch read a year ago. It was to this effect: that "somebody who was not deterred by bugs and low prices from planting a full crop, would probably make a good thing of it the coming season," and, as you are now aware, somebody did that very thing; though fewer than was desired. Now here was a fulfilment of "historical prophecy" worthy of your observation, and of your attention to future predictions. But why speak of this proof of my successful predictions? Is it not always the case that "a prophet shall have honor, save in his own country"?

It was customary in former chapters to describe in connection with agricultural affairs, the weather, on which they are so dependent. Now since you have a meteorologist of your own who comes before you with his report, sanctioned by the National Signal Service Bureau, these pages may be spared from the usual weather observations, except those of the Assistant Historian; she remarks that thunderstorms were unusually prevalent and severe in the 5th month; also that the heat of the 7th month was excessive, and the cold of the 12th unexampled; while the sleighing consequent on the steady severity of the first two winter months lasted continuously for forty-four days.

In reference to business concerns, other than agricultural, it is proper to mention the subject of the neighborhood mills, and the improvements effected during the year in these important structures. On the Patuxent, an old mill has been refitted, and operated by the hands of two enterprising young men of the Lea family, with a vigor and energy deserving success. In the central part of the neighborhood, the steam mill of B. Rush Roberts, which has been of such great benefit to the public, meriting record in our history as an institution of which we may well be proud, has also been revised and improved. If it should ever be suffered to stop, we would complain more of the privation than we manifested gratitude at the establishment: such is mankind.

There remains still another mill, a greater novelty than either of the others. A turbine wheel was fixed up—I might almost say constructed—by Charles F. Brooke, whose inventive enterprise was, doubtless, sharpened by that trip to the far West mentioned in a former chapter. The wheel strikes us as being a queer little fellow, whose effective power is another proof of the old saying, that strength is not always in proportion to size; that "cunning is better than strong."

Another evidence, in the way of business prosperity, that Sandy Spring is not ready for its Gibbon, is afforded by the continued, gradual growth of the "Savings Institution," whose deposits (though its most active founder, J. T. Moore, tells me I must not call them "deposits," but "its total funds on hand,") have risen in the year from $60,000 to $70,000. It is a gratifying feature of our Institution, that a considerable portion of this fund remains in the county to push on the wheels of progress.

Under the head of material improvements would properly come a statement of the condition and prospects of the railroad, which has been spoken of several times before, and which shall continue to constitute one of the subjects of this history so long as the present writer holds the pen. This is about all that he has to say at this time. Better luck next time.

It is well remarked by my Associate that the events of the year, as far as they are matter of record, are all summed up, and nearly all swallowed up in one comprehensive word, "The Centennial." It will be of interest to state the number and names of those who went from Sandy Spring,—the person who did *not* go became a curiosity. Beginning in the 5th month, at the very opening, the stream of visitors from our neighborhood kept up the flow through the whole season. Some of these, on the 10th of May, saw the great Corliss engine set in motion by the President and the Emperor, and looked, November 10th, upon the last revolution of the immense wheel, slowly, slowly dying away! In many cases the visits were repeated a second and a third time; and who is there that regrets having gone? whose brain was not enlarged and filled with pictures and ideas that will be a treasure while life remains? The information imparted to the mind, and the life and energy given to the spirit, by one of the greatest of human achievements, are full of compensation to the individual and to the nations for all it cost. Perhaps the comparative degree of attendance on the Centennial by different country neighborhoods is a fair criterion of their intelligence and progress.

The event which we are next bound to record is of very different character. In common with most other rural communities, we have been *pestered* by the invasion of tramps, in unusual numbers. While we are obliged by our reason and better feelings to make some allowance for a throng of disagreeable visitors, of whom many come because they have no place in the wide earth to go, since the depression in business has closed the avenues of industry, their coming among us is none the less unwelcome on that account. But there were some who came to hide themselves from the avengers of their crime. Two of these, guilty of atrocious murder, dropped last summer into our midst and went to work in ditching for some weeks, without giving the least suspicion for some time of the horrid characters we were harboring in our kitchens and tenant-houses. Then Sandy Spring store was broken open and robbed. Other burglaries followed; but the avenger was on their track. He came; and with assistance freely and efficiently rendered, secured the culprits. The capture required no little contrivance to plan and courage to execute.

It is only the truth to say that great credit is due to those whose courage and contrivance delivered our community from dangers certainly to be apprehended from the presence of such miscreants. And it is great satisfaction to have this proof that Sandy Spring is not a safe place for men of that character. Neither is it the first time she has showed that she nourishes within her quiet borders the spirit called for by the occasion. Of course we are a peaceful people; but still we would rather keep with us the sort of young men who have the spirit which the occasion calls for. This is very useful sometimes, and not really un-Quakerlike.

Another important event of the year remains to be referred to; I allude to the Presidential election of 1876. This event is rendered conspicuous in our annals, chiefly by the circumstance that it produced a division in political sentiment, such as, I suppose, has never before occurred among us. Yet there is not much harm apparent from it so far; the disputes have been lively, without being violent, I think. And then—may I not say?—"there is a little bird in the air" that sings of a coming lull in the waves of party strife.

Now having disposed of mere events and material concerns, let us turn to those beacon-lights of true progress shining forth from our intellectual, moral, æsthetic and industrial associations (for we have them all). Let us begin with the Lyceum as the central point for developing literary and scientific progress. Should the gains therefrom seem small, the deficiencies cannot be imputed to the president and directors. There have been lectures and exhibitions of various sorts and of different qualities; the attendance has been large at times, at other times small; with this unfortunate circumstance that some of the best lectures ever delivered here have had a meagre audience, while throngs have come to see and hear those which professed only to offer entertainment.

Such preference palpably paid to passing pleasure drew from one of the fathers and steady friends of the Lyceum the caustic censure that "a monkey and hand-organ would soon be the only sort of attraction sufficient to fill this hall." Too severe this, perhaps, but like all honest severity, much more wholesome than flattery. It is proper, however, to acknowledge that our people are not peculiar in preferring entertainment to instruction. Why do they come, if not to be entertained? Still the fact remains, that it is best of all to give each demand and faculty of our nature its proper place. A laugh is good; something to feed the mind with thoughts that inform and elevate is better; and, in the end, higher and more enduring pleasure will come of the latter. A proper mixture of instruction and entertainment is what this Lyceum was built for; and if your historian is not mistaken in apprehending that a disproportionate place is being given to the comic and the droll, this is the right time and place to sound the alarm. Instead of continuing the process of scolding, to which there are always great objections to be made, let me recommend that our young people shall take up a course that may lead to solid acquisitions worthy of their character for intelligence, and the times they live in. Let them form an association for the promotion of science, art, and the study of history. Books alone will not answer. A society is wanted to cultivate that acquaintance with the history of past times, without which no solid judgment can be formed of the present. Such knowledge is absolutely necessary in order to correct the raw, crude notions formed of passing events, from prejudices instilled by the passions and excitements of the parties of the day. An association for the promotion of science among us—science, that queen in the realm of mind whose power goes on more and more rapidly dispersing old clouds of darkness, and bringing the light that shows the true nature and meaning of all created things, from starry universes down to the microscopic germs floating in the invisible air and bringing the seeds of pestilence and death—science, which as now being investigated and utilized, comprehends simply all that is worth knowing—all there is to know.

Lately while groping in that mine of wisdom, the Life of Benjamin Franklin, I was impressed with this idea of a new association such as I have just mentioned, and from his success in getting up a similar society in Philadelphia, which has grown to be one of the most illustrious in the country, I drew the conviction that such a man, with the material he could find in this neighborhood, might organize an association that would overtop all others in usefulness and intellectual benefits.

Alas! we have no Benjamin Franklin. We shall have to wait until the hunger for knowledge—"the longing to know"—shall become so strong as to be irresistible.

In the meantime the various associations which we at present possess are going on in their quiet way, doing their accustomed work; a part of which doubtless is "to spread peace and good will amongst men." Notwithstanding the eulogy just passed upon science, this tendency of the various societies kept alive so long among us is even better. Science is wholly an affair of the intellectual part; the other—the emotional part—the feelings, constituting at least three-fourths of our being, and a still larger proportion of our happiness, is consequently of greater importance. All of our varied societies, in different degrees, while promoting the culture of the intellect, have served also to animate and keep alive the principles upon which society mainly depends.

My loose sheets, like the evening hour, are running out so rapidly that I have not time or space to describe more particularly the meetings of the Societies, further than to say, in the language of the Discipline, "I believe they were all held, and attended by most of the members." Also to notice the pleasing arrangement by which they succeed one another. Last week the Debating Society (of Centennial origin, which has not only kept up well, but has developed new and growing talent), held its last meeting for the season; while the Horticultural, which slumbers through the winter, along with the flowers it cherishes, blooms again into life to-morrow evening, in that respect rather anticipating the birth of its sweet children. The Sociable too, in which no decline is admitted by its faithful members, soon comes to its annual pause. The Clubs engaged in agricultural pursuits have all been faithful to their duty, the elder of the three maintaining its place at the head of the column. At least this claim appeared to be supported by the comparative exhibit of principal crops made at the Annual Convention. The "Farmers' Club" excelled in the return of wheat, corn and hogs; not descending to compete in respect of potatoes, dairy products and other small matters, in which the other two went far ahead. Indeed, the original Society acknowledges, and with entire satisfaction, the greater enterprise of the parties animated by younger blood, being well pleased to see our improvements carried on and exceeded by those who must naturally take our place. No earthly prospect could be so gratifying as the assurance that our sons shall make as great improvement in the next thirty years as we have done in the last.

However it may be that the elder class of our farmers have still done their proper part in their respective fields of active usefulness through the summer season, they can show few results for the past winter—a season which appeared to exist almost solely for the use of the young. Sleighing of nearly seven weeks' duration kept up and increased the whirl into which the Centennial had plunged the youthful mind. Louder and louder swelled the cry—

"Then top and maintop crowd the sail—
Heave Care o'erside!
And large, before Enjoyment's gale,
Let's tak' the tide!

"Oh! Life—how pleasant is thy morning!
Young Fancy's rays the hills adorning,
Cold, pausing Caution's lessons scorning,
We frisk away,
Like schoolboys at the expected warning
To joy and play.

"We wander there, we wander here,
We eye the rose upon the brier,
Unmindful that the thorn is near
Among the leaves;
Although the puny wound appear,
Short while it grieves."

An observant young lady declared with meaning significance, "If that sleighing had lasted a little longer, something dreadful would have happened!" Perhaps she referred to the-used up condition of the horses, or the health of the young, or patience of the old. The sleighing certainly lasted long enough to become historical.

And yet the year has but one wedding to commemorate. Eleventh month, 16th, 1876, John Thomas to Kate Vickers of Baltimore. Here we *gain* a sister without *losing* a brother. Only *one* this time, but just wait till next year!

In the field of pleasure, as in the field of labor, the old and the young occupy a different and contrasted place, but our next leaf unites both,—all ages, without distinction, in the grave. No difference, no separation, there!

5th month, 8th, 1876, the remains of Anna Stabler were brought from Philadelphia and laid in Leawood Cemetery. The deceased deserves more than a passing mention. Her energy in the performance of duty was remarkable through life, and the conscientious care which she took of her motherless nieces and nephews will long be gratefully remembered by them. Among her active enterprises the cause of education obtained the most earnest efforts; and while engaged in the labors of a boarding school, it is worthy of memorizing that the first stage run from this neighborhood to Laurel was started by her about the year 184—. It made weekly trips, and was justly acknowledged to be a great accommodation. In the latter part of her life her health gave way and her mind was clouded.

7th month, 18th, Howard Stabler, after a sad and distressing disease, died before reaching the middle point of life.

8th month, 5th, Samuel Miller, of Alexandria, died at

the house of his nephew, Warwick P. Miller, and was buried in the stone-walled enclosure of his family burying ground. In a quiet way he had led an active life for more than the full span of man; his friends many, his enemies few or none.

9th month, 2d, Caroline B. Scott's mother died at her house, after a short illness, having come to live with her daughter.

10th month, 29th, Harriet Iddings departed this life at a very advanced age, surrounded by all her children. A blameless life and conscience void of offence were hers. The first obituary record of this history is of the death of her husband.

12th month, 27th, Anna Holland passed away very suddenly, to the spirit land. Her death was a great shock to her family and friends.

2d month, 20th, 1877, "The dear little infant," its grandmother writes, "closed its eyes in dreamless sleep, at Norwood, after a few hours' illness."

Second month, 21st, 1877. The same pen writes, "Deborah Paxson, sister of Charles Iddings, died at his house, struck down in a few days by a strange, severe illness. She had lived with her husband many years in California, and they were spending the winter at Riverside. She was a very lovely and attractive woman, and much respected by all who knew her, following her aged mother after a short interval to the same spirit land,"—the "Beautiful Land" (friend Moore well expresses it), for she was certainly one of those who *make this earth beautiful*, even when lying wrapt in her shroud, strewn with white flowers, fit emblems of the purity and loveliness of the form they covered and the soul gone up to heaven.

Third month, 21st, at Oak Grove, Hannah Birdsall, in the

seventy-fourth year of her age. The present writer remembers forty-five years ago, when first he began to be interested in looking at such groups of human beings, that the three sisters Sarah, Hannah, and Lydia resided at Mount Airy, assisting in dispensing the known hospitality of their father, Bernard Gilpin. The sisters, as is the destiny of women, were widely separated for many years; Hannah returned to her old neighborhood and the society of her elder sister, sharing with her the dutiful attentions and tender cares of near relatives and friends.

The number of deaths this year is unusually large; of whom seven only belong to the statistical record of this neighborhood. Number of births, 8.

Some miscellaneous contributions from one of my associates are very properly annexed to the foregoing, as pertaining to the annals of the Centennial year.

On alternate First-Day evenings, meetings are now held in rotation at the houses of several friends, and attended by a large and appreciative class, coming to listen to Bible readings and expositions, chiefly by Edward J. Farquhar. This outcome of the First-Day school appears to have been kept up with a spirit and interest characteristic of a revival. Collections are being made for repairs to the Meeting House, not before they are wanted.

We conclude with a list of persons visiting the "Centennial" from our neighborhood, prepared by Mary B. Thomas. Of these visiting friends the Stabler family furnished 36; the Miller, 18; Hallowell, 15; Thomas, 15; the Brooke family, 14; Moore, 13; Farquhar, 12; Lea, 11; Gilpin, 10; Bond, 9; Schofield, 7; Bentley, 7; Kirk, 6; Janney, 5; Iddings, 5; Ellicott, 4; Roberts, Porter, Hopkins, Stone, Scott, Chandlee, Hall, Holland, each 2; Magruder, Snowden, Hartshorne, each 3; Leggett, Jackson, Taylor, each 1; comprising in all, 215; with many colored persons.

Enthusiasts consider this a record of honor.

CHAPTER XV.

FROM FOURTH MONTH, 2D, 1877, TO FOURTH MONTH, 1ST, 1878.

Progress of the History — The story of the world — Repairs of the Meeting House — Its great influence — Increase in wheat crop — "Dear Old Fogy" — Favors of the season — Former remarkable seasons — Our Bank — Telephone instead of telegraph — Steam at Brooke Grove Mill — Improved roads — Immigration of Baltimoreans — "Human degradation" — First step to co-operation — Fifth Month Quarterly Meeting — The Book Club — Improvements in schools — The Lyceum again — Agricultural College — Preachers — Sweet marriage ceremonies—Character of the obituaries in this History.

The suggestion made by Francis Miller at our Annual Meeting fifteen years ago, that a "Historian should be appointed to make a record of neighborhood events," seemed at the time to some of us a mere fancy; but it was regularly carried out, the yearly record growing by degrees, from nine pages up to twenty; sometimes written on loose, detached leaves, and never in a condition adapted for preservation. Several members of the Lyceum, among whom B. Gilpin Stabler is remembered as most active, became dissatisfied with the situation; and it was resolved a year ago that these sketches contained matters of permanent interest to the families of Sandy Spring neighborhood. In accordance with that resolution, a handsome and durable bound volume has been procured from Cushings & Bailey, containing 400 pages, of which the previous sketches occupy just 200, leaving the same number to be filled with future history. The back and sides of the book, which is now your property, bear the inscription, suggested by H. C. Hallowell, in letters of gold, "Annals of Sandy Spring."

Thus raised to new dignity, the work of your historian demands increased care and pains. Just consider the situation! it is certainly a novel one. The writer has now to address an audience, many of whom in the early days of the History were too young to understand the significance of the word. They have grown up under the influences of a period fuller of change than any other since the world began: new views of life, its objects and pursuits, and especially of its *pleasures*, are naturally theirs; while the lessons of experience which comprise the chief practical benefits of history, are less likely than ever to secure their proper authority in the youthful mind. When told as it might be, and sometimes is, history is by no means wanting in entertainment, which, however, is never its chief purpose; and those who take it up with such view are very apt soon to lay it down. "I don't want to study history," said a bright boy of ten years old to his aged parent; "tell me about the things that happened when *you* were young!" "All right," replied the father, "that *will be* History; the most important and interesting events of common life make up the best part of that grand study; the best and most instructive." I will close this preface with a short, solemn extract:

"The story of the world has yet to be written. Pray you that have children, not that they be strong, or clever, or comely, or ambitious, or wealthy; but that they have sense to know how to live!"

This is the science of sciences; all studies should be auxiliary to that.

The first event noted in the minutes kept by the historian refers to the central point of the neighborhood and to the repairs made there. The roof of the meeting house, which had sheltered it for sixty years, was replaced with new shingles, and the ceiling of the interior made sound and safe with fresh plastering where required in consequence of injury sustained from the leaky roof. Who of those here present will see that the next roof is put on in proper time? The moral of this event seems to be—and you all know your historian is nothing if not allowed to moralize—that we who sit reflecting below that roof may remind ourselves that things which are *old* are not always venerable.

As was stated, this year's narrative begins at the centre; yes—for it is simply a historical fact that yon building, now of brick, formerly of timber, is originally and essentially the central point of this peculiar neighborhood. Without it—I mean without the *influences* which erected and sustained it, and which have been sustained by the administration of its proper office—there would have been, doubtless, a community in this part of Montgomery County, but one different from this. Sandy Spring, with the peculiar features that mark its character, would never have existed. The efforts and sacrifices made to advance toward a higher life, an improvement infinitely more valuable than houses and land, are due to the high social, moral and religious principles of the founders. Whatsoever advantages are now possessed were built upon that only sure foundation; and whatsoever hope can be justly entertained of their continuance and progress depends upon the degree in which those principles shall be substantially maintained. *Principles,* I say, not *forms* that necessarily vary with the passing years; changes in *them* are essential to growth, and therefore to life; but life and growth depend upon the sound heart.

It is proper to mention, as connected with the Meeting House, the purchase for a hundred dollars of a piece of land adjoining it. Our careful managers have shown a proper foresight in this matter, and our people were reasonably quick to respond with the necessary supply of funds—being more prompt than in the case of the roof. Thus one improvement suggests another; it is only necessary to make a good beginning.

It is usual to make early reference to the experience of the past year in regard to farming operations, as being the chief interest of a material character. Beyond question that interest centred this year on wheat. It began a year ago. A mischievous speculation took the price up last April above the point where it could be sustained. A few profited by it, while the chief mischief was stored away in the farmers' minds by inducing very many to decline a fair price in the fall, hoping that a rise would occur again this spring. At the present writing the appearance of such good fortune is not near so bright as the appearance of the growing wheat and the almost unprecedented show which it makes for a good crop. Owing to early sowing, and the wonderful mildness of the season (up to a very recent date), we have now in the wheat fields a growth of stem and leaf which may, perhaps, be considered superfluous. It looks very beautiful now; whether the harvest shall be in proportion must be left to the next chapter to relate. Experience is said to be against it; but experience is sometimes an old fogy—though, in the long run, a very dear old fogy. For some reason which has not been satisfactorily assigned, the wheat crop of last year was large in almost all parts of the country; the same may be said of most other crops, the single failure being in apples. And notwithstanding some disappointments in the matter of price, the agricultural outlook has been, and is, brighter than usual. Health generally good—weather never finer—and spirits (if you look at the younger and more numerous class) higher than ever before in this part of the world. This fact is the more remarkable as there was *no sleighing* to speak of; a merciful dispensation, doubtless, for the preservation of health and horses.

Although the subject of weather has been fully treated statistically, it may be interesting to record that the season is a very forward one, and to make some comparison with former seasons, I copy here a few records from my diary of the year 1842.

"January 1st. We have had by far the finest weather through this month that I ever knew. February 28th. I must repeat of the winter just gone, that never in my recollection have we been favored with so much fine weather. March 3d. A most beautiful Spring day; the robins sing lively; grass getting quite green; lilacs showing considerable leaf. March 4th. Thermometer nearly 80°. March 10th. A little peach tree in front yard, with south exposure, has full bloom on it. Apricot is in bloom. March 20th. Damson and cherry come out very full. Anemone in bloom. For nearly a week in the early part of this (March) month we sat without fire." So far the mild climate was unprecedented, but on "the 29th of March, thermometer fell to 29°. Peach blossoms killed in many places. On the 31st the wind blew lion-like. April 16th. The season has made very little progress in the past two weeks." But on May 1st (still in

1842) I write: "Nature wears to-day such a dress as would accord with the poet's prettiest fancies about May-Day. The locust is coming out in bloom." The presumption that people must be interested in a theme which they talk so much, is my excuse for dwelling on the subject of the weather so long. Certainly it passes through strange modifications, as will be proved by records carefully kept.

I believe that in great business centres people look to the banks as an index of the situation, showing the rise and fall of the general prosperity. It can scarcely be claimed that our Savings Institution has acquired as yet all the high powers and functions of banks. Being only 10 years old (the first meeting to organize it was held on 22d of February, 1868) and not meddling with the critical business of discounts, its influence is of course limited, but so far as it has gone the indications of success are favorable. The amount due depositors increased during the past year, in round numbers, from $70,000 to $80,000. Notwithstanding the distressing failures everywhere of savings banks, and our lowering of interest from 6 to 5 per cent., the amount withdrawn during the past month indicates not the least diminution of confidence among the people. The Bank is on a solid foundation; its Directors have learned useful lessons in finance in the past ten years, and to say that its officers are honest men is only to say what everybody knows. Nothing is required but a *continuance of confidence* to establish this Institution on a basis of permanent usefulness, widening gradually every year, and striking its roots deeper as it grows.

During the past year we have to note a serious loss in the facilities of intercourse with the outside world. The Western Union has removed the telegraph, which so often served our purposes of business convenience, and the more precious object of keeping up instant communication with dear and distant friends. Now this *losing* advantages is something we do not like at all. It seems like "going back," which does not belong, and never has belonged, to the neighborhood of Sandy Spring, whose honest pride and stirring aspirations point naturally forward. It is some comfort to know that the privation, however much to be regretted, is not from any weakening on our part. We are no more responsible for the *undoing* by the Telegraph Company than for the *not* doing by the B. & O. R. R. Company of what they often promised should be done. The Railroad has fallen into troubles never anticipated, so we must let it off for awhile, trusting that a way will be found to supply the longed-for communication.

But we rejoice to learn that a cheering exhibition of an enterprising spirit has been afforded recently in a similar direction to that we have lost; an affair wholly got up by our Sandy Spring boys. The Telegraph set up by people from outside is taken away; the Telephone, which is to the Telegraph as Raphael to a house-painter, has been erected, actually placing in closest and tenderest connection the two historical mansions, Sharon and Brooke Grove.

Happy is the man or the neighborhood that never looks to another to do what can be done by the energies at home. It were something worthy the reputation of Sandy Spring to produce a telephone connecting with the nearest telegraph station of the B. & O. Railroad, provided that such an enterprise should be found, after making a prudent estimate of cost, to be within our reach.

In close vicinity to the operating telephone another recent exhibition of energy is puffing away in rather louder tones. The junior partner of Brooke Grove Mill has added a steam engine to the water power. We entertain a lively recollection of repeated floods in that stream the past season, causing such destruction as to induce the neighbors, who could not afford to dispense with the use of that mill, to turn out and make a frolic of repairing the dam. Those floods of the autumn of '77 left their mark on many a wheat field and common road.

The statement has often been repeated that nothing shows a better spirit at work for the benefit of a farming community than the improvement of its roads. In this respect, more than usual has been done the present year. The Ashton turnpike is kept in excellent condition, while individual contributions have been made toward other roads. A peculiar act of benevolence was manifested by a private gentleman who placed a thousand dollars in the hands of another private gentleman, for the improvement mainly of the Laurel road, being extended also to the centre of the neighborhood. The donor of the benefaction was John S. Miller, not long a resident, who put it into the right hands when he gave it to Caleb Stabler. This affair well deserves a place in the history of a rural community, reflecting as it does nearly equal honor on both gentlemen.

Before leaving the narrative of improvements (among which must not be forgotten a fine barn on the "manor," whose building was compared to the blossoming of "Jonah's gourd"), it is pleasant to mention an addition to the neighborhood of another sort—one to which Sandy Spring has often been greatly indebted for the estimation in which its social qualities are held. The family of the late Henry Tyson, who was closely connected with our people, have come among us, whether for permanent settlement or not it is too soon to determine.

Those additions and improvements constitute what may be termed the bright or "day-side" of the history. Unfortunately, there is always a dark or night-side too; and as truth forms its whole value and highest quality, the latter cannot be wholly omitted. You must not fall into the natural error of supposing that the "night-side" here meant is intended to apply to the turning of night into day (or day into night, which?) by young folks in pursuit of pleasure; that belongs to another concern. What is now meant refers to the doings of tramps, and of native pilferers, worse than tramps, whose nightly performances almost keep up with honest business. In the early part of the year some steps were taken toward forming an association for the suppression of these nuisances. But that remains, as it has always been, a most difficult undertaking to accomplish. It would seem that the progress in science, morals and humanity, in all that most elevates a community, only serves to widen the chasm that separates between the vicious and the virtuous classes, rendering it more difficult to devise effective means of redress, such as will not shock the higher principles of Christianity. The Convention which met in Baltimore last winter to consider these questions failed to present any sort of acceptable legislation; indeed, the remedies proposed were worse than the disease. I append an extract which contains a sentiment that ought certainly to go down to posterity as being the principles of Sandy Spring:

"Human degradation.—In casting the vote which defeated the whipping-post bill in Kentucky, the Lieutenant Governor put his decision on the broad ground that humanity is already too much degraded, and that no amount of saving in criminal expenses would warrant the State in promoting human degradation."

With that golden extract, and another, that "Error is oftener the child of ignorance than of evil intent," let us "pass into the sunshine, out of the shade."

If our neighborhood is more distinguished for any one thing than another it must be for the number of its Associations. I suppose it is also generally understood that all these had their origin in the old Farmers' Club. The discovery was then made that it is a pleasant thing to come together and discourse on subjects of common interest, enjoy a good supper and get home to our families in good time. Behold the programme containing all the essentials of a rational and successful rural association; this being modified to suit circumstances (too much *modified* in the last particular), has formed the basis of all the successful efforts at social combinations. The benefits resulting from that first step toward co-operation can scarcely be told. Without the Club of '44, would there have been a Mutual Insurance Company of '48; a Lyceum of '58; a Turnpike of '60; a Savings Bank of '68; and the whole host of delightful and profitable associations of both sexes, which form a large part of our social existence? Certainly this is a triumphant illustration of a great historian's assertion that "progressive human civilization is the result of learning to act together for a common end."

There is so much of interest and instruction in the career of different societies, in observing the various features that distinguish them, their successes and occasional failures and the causes thereof, I am inclined to offer the suggestion that each permanent association should have a historian for itself.

So much is lost because it is impossible for one person to discover what is said and done worthy of record in the various assemblages. This view is confirmed by the "assistant historian," who suggests that it would be well to have the help of correspondents in different portions of the neighborhood to gather up interesting occurrences, so that nothing may be lost. With the aid actually furnished I am enabled to note down the following several particulars: The Quarterly Meeting held for the first time in the 5th month is described "as a very good one; we were highly favored in doors and outside too; the weather being very pleasant, and the country appeared beautiful, dressed in its early green." But it is added, "the attendance was much smaller than usual." The change of season for holding it not being satisfactory, the former date is to be restored in the 6th month.

There has been an omission hitherto in noticing the existence of a circulating library, known as "The Book Club." This addition to the reading material is said to be "in healthy condition, with twenty-eight members." The idea had got about that it was composed chiefly of works of fiction; but this could scarcely be the case, else the term "healthy" would not apply. There should be, of course, a fair admixture of instruction and entertainment in such libraries; but the success of this Book Club certainly confirms the view held and carried out by the founders of the old "Sandy Spring Library," to the effect that it was not necessary to include works of fiction, because a sufficient supply would be sure to find their way into this lively neighborhood.

From books to schools is a natural transition. Our Public School enjoyed for a while the valuable services of an excellent young man, George W. Israel; although here for a short time, he seemed to drop very naturally into the social circle. On the subject of schools there will probably be something further to record at the next annual meeting. In passing from it, I take pleasure in noticing a delightful little May party with which Lizzie Bond brightened up her youthful pupils, and their friends too. Oh, you school children of these days! How is the path of learning bordered for you with flowers!—contrasted with the thorny road your predecessors had to pursue in old times, how thankful you ought to be! Assuredly it is an improvement which cannot fail to be twice blessed; first in the character of the child; again, and for life, in that of the woman and the man.

The historian of the neighborhood speaking in this hall cannot avoid giving due place in his truthful narrative to the affairs of the Lyceum itself. To leave that out were indeed "to play Hamlet with the part of Hamlet omitted." One of my assistants shows a proper anxiety (though speaking in rather an apologetic strain) that we should all be reminded of the various useful services rendered by this building during the past year. Although the hall was prevented from putting on the sweetest aspect of beauty which it ever wears, owing to the temporary suspension of the Horticultural Exhibition, yet we had the annual Convention of the Farmers' Clubs, which showed no abatement of general interest. The Dairy Association continued its quarterly meetings, and the Centennial Debating Society with unflagging spirit kept up their discussions in such manner and upon such questions as to extend the interest outside these walls. Its last meeting, to which the public were admitted, was well attended, and the decision arrived at that "England is wrong in meddling with the Turko-Russian affair," will be confirmed by the majority of the American people—though Earl Beaconsfield sees the question in a different light. The President of the Lyceum performed his part; he secured promises from able men to deliver lectures here, but wisely concluded not to expose them to the mortifying ordeal of empty benches. Our young folks seem really not to have time to attend lectures; other entertainments are more attractive now. The repetition of "Buck Fanshaw's Funeral" brought crowds, but then a blind man was the speaker, and it is a duty to assist the blind. These sarcastic remarks are unprofitable; facts are the historian's proper business, and to them I propose to confine myself. The Lyceum has latterly fallen off in accomplishing the purposes for which the building was mainly erected. These purposes are clearly set forth in the definition of the word. Worcester's Dictionary gives four definitions of "Lyceum," every one implying "an institution for literary or scientific instruction and improvement." While these objects were designed by the founders to be kept in the forefront, there was no thought of excluding the idea of entertainment. For those who believe that amusements occupy a rightful and important place in the education of human beings, it is only when they interfere with the improvement of the mind or with health of body, or with other duties, that any objection can be properly made. In the case of our Lyceum no objection is made to anything *done* within its walls, but for what has *not* been done. It must be acknowledged that the advocates of amusing entertainments can make a very strong case in their favor. According to reports of the Treasurer, the finances of the Lyceum company had run to very low ebb. Obliged to borrow money to pay necessary expenses, it was relieved from this sad condition by the kind offices of the lively and flourishing society called the "Sociable," whose distinguished efforts not only relieved us from debt, but left us with a comfortable surplus. From this it would appear that the efforts of the Lyceum to give *instruction* were rewarded with *insolvency; amusements* brought wealth and prosperity. Does it not remind you of the question lately stirred up through the State, relating to the Agricultural College? While endeavoring to teach agriculture, it fell "over head and ears" in debt; transferring its efforts to the preparation of boys for West Point and the Naval Academy, it now exults in entire freedom from debt, with triumphant success in all respects, excepting the one object for which it was built! Perhaps the parallel drawn between the Lyceum and the College is scarcely fair. The only complaint which can be made of the former is that spices and seasoning are being used in too great proportion to solid viands that afford nourishment essential to true life. So far from objecting to the late evening entertainment which thronged this hall up to if not beyond its utmost capacity, the judgment of your historian regards the influence of music, which formed a principal part of the novelty, as a favorable element introduced into our modern society. As it is not apprehended that the cultivation of this one of the fine arts is likely to be carried to any great excess among us, let it be welcomed to its proper place. "The possession of a faculty is the divine warrant for its exercise," and the many of us who do *not* possess it have only not to try to exercise, nor to condemn.

One more suggestion regarding our Lyceum. In its early days a full attendance was secured by disposing of tickets to a lecture course, at the commencement of the season. Let us use the same method again. There is something so divine in purely *mental* pursuits, it will never do to slight their paramount claims. Direct the overflowing streams in the minds of the rising generation into worthy channels, and all will be well.

It is a natural transition to pass from moralizing to preaching; and it seems entirely proper to refer to the discourses of two ministers, who favored us during the past year with no commonplace sermons. The first was a lady friend from West Chester, Pa.; her communication was remarkable for the beauty and propriety of its language, and for the earnestness with which she urged the duty of taking wise care of our bodily health, and of every good gift from the Heavenly Father which tends to promote the happiness of life.

The other discourse was by Sunderland Gardner, who expounded with great clearness the simple fundamental principles of our Society, impressing with deep conviction their full sufficiency, if properly maintained, not only as a guide through the paths of duty, but as a means of evolving and developing all the better powers of our nature, up to the highest perfection of which they are capable. The opportunity of listening to such teachers is one of the noteworthy events of the year.

Another occurrence, so agreeable to the present writer that he can in nowise refrain from recording it, was the meeting last 5th day at his house of the "Ladies Association for Mutual Improvement."

The allusion to these eighteen excellent women, all save three in the present possession of happy husbands, opens a clear way to congenial events next to be recorded. The predictions made a year ago, of the probable consequences—at least *sequences*—of all that winter's sleighing, were to a certain extent verified—there being three marriages to record:

Fourth month, 10th, 1877, Samuel Hopkins to Patty Smith. The blow was softened to her friends, in that the sweet bride was not taken entirely out of their social circle.

Tenth month, 18th, 1877, Granville Farquhar and Patty Thomas. The hundred witnesses of the dignified and beautiful ceremony by which these two "took each other as loving and faithful companions for life, with mutual declarations of perfect equality, forming the truest foundation for permanent happiness," agreed that they had never seen this wedding surpassed.

First month, 10th, 1878, Alban Brooke and Sarah Pleasants. This number, three, for marriages, has never been exceeded in our neighborhood in the last 15 years. Only three births within the year; less than half the average number.

In writing the obituary notices which form an important part of these records, it has been the aim of our historian to state a few leading traits of character known to him, which may serve to recall the deceased to your minds and to leave a pleasant and *true* impression of the departed; without illusive coloring, "to keep their memory green."

Fifth month, 23d, 1877. The first name on the mournful death-roll is Mary Chalfant. Few children of her age among us had excited so warm an interest in life, and so much sincere grief in death. Tears from many, even those not connected by near relationship, bedewed her grave. Yet sad as it was to lose her, it is a pleasure and privilege to think of her, not as "lying under the daisies," but as a little fairy dropped down into the dull precincts of the village, and brightening them up with a transient gleam.

Seventh month, 26th. How wide apart, how strangely distinguished are the marks on which death's arrows in succession fall! Elizabeth Pleasants departed next, after a lingering and painful illness. Long afflicted and distressed, she had been unable of late years to occupy the place in general society which she once adorned. Only those whose acquaintance dated back to periods of the "far past," could fully appreciate her qualities of gentleness, lively wit and intelligence, delicacy of feeling and crystal purity, never exceeded in any person we ever met. While we live, the influence of her quiet spirit will not pass from earth; emotions of deep tenderness will ever rise at the mention of her name.

Ninth month, 7th, Benjamin Hallowell closed his long and useful life. If that picture, looking down on me with its benevolent expression as I write, could speak, I believe it would say, "Write no more; let that simple notice suffice!" But when we remember how closely this eminent man was identified with our neighborhood, it seems natural and proper to give his memory a fitting recognition in the "Annals of Sandy Spring." It was here he brought the first fruits of his labors in the great cause of education; and it was here, after that life-work, exerted for many years with all the strength of his powerful nature, and crowned with distinguished success, here he returned with the ripe fruits gathered, to continue while life should last, serving God and man as "truth opened the way." Here his remains rest under the overshadowing poplar, near those of his Margaret—his life companion—whom he had loved so long and so well.

A gifted son of genius, now resident in England, writes thus of the impression made on his mind by the man whom he had learned to reverence long years before. It affords me much satisfaction to find a place for part of his letter in the present memorial. He writes from—

LONDON, October 22d, 1877.

MY DEAR MRS. MILLER:—I have just heard of your beloved and revered father's death, and cannot forbear writing you to say how deeply I feel this event. All sorrow at the death of such a man as Benjamin Hallowell is overarched with a bow of hope. He remains so immortal in our grateful hearts that we cannot think of his life as closed and ended; he only rests from his labors, as *we* knew them; and where our own weak wisdom valued him so much, we cannot think the Great Wisdom will value him less, but much more.

After long years of contact with sects and their dogmas, I find that at last I have a creed—and it is written in such lines and hearts as your father's. The faith that can produce such men is the faith for me. With one Benjamin Hallowell I will outweigh all the theologies ever written. Dear old Sandy Spring—how I love it!

I have over my table, in a frame, sent from India, one leaf of the "Holy Bo Tree"—the tree under which, it is said, Buddha sat down a Prince, and at last rose up a Prophet, an "Enlightened Teacher," 500 years before Christ. As I look at the leaf, it seems to be transformed to many—to an old oak grove with Sandy Spring Meeting House in the centre. There I sat down a Methodist preacher, and rose up with faith in "the Inward Light." We must all have our own Bo Tree before we can reverence that of another; and though I am not a prophet, nor very "enlightened," I can see the light, and as Paul says, "follow after."

[Signed] M. D. CONWAY.

Last on the list of the valued dead of the year is Sarah T. Brooke, who closed a blameless life, of nearly 83 years, on the 1st of the 10th month, 1877. She was throughout life a good woman, who tried by example and precept to do what she thought was right. Failing health confined her to the house some time before her death. She had always lived in her native place.

In closing up such a document as the foregoing, there are sure to be left some loose ends to gather up, of interesting facts, omitted in their proper place. One that comes up now is a very recent enterprise—a printing press of A. G. Thomas, which already exhibits such neat work as to deserve the encouragement which it can scarcely fail to receive.

The word with us still is Onward!

As the "Nutting," alias "Montgomery County Tichborne case," was noticed in a previous Chapter, as an element of threatened disturbance, it is gratifying to state that it ended as all such cases ought to terminate—in smoke.

Another striking feature of the past summer and fall was the revival of athletic exercises in the most intense form of base ball.

STATISTICS FOR THE PAST FIVE YEARS.

	Marriages.	Births.	Deaths.
1874	0	9	2
1875	3	8	2
1876	1	5	6
1877	1	8	7
1878	3	3	4
Total last 5	8	33	21
Total last 15	33	112	61
Average per year	2⅕	7½	4+

CHAPTER XVI.

FROM FOURTH MONTH, 1ST, 1878, TO FOURTH MONTH, 7TH, 1879.

Census of the Neighborhood — Prosperity and adversity — The great hailstorm — A cold May — Failure of fruit —Stanmore boarding school *removed* to Rockland — Base ball vigorously renewed — Celebration of Eliza Kirk's birthday — Pleasure tours in new directions — The five crops abundant — Relief to yellow fever sufferers — A new party — Fears for the corn needless — A bad sport —Establishment of the "Benevolent Aid Society" — Election at Mechanicsville — Bible readings resumed — The Oysterman, a welcome arrival — Bad conduct at "Sharp St." — Fire-crackers banished from the stores at Christmas — Big fires, kindliest assistance.

Census of "Our Neighborhood," (*Sandy Spring,*) taken April 1st, 1879.

Families.		No. of Persons.	Families.		No. of Persons.
1	Charles H. Brooke,	6	25	James Holland,	4
2	James Stabler,	2	26	Amos Holland,	2
3	Roger B. Farquhar,	7	27	G. W. C. Beall,	4
4	William S. Brooke,	4	28	George E. Brooke,	4
5	Roger Brooke,	6	29	James P. Stabler,	7
6	Sallie Brooke,	3	30	Mary G. Tyson,	6
7	Alban G. Brooke,	4	31	Bernard Gilpin,	3
8	Mahlon Kirk,	6	32	William H. Farquhar,	4
9	Sarah B. Farquhar,	4	33	Alban Gilpin,	3
10	Richard S. Kirk,	5	34	Clara Chalfant,	4
11	Granville Farquhar,	3	35	Wm. H. Stabler,	5
12	Dr. Wm. E. Magruder,	8	36	Edward Stabler,	4
13	Henry C. Hallowell,	9	37	Arthur Stabler,	2
14	Francis Miller,	6	38	Richard T. Bentley,	5
15	Joseph Wetherald,	5	39	B. Rush Roberts,	2
16	Robert S. Moore,	7	40	Charles G. Porter,	4
17	Samuel Bond,	5	41	Benjamin H. Miller,	5
18	James H. Stone,	2	42	Philip T. Stabler,	3
19	Joseph T. Moore,	9	43	William Schofield,	6
20	Wm. W. Moore,	5	44	John Smith,	5
21	Robert R. Moore,	3	45	Sally Lea,	2
22	Caroline B. Scott,	7	46	Mary Chandlee,	5
23	Benjamin D. Palmer,	3	47	Edward Lea,	4
24	Penuel Palmer,	2	48	Elizabeth E. Tyson,	1

Families.		No. of Persons.	Families.		No. of Persons.
49	Charles A. Iddings,	5	68	William S. Bond,	6
50	Harry T. Lea,	3	69	William Kinnaird,	4
51	Edward C. Gilpin,	6	70	Gideon Gilpin,	7
52	Thomas J. Lea,	5	71	Francis Thomas,	4
53	Isaac Hartshorne,	6	72	John Thomas,	4
54	Harry Stabler,	4	73	William John Thomas,	2
55	George L. Stabler,	6	74	Edward P. Thomas,	7
56	Edward Pierce,	5	75	Samuel P. Thomas,	3
57	Sam'l A. Janney,	8	76	Charles Stabler,	6
58	Henry Chandlee,	2	77	Mary P. Thomas,	3
59	Mahlon Chandlee,	3	78	Hetty Stabler,	6
60	Samuel Ellicott,	4	79	Dr. Edward Iddings,	6
61	James S. Hallowell,	7	80	Alban G. Thomas,	5
62	E. J. Hall,	7	81	Llewellyn Massey,	5
63	Frederick Stabler,	5	82	Henrietta Snowden,	5
64	Robert M. Stabler,	8	83	Walter H. Brooke,	6
65	Asa M. Stabler,	7	84	Samuel Hopkins,	3
66	Warwick P. Miller,	11	85	Thomas Lea,	3
67	William Lea,	5			
	Families 85.			No. of Persons 407.	

An important part of the history of a people is contained in information of a statistical character.

In order that statistics should be of proper value, they must possess definiteness and precision. It may be justly claimed that a considerable degree of care has been exercised in drawing up the statements made in this volume of the births, marriages and deaths, with other statistical matter pertaining to "our neighborhood"; still there has prevailed all the time a slight degree of indefiniteness in regard to the exact names and number of the individuals of whom "our neighborhood" is really composed.

In accordance therefore with the spirit of progress which we claim, it has been thought by your historians advisable to prepare a regular census of the people referred to all along in our Sketches of Sandy Spring. The lines that include them are lines neither of sect nor party, of latitude nor longitude, extending from Charles H. Brooke on the west, to Samuel Hopkins on the east (but not taking in all between), the boundaries being of a social character, rather spiritual than material.

The work of this census was not without its difficulties, such as are always experienced in *drawing lines* of this nature. In general, it was thought better to avoid the extreme of exclusiveness. Of course the performance is imperfect; but from long experience in census-taking (as you know), your historian ventures to express the opinion that it is not any fuller of errors than are most other censuses.

The observation was made to me lately that I would find a great deal in this year to recount, as there was an idea prevailing that the current of neighborhood activity was running with more than usual force and life; perhaps this is the case, in some directions it certainly has been so. Prosperity was mingled with a full proportion of adversity. Within a month from the beginning of our "record year" a most disastrous hailstorm crushed into the ground the reasonable hopes of some of our best farmers, and a month before the end the still greater calamity of fire struck on the farmer's tenderest spot—the *noble horse* and the capacious stored barn. The year belongs to the category of those that are not soon forgotten. Its ample blessings showered down in liberal abundance shall have their place in a subsequent part of the story.

We know that time is not measured by months nearly as practically or impressively as by events; "Fifty years of Europe are worth a cycle of Cathay." Substitute "Sandy Spring" for "Europe," remembering that nothing is more promotive of progress than the full belief in it, we can make out a very fair exhibit for the year just closed. The neighborhood has certainly been *alive*, and life is activity. Whether it has always been of a beneficial sort is a circumstance yet to be developed. However that may appear, the truth still remains, that all pleasures which promote neither vigor of body nor elevation of mind are a waste of that energy by which alone progress is promoted. Your historian must again repeat that he set out in the beginning to make his record consist almost wholly in relating the essential progress of our beloved neighborhood. Other circumstances were scarce worth the pains to record.

It affords me real pleasure to follow the good example of my senior assistant in taking up the story of each month in succession, as the rolling year brings one after another into view, into (we may say) the materials of our life; for so it is made up.

I begin these notices by copying the first minute made by the junior assistant, whose mind excels in portraying the beautiful, as well as in registering with precision the actual dates and events of the record. She writes: "On the morning of the 14th of the 4th month, I saw, between the hours of 5 and 6 o'clock, a very beautiful and perfect rainbow, a rare event in the morning. The arch was without a fault. I would have liked all my friends to see it." Thus you see we begin with that most beautiful of nature's displays, beautiful indeed, but oh, so transient! Still a lovely omen, this bow of promise, for what the year was to evolve, promise for some, while soon for others

"A transient form,
Evanishing amid the storm."

On the 28th of this same month of April, 1878, occurred the great hailstorm, which is certainly entitled to have its memory preserved by the following description made freshly at the time. The account is from the pen of our junior historian, who might truly say, if she indulges in Latin, "*magna pars fui.*"

On Sunday, April 28th, 1878, occurred the most terrific hailstorm ever known in this latitude by the present generation. The morning was lovely and the landscape lay green and smiling until noon; the sky became overcast soon afterward, and clouds of a singular brassy tint appeared in the southwest. In a few moments a dense gray wall moving swiftly from S. W. to N. E. swept over a district of eight or ten miles in length by from three-quarters of a mile to a mile and a half in breadth. The hail fell for nearly half an hour without an instant's cessation, and during most of that time it was impossible to see one inch beyond the window pane. The noise can only be compared to the roar of Niagara, persons in the same room having to shout in order to be heard. When the storm ceased, what a scene of desolation met the eye! Wheat tall enough to conceal a post-and-rail fence was mowed down to stubble on a level with the lowest rail (it put up stalks afterward that produced eight bushels of wheat to the acre); fruit trees heavy laden an hour before, were not only stripped of every apple, peach and pear, but in many cases not a leaf was left; gardens were as bare of green and growing plants as a floor; cattle that had *waded* in pasture in the morning, stood lowing for food until they received their supper from the barns. The ground was covered for miles to a depth varying from four inches to two feet, and hail was found in sheltered places one and two weeks after the storm. Most fortunately the hail stones were of moderate size.

The loss to the community, which suffered in growing crops and orchards, can scarcely be estimated, going up easily into thousands of dollars. The principal losers amongst those included in this history, were William Lea, William S. Bond, William Kinnaird, John Thomas, William John Thomas, Dr. F. Thomas, Edward P. Thomas, Charles Stabler, A. G. Thomas, Llewellyn Massey, Walter Brooke and Samuel Thomas. (All these names will be read with increased interest in future years.) Carriage loads of people came from distance of miles to witness the destruction. As the season advanced, the stricken forest put forth a few leaves, which on some oak trees grew to an inordinate size and of singular shape. From elevated points at a distance, the "burnt district," as it was termed, could be distinguished far and wide.. Nor must we omit to mention the timely, generous assistance in farm work, given by those who escaped the afflictive visitation—friendly aid not to be specially recorded here.

It must be interesting to compare the hailstorm of 1878 with one that occurred in 1799, also within our neighborhood, as recorded in a letter written by Mrs. Chandlee, the grandmother of our young ladies of that name, under date "Black Meadows, 5th month, 26th, 1799." It appears from the writer's statement, that the storm broke out in the evening of the 24th of May, about six o'clock, "continuing three-quarters of an hour with incessant flashes of lightning and constant peals of thunder. The devastation of timber, loss of grain, clover, outhouses, gardens, &c., is almost past description." She says the trees were nearly stripped of leaves, many having merely the stem left with a brown crust around it, as if scorched by the lightning. The danger to the house was very great; glass from the windows, and the hail flew over the house in such a manner that there seemed hardly a spot large enough for her babe and herself to find shelter, the roof being part blown off.

This storm, described in the letter as resembling the hurricanes of the West Indies more than our tempests, appears to have exceeded our hailstorm of last year in violence.

Perhaps you have now had a sufficiency in the way of storms; but my attention has been drawn to the description of another that occurred in our county, a few extracts from which will serve to furnish an additional comparison offered by these interesting natural phenomena.

The hailstorm referred to (according to the account in the paper of the day), desolated a tract between Rockville and Clarksburg, breaking out on Sunday, the 7th of June, 1818, sixty years before our own. "It approached from the southeast accompanied by a confused rumbling noise. Fortunately it did not *drive* much, or the mischief must have been much greater, as some of the hail measured fourteen inches in circumference; a large hog was seen to fall dead from receiving one, and the backs of the cattle were so lacerated as to cause the blood to run down their sides. Generally they were the size of a goose egg, and were of irregular, conical form. Some farmers had their prospects blighted in seeing their towering fields of grain laid prostrate to the earth." (From the *Federal Gazette and Baltimore Daily Advertiser.*)

I was somewhat surprised to see in the advertising columns, the notice of an auction sale of Alderney cows.

Returning to our neighborhood annals, it is noted that the month of May was a rather remarkable one. The weather changed cold, so that the early progress of the season was interrupted. Actual frosts produced injury in many places; but their chief disastrous effects were upon white wheat, which appears to have blossomed at the critical period, and was thus cut short to a degree sufficient to discourage most farmers from sowing it again in the following autumn. A green bug (*aphis*) swarmed in great numbers on the wheat head, producing some alarm, but without doing notable injury. The worst feature affecting the wheat crop was the distressing fall in price.

June came with continuing abundance of moisture, and cool to an extraordinary degree. The apprehensions, which our farmers had been abundant in expressing, as to the prospect of crops, were gradually removed; a full crop, barring white wheat sown in corn stubble, was harvested. An unusually heavy hay crop was cut, which had throughout the year an extremely depressing effect on the market. Abundance prevailed in nearly all the main farm productions, with one sad exception, which was in the case of fruit. Perhaps no worse exhibit is made of that great article of comfort and luxury in any part of these annals.

This month was brightened to a number of our people by an interesting marriage that took place at Bloomfield with numerous festivities. Boarders came from the city, though scarcely in such numbers as usual; and our young farmers enjoyed all the gay recreation required to relieve the monotony of hard work. The close of the month of June was distinguished by the final breaking up of "Stanmore Boarding School of Girls."

July is regarded by my statistical correspondent as being "quite uneventful"; although it witnessed the renewal of the game of base ball with renewed zeal. Some queer difficulties arose in the preliminaries, showing that our young men are already up to the mature politicians. As those latter use party-spirit to accomplish what they profess to make their object, namely, the public good, so in "officering the nines," did the former employ the same unblest means for spoiling their pleasure. Party spirit, alas! has just about as much to do in good government as in sportive games. None the less was there expended in yonder pasture-lot, agreeably to close mathematical calculation of the "Correlation of Forces," an amount of muscular exertions, which being converted into another form of power, might have cut and secured all the harvests of the neighborhood! Whether this is to be considered, in mechanical phrase, a waste of power, is for you to judge. A deliberate conclusion would be—that sport becomes waste of power just when it passes the point where it runs into excess. All must admit that the escape from serious injuries, by bat and ball, was cause for much gratitude and satisfaction.

The 1st day of August was pleasantly commemorated by a celebration at Woodburn, of the 84th birthday of our much-loved and respected friend, Eliza Kirk. Her children, grandchildren, and numerous old friends were around her, and left nothing undone to bring to her affectionate heart the gratification so well merited by her long and useful life.

In August were continued the tours in pursuit of health and pleasure, begun in the preceding month, with more than usual satisfaction to several parties. The Virginia springs and the seashore, away up to the island-mountain of Maine, were the choice spots visited.

By the end of the month, the perfected corn crop completes the almost unprecedented abundance of all the five chief crops of our neighborhood, viz., grass, wheat, oats, corn and potatoes. But welcome abundance is attended with the natural accompaniment of low prices, which takes off considerably from the satisfaction of the producer. It seems that we can rarely have both blessings at once.

Another blessing must be noted, namely, the prevalence

of good health among us, while the Southwest is so terribly afflicted with yellow fever. Liberal contributions were made to relieve, so far as in our power, the sufferings of our fellow-countrymen.

September. Apprehensions entertained lest the corn should not harden; but by the middle of the month it was cut and set up in excellent condition, affording ample time for preparations to sow wheat. A few began that important work in this month. There was a decided disposition among some to experiment with new fertilizers. Wheat very steady at $1.00. The New Party, got up to make money more easily and expeditiously and abundantly, attracts notice in the crowd.

The Horticultural Fair was held at the Lyceum, after the intermission of a year. The vegetable exhibit was not remarkable any way except for the diminished figure cut by the pumpkin tribe, but the display of flowers gave shining proof of the increased devotion of our ladies to the charming department of horticulture. The success of the Fair as shown by the large number of visitors, and by its general management, was every way encouraging.

The history of September, 1878, cannot be closed without referring to the establishment of "Rockland Boarding School for Girls," which seems from its position and management rather a transfer of "Stanmore" than a wholly new concern; my assistant adds that "it was hailed with such satisfaction by us young mothers as to deserve special recognition."

October furnished less material than usual in the way of gay and brilliant foliage to deck the parlors with autumn wreaths, but it was good for sowing wheat, digging potatoes, and commencing the husking of corn; the dryness of the latter disappointed the croakers of the previous month, as so often happens. Those useful labors being well finished, who shall blame us for indulging in a little "high sport" (?) when a party of "old men and boys, and loving friends, and youths and maidens gay," met to enjoy the excitement of a "bag fox-chase." Any one desirous of information as to particulars may know where to inquire, but they need not go to the genuine old sportsman, who considers such fox hunting like box pigeon shooting, *beneath the chivalry of true sport.*

This month was signalized by the establishment of "the Sandy Spring Branch of the Benevolent Aid Society," which made a good start under the presidency of Caroline H. Miller, and being conducted almost exclusively by ladies, increased until about a hundred names were enrolled. Meetings were held twice during the month throughout the cold season, and it is believed much good was accomplished.

November was ushered in by the performance of the great civic duty of voting at a new place, Mechanicsville, the larger part of our neighborhood being thrown into the newly organized eighth district of the county. There came, or were at liberty to come, about 70 out of the whole number of voters in the neighborhood census, their political sentiments being expressed nearly thus: 50 republicans, 10 democratic, 5 "the new party.".

A wide circle of our friends was shocked at hearing of the sudden death on the 5th of this month, of Anna T. Hallowell, widow of the late J. Elgar Hallowell. For a number of years she had lived among us, endeared to the hearts of her relatives and numerous friends by her lovely traits of character and winning face and manners. Though not properly a resident of Sandy Spring for the last sixteen years, she felt so near and dear that we never ceased to claim her as one with us. "Her place is kept" in many a warm heart.

In this month were resumed the bi-weekly meetings for Bible reading and other religious exercises, conducted by E. J. Farquhar, at the house of Benjamin H. and Sarah T. Miller. The number who attended with considerable regularity was sufficient to produce the impression that there is among many of us what may be termed "a ground swell" of fresh religious feeling. Every serious thinking person must desire that it may not be smothered, but may find the proper direction that will conduct to peace and the higher life.

In this same month the two societies, the "Debating" and the "Sociable," recommenced the performance of their interesting functions. In regard to the success of the latter, no doubts or insinuations are admissible. The crowded meetings, the high style of literary proceedings, declamatory and written, the *power* it has twice exhibited to fill this Lyceum hall when it gracefully consents to aid some struggling effort in a good cause, finally its manifest reluctance to adjourn for the season, all these are clear indications of a brilliant success.

In addition to other pleasant things November has also brought round the *oysterman* to give us countrymen a taste of city luxury—a welcome arrival, but of course it costs.

December. Early in this month occurred a very ugly fracas at the colored people's church. The number of their young men going round with nothing to do is becoming a source of increasing concern, though nothing could be better punishment for one guilty of the grave offence of knifing a rival than a year in the House of Correction, lately awarded by our Court. As "idleness is the great mother of mischief," it becomes a matter of serious moment that the employers of labor should look round more diligently, and exert their efforts more efficiently to find work for all persons seeking labor. This is a duty whose neglect will insure future heavy penalty.

On the 15th died John S. Miller, a citizen of Philadelphia, of whom honorable mention was made a year ago, for a large contribution to repair of public roads. He had reached an advanced age, and accumulated a large property which was divided in an equitable manner among his relatives. So considerable was the amount that ought to flow into and swell the current of Sandy Spring business activities that apprehensions were entertained by some of the apprehensive sort, lest mischievous effects might arise from the sudden influx. It is proper to state that no such injurious effects appear thus far to have been produced.

Christmas was pronounced to have been more than usually quiet, especially around the stores, whose proprietors manifested great and disinterested regard for the peace and safety of the community, by withdrawing from sale all fire-crackers, torpedoes, and such nuisances peculiar to the season.

Another reform, well worth recording, may be claimed for the holiday; there was less drinking among those who have been in the practice of indulging in that way. It is due to the truth of history to state that this improvement was attributed by certain disbelievers in progress, to the fact that the continued low prices of produce, especially of hay, had left people too poor to indulge in dissipation; if it was so, it was a blessed poverty; but the idea had little or no foundation. Considerable ice was stored away in Christmas week.

January, 1879. This, the 10th month of our year, was

distinguished for a spell of very cold weather. The thermometer sinking on an average through the neighborhood, only to minus 3° and 5°, was but a partial test of the severity of the cold. "The wind makes the weather," is an old saying, which was true this time. The frost-king managed to penetrate cellars and potato caves, with disastrous effects. On the other hand, ice houses, not being large enough to hold all the ice desired, new ones were made above ground. From notes made in this month I observe it stated that "society revives in full feather"; frequent parties restore the social character of our young folks, which was accused of a falling off in the early part of the winter.

Another revival, truly worthy of the name, came on in its turn. The Lyceum, our pride of former years, monument of our earliest efforts to raise the standard of intellectual improvement, had threatened to become a *monument* indeed. Several preceding pages of this history complain in mournful words of the lukewarmness which had crept over our better aspirations. Our officers had done their duty in making efforts to provide high-class entertainment. The people would not come; they appeared to grow weary; cloyed with such substantial aliment of mind, and wanting something of lighter sort. A new plan was used, or rather an old one revived. Tickets were sold in advance by interesting little children. The effort was a success; for who could refuse the cherub applicants? Lectures were started again, and went on. On the 16th, Hon. Alonzo Bell favored us with one of the healthy sort, worth listening to, for it was bracing to the soul. Every person was pleased, and many observed "This is indeed an old-time Lyceum audience"; for the room was filled. Other successful lectures followed.

Capt. Tyson, a man of words as well as deeds, but of deeds surpassing his words, displayed to a crowded audience at the next meeting in February, a graphic picture of that fascinating Arctic scenery, with the still more moving qualities of true manhood in mastering its dangers and terrible sufferings, in a way to fasten the attention of old and young, sedate and gay; also the best order was observed. Interest the people; they will listen.

It was observed throughout this exceptionally severe winter (as we must continue to regard it), that the health of our people was remarkably good as long as the severe cold lasted; so soon as there came a partial thaw, catarrhs and neuralgia began to be very prevalent, with tendency to pneumonia. But with the one exception of James Stone, there was no severe case. Taking the year through, the general health was fairly good. The preservation of all the numerous tender children is indeed remarkable, and, as my venerable sister justly writes, a cause of devout thankfulness. But we have to note an unusual number of accidents; six having occurred. The sufferers were Robert R. Moore, from the stage running away; Charles F. Kirk, from the horns of a horrible bull; E. P. Thomas, from *gravitation;* Charles H. Burke, a broken bone; Llewellyn Massey—and a dreadful wound by a gun in his own hand, that caused the death of Frank Sullivan; and the fall, at a later date, of Rebecca Thomas, not severe, but slow of cure.

The Convention of Farmers' Clubs, held at the usual time in January, was well attended, and served to bring out the various qualities of the respective tribes. The amicable competition thus exhibited appeared to afford amusement without any serious opposition. More important measures were started by a resolution unanimously adopted, looking to a reform in the management of county affairs; a rolling stone which appears to be gathering moss.

It is supposed to be the province of historians to record the joys, sorrows, and misfortunes of others, not their own. Now it is the singular office of two out of three who contribute to these annals, to tell of disastrous events affecting their own case.

A fire broke out in January, which threatened to destroy the dwelling of Edward P. and Mary B. Thomas; it was checked in time. On the last day of February the barn of Wm. H. Farquhar with all its contents was wholly destroyed. The building had stood for 60 to 70 years; within half an hour it was reduced to smoke and ashes. No reasonable doubt exists that the source of the mischief was the smoking-pipe of the hired man. No comment is needed to enforce the lesson: Beware of pipes! An attendant feature of this very serious calamity well deserves a more extended notice than I feel able to give it; *before the flames of the hay, straw, and fodder were extinguished, two loads were seen coming* up the road from a *neighbor's barn* or stack, sent to supply the remaining stock with necessary subsistence. One horse, the most valuable, was consumed in the fire; another neighbor took in the dry cows "to keep in his barn till the grass should come." The day following many loads of fodder were deposited in such quantities as to elicit the remark of a relative, that she had never seen corn *grow so fast* as it did that day in Uncle William's barnyard.

It would take more room on these pages than I have to spare, to recite the evidences of neighborly kindness which were drawn out by the calamity. And it would be ungrateful and unjust were I not to add, that the kindnesses were by no means limited by the bounds of *neighborhood.* When the new building now being constructed, shall rise on the ruins of the old, its figure from roof to foundation-stone shall be while it stands, at least for me and my children, an enduring monument of the brotherly kindness shown by the members of "Olney Grange," as well as by the nearer neighbors of Sandy Spring.

The record of the year touching matters of business is not very different from the country generally, only rather less depressed. The Savings Institution still continues to show an increase of deposits, though of smaller amount, with a stronger basis than a year ago. A test of the neighborhood life is shown by the operations of the Post-Office. Samuel Bond, Assistant Postmaster, has kindly forwarded the following report:

During the twelve months ending April 1st, 1879, were cancelled $793 of postage stamps, which being reduced to single letter postage, would make 26,433 letters sent *from* the office, but of course there were circulars, cards, &c., included. During the same period were sold here 7085 postal cards, against 3400 sold in 1874, the year they were introduced. Of money orders issued during the year amounting to $2845, *sent away*—$1287 sent here—excess *sent out* $1558, against a difference in same direction of $1727 in 1871.

As another feature showing progress in our neighborhood, my Junior Assistant very properly suggests that notice should be taken of the great increase in the number of cows, which she estimates as being four times as numerous as they were ten years ago. Also the recent opening in the forests affording views more extended, besides the substantial benefits from an increase of arable soil. Then there is now going on a planting of hedges;

numerous bay-windows and conservatories are added to dwellings, while the paint brush is more used than of yore; all of which are tokens of improved civilization. Mention is also made of the pleasant incident of a "house-warming entertainment," presided over by Mary P. Thomas, which afforded sympathetic gratification to all the old friends who rejoiced that the parents had come into such agreeable quarters in their declining years. At the very close of the year we were indebted to the contractor for establishing a new mail. That "herald of a noisy world" now comes twice a day; when I was Postmaster it used to come twice a week.

The closing pages of this year's history have room for only one more line—the most important of all.

Within the limits now defined as constituting "our neighborhood," the statistical return is: marriages 2; births 14 (9 boys and 5 girls); deaths 1.

CHAPTER XVII.

FROM FOURTH MONTH, 7TH, 1879, TO FOURTH MONTH, 5TH, 1880.

The largest tree — Changes in men — The spirit remains — A year of action — New buildings — April an important month — Barn raising — Pleasant Quarterly Meeting — Help to sick harvesters — Early sound of the steam whistle, for threshing — New games, the Archery — A new Bible class — Numerous premiums at Rockville Fair — The Great Cyclone — Remarks on Monthly Meeting — Reflections — Sanitary facts — Dr. Hartshorne's book — Mild winter — A house warming — The ladies' success at the Lyceum — The Dickens Calendar — Amanda Dèyo — Revising the Discipline —Two new Societies — The Farmers' Club conclude to use the moonshine.

There are many trees still standing in our neighborhood which were growing when the first white settlers made their way gradually and *cautiously* along what is now called the Laurel road, leading then, as now, from the lower counties where settlement began. The chestnut tree standing nearly in front of Cherry Grove, largest tree in this part of the country, being thirty feet in girth at the ground, and twenty-two and a half feet at five feet higher up the trunk, probably did not attract the attention of the adventurous travellers nearly two centuries ago, unless indeed a panther was hanging to an upper bough, or a bear was hugging the trunk with arms which might then readily enclose it.

The appearance now presented by these remains of the ancient forest differs greatly from that which it bore when first viewed by the eyes of our forefathers, who, nevertheless, failed to perceive the changes as they proceeded from one year to another. The full life of a tree far exceeds that of a man; yet even in his case, the change annually produced in the man, although really greater than in the forest, is scarcely perceptible, or at least is apt to be denied by him, and by the friend who good-naturedly compliments him with the assurance that "he is looking just the same as he did years ago." This may safely be called a pleasing delusion on one side, and perhaps an innocent fraud on the other. For all the time, alike in the man as in the tree, continual, eternal change is remorselessly proceeding onward, with results—not now to be described—the time inevitably comes when neither self-delusion nor friendly compliments can hide the unwelcome fact. Such is the law with every individual thing that has life. Some writers say the same law prevails with nations; asking of "Assyria, Greece, Rome, Carthage, where are they?" Modern scientists agreeing with Scripture at least on one point, claim to have settled it beyond doubt, that the whole universe is passing and bound to pass through the same career; that the time must come when "the Sun himself shall grow dim with age, all Nature sink in years"; but here the bard and prophet, inspired from a higher source than material science, come in, assuring us there *is that* "which shall flourish in immortal youth,

> Unhurt amidst the war of elements,
> The wreck of matter and the crush of worlds."

In plain simple prose, there are two distinct realities which the mind has to keep in view, if it would arrive at truth; one, obvious to the senses, consisting of things changeable and perishing; the other, relating to something just as *real* as the former, but requiring the use of a different part of our nature to comprehend and appreciate. The individual tree dies, but the *principle of life* remains. The individual men and women who composed the nations of Greece and Rome are not to be found there now; but if it is asked "Where is the spirit, the essential part that constituted those nations?" the true answer comes—"It is *here*, around and within us, in our books and our lives, diffused over the civilized world in the things that make it refined and beautiful, as well as in the law and order essential to its government." This order and beauty, like all *essential principles*, belong to the spiritual, that does not perish. Every *real existence* is endowed with it. Therefore, as was shown on a former page of this history (see Chapter VII), that this neighborhood is such a real entity, an existing thing, our object should be to get at its essential, its spiritual part, which includes the life of the place, and *on which* depends the problem of its present condition and future destiny.

It may now be perceived that in selecting material for

our Annals, the principal effort is to describe such events as appear to have closest connection with permanence of condition and character; not slighting, however, everyday incidents, such perhaps

> "As have no slight or trivial influence
> On that best portion of a good man's life,—
> His little, nameless, unremembered acts
> Of kindness and of love."

Preliminary remarks being at last disposed of we come to the events of the rushing year. A year of action and life it has been; one sharing, too, in the prosperity of the country. True, it has not passed without visitations from the "pale messenger," but in each case it was the "ripe fruit that was shaken from the tree."

This general activity was shown in a shape which is perhaps the most striking. New buildings are exceptionally numerous and fair to look upon. Three large barns, which naturally come first, seem to claim, from the high position on which they are erected, that degree of respect always accorded to them by a farming community. The year boasts also of two fine new dwellings; one, a neat and comfortable addition to the aspiring village of Ashton; the other exhibiting, near the shore of Rock Creek, a specimen of ornamental architecture such as was not previously attained in our section.

As the erection of good houses and barns is one of the most important evidences of improvement in a country, it is a fact worthy of record, to state that within the period embraced in this historical sketch (a space of 16 years, or since the war), we may count up, among buildings either wholly new, or so much repaired as properly to be reckoned among the new ones—of houses 30 (not counting a number of tenant-houses); of barns 22 (beside 25 stables, wagon-houses, shops and such). These are the property of our 85 families. There are at least 20 new additional houses within the circle bounding our neighborhood.

Taking the months in regular course, we note in regard to April (a very important month to farmers; once let "Time's forelock" out of your hands during this precious month and you will have trouble enough to catch up with the old fellow—but this is a digression). Last April was steadily cool, and not so favorable to the rapid advance of vegetation as it was to plowing and building. The youthful class enjoyed themselves in practising on old amusements and in organizing new ones. The Sociable closed for the season. The Horticultural made a bright commencement at Norwood. Fruit was full of promising bloom. But while this month was full of animation to others, it was made very sad to our elder historian, by the death of an only sister and brother. Nearly the same loss fell during the year upon him who writes this.

May. The month came in cool, and continued so rather steadily, the thermometer on the 3d being at 37°. Instead of raising a May-pole, our young men spent May-day in raising a big barn for William Lea. The new style of making barns, 20 to 25 feet to the square, and the introduction of new machinery, render this old business somewhat different from what barn-raising used to be. Still the crowd assemble in numbers of 100 or more, and partake the abundant entertainment, very much as they did in the olden time. Everything went on satisfactorily, to the great relief of many who looked anxiously on.

The same proceeding with nearly the same method, and nearly the same favorable results, was repeated on the 14th of the month, in raising the barn of Wm. H. Farquhar, on the site of the conflagration described in this story a year ago. A cheerful, vigorous crowd, over 70 in number, lent their willing hands; and though much was said about the folly of using such a superfluity of men to accomplish a work that is done in some places with one-tenth of the number here employed, the impression produced on my mind was very favorable to the scene before me. There was so much of the hearty hilarity and social feeling described as belonging to the "good old times" we read of. Nor must it be forgotten that some 30 to 40 of the gentler sex brightened the scene by their presence, doubtless imparting vigor to the muscles whose activity was needed.

To this month belongs another scene, of very different order, in which that sex bore the most conspicuous part. As a memento to be handed down to future generations (it would have astonished the former), the programme is hereto appended. See

A LYSTE OF YE PSALMS AND WORLDLIE SONGES.

1st PARTE.

1. Auld Lang Syne, by ye whole Companie.
2. Dost Thou Love Me? by Sister Ruth and Brother Simon.
3. Hail Columbia, by all ye Syngers.
4. Ye Bloom is on ye Rye, by Brother Caleb.
5. Ye Dearest Spot, by Every One of ye Syngers.
6. Within a Mile of Edinboro Town, by Phœbe Mayflower.
7. Yankee Doodle, by ye Mankind Syngers.
8. Coming through the Rye, Rosa Belinda.

2nd PARTE.

1. Home Again, by All ye Syngers.
2. Ye Old Sexton, by Brother Zachariah.
3. AMERICA, by ye whole Companie.
4. Auld Robin Gray, by Phœbe Mayflower.
5. Cousin Judediah, by All Ye Syngers.
6. Old Folks at Home, by ye whole Companie.
7. John Anderson my Jo, by Rosa Belinda.
8. Marseilles Hymn, by every one of ye Syngers.

Sister CAROLINE POUNDKEYS, from ye village of Baltimore, will sounde on ye Spinet for ye Syngers.

Lively and innocent amusement was made the means of filling up the empty coffers of the Lyceum.

June. "A very pleasant and good Quarterly Meeting," is the first record of this month; attended with none of those objectionable disturbances which have sometimes been made by rude visitors from town. This month, though decidedly cool for awhile, was distinguished by its favoring weather, there being just enough rain in the early part and becoming dry toward the close, so as to make a good time for harvest. Wheat ripened fast, of a quality and quantity not to be complained of; and the grass crop came out all right. "The boys," besides doing full duty at their respective harvests, rendered acceptable help to one who was sick; making with the aid and presence of the "girls," a choice frolic.

July. As usual, many boarders and strangers came to the neighborhood; of whom nothing remarkable is related. There was about the average of summer travel by our people; a number were to be seen paddling in the ocean deeps (or rather "shallows"), while others with alpenstock in hand, climbed Mount Mitchell, mightiest peak of the Alleghany range, returning with such glowing accounts as to turn the attention of tourists in a new direction.

At an early period in the month the now familiar sound of the steam whistle began to be heard, token that threshing was begun. This music, very animating if not melodious, was rendered still more exciting by prospects of the increased price of wheat. Those who sold gained no great advantage by their haste, but had the satisfaction of superior energy in being *ahead.* They will be very apt to do the same next year, and probably make a successful hit. The hay crop came out much better than was anticipated, proving a source of profit to those who did not make engagements too hastily.

And now, the "labors of the harvest being ended," our young men who had stood up so faithfully to their work, "bearing the burden and heat of the day," are quite ready for recreation—for recreation that will recreate most effectually. Dropping the old game of base ball, whether the relish for it was outgrown, or because the old ground had been plowed up, where should they turn? In this age of progress it could only be to seek for comrades in sport of a higher order; comrades, who formerly were merely spectators, *now* to be indeed *comrades* in the game! But in order to do justice to the subject, it is absolutely requisite that I should "drop into poetry." The subject demands it; your historian's known æsthetic predilections must not be stifled. What shall it be? Nothing appropriate occurs but these lines:

> "Forth from the pass, in tumult driven,
> Like chaff before the wind of heaven,
> The Archery appear!
> For life, for life, their race they ply—
> While shriek and shout and battle-cry,
> And plaids and bonnets waving high,
> And targets flashing to the sky,
> Are maddening in their rear."

The only excuse that can be made for introducing such inappropriate verse as the foregoing, is the fact that the lines *would* keep running a race in my head. Could anything be *less* appropriate to describe the archery meetings of last summer?

A green lawn; gayly colored target, with circular divisions pleasing to the eye; long bows, curved in the line of beauty; fancifully decked arrows; lively maidens, bending with native grace the bow which impels the arrow against—no *vital* part; sport "that owes no pleasure to another's pain"; all these, in the fresh air and under the blue sky—how could a young farmer find a recreation more delicate, more refining, more innocent?

And yet ancient faith requires a glance at the other side. So powerful is the influence of amusements on the tone of society; their quality is regarded by historians as such an indication of the rise and progress, or the decline and fall of a community, that new ways are not to be passed over. In reference to the sports of archery, there are some observing critics who view them as out of keeping with rural life; affording a measure of exercise to a class not specially in need of it; involving expensive preparations; communicating no new ideas of value; and being severe on delicate fingers. Since pleasure is something not to be measured by rules of science, the true worth and nature of archery as a farmer's game must be left to the parties most nearly concerned, who are not entirely oblivious to the comfort of others outside.

The weather of July was somewhat peculiar, and extremely variable. About the 25th there fell some heavy rains, following distressing drought, which completely changed the face of the great corn crop; a dearth had threatened, but the deliverer came, leaving some disagreeable mementoes, in deep scratches in plowed fields.

August came in hot and growing. Rain fell in excessive abundance. This being comparatively a leisure month with farmers, the tourist feeling took possession of a number. Amusements grew more and more lively—archery fairly boomed. Sport of a more doubtful character began to exhibit a degree of excitement among some of the young ladies, which elicited from an old bachelor (of course) the sharp remark that "the sex, grown weary of being hunted, would now a-hunting go." On the other hand, a new Bible Class was formed in this month; so various and multitudinous are the ways of this neighborhood getting to be.

In this month William Henry Gilpin died—a happy release for him—his life was a sad one; deprived from early years of the faculties which alone render persons responsible for their actions.

It is proper here to record that at the close of the month many of us were saddened to hear of the very sudden death of Gerard H. Reese, in Baltimore, who had been closely knit by ties of friendship and kin to a large circle at Sandy Spring.

September. This is the month of Fairs, and our people bore a full part in the two that most concern them. They swept numerous premiums at Rockville; and at our Lyceum they made the Horticultural Fair a complete success, as regards the chief purposes for which it is designed, viz. the assemblage of a friendly crowd, and the unequalled exhibition of flowers and fruits, with the no less æsthetic triumphs of culinary art.

On the 3d of September, 1879, occurred one of those tremendous sports of our atmosphere, which are fortunately exceeding rare in any one place. The first Cyclone mentioned in the history of the neighborhood passed several miles through what may be called its western interior, or very nearly its centre, with a varying width of thirty to seventy yards. *Coming down* (for that seems to suit the course that cyclones take) between the land of Stephen Holland and that of the old Cashell family, it struck and twisted in cyclone fashion the limbs of a cherry tree, and went on scattering heaps of manure in the adjoining field, then into the quiet abode of the ancient dead, where the heavy tombstones of wife and husband were flung, one to the east and one to the west,—passing on through a gap in the cornfield (made by itself), at the edge of which it dug up some potatoes, and even the weeds of the patch; after this low freak, its course was ascending, for a few hundred yards merely brushing the tops of the forest trees. Again dropping into a field of Augustus Cashell, it lifted three or four stones out of their bed; for a space of half a mile its track was barely discernible, then skirting the land of Penuel Palmer, it struck with tremendous force into the woods of Frederick Stabler, prostrating the largest trees; next, after an interval, it passed into the woodland of Joseph T. Moore, playing havoc there (perhaps the most destructive on the whole route), then into William W. Moore's cornfield, *scraping* the very earth, and close by a tenant-house which escaped serious injury. Still on, preserving very nearly the same direction of north by east, it came to James Powell's, where it moved the corn-house from its foundation so gently as scarcely to spill any grains from an open barrel of wheat which it carried along. James H. Stone and William H. Farquhar were the next victims of the tornado, suffering just alike in the orchard and the front yard. The last named lost a half dozen of his most valuable apple trees, and had the symmetry of his ornamental trees sadly and lastingly impaired. After leaving this place the cyclone made one more tremendous dig into some large trees on the public road west of "Charley Forest," taking down an apple tree or two of Si. Bowen's; its further track could be just followed, until near the field of Mahlon Chandlee, not far from his dwelling, the whirlwind went up into the higher regions whence it fell. This rising and falling of the cyclone was a very peculiar feature; viewed from the hills, the double cones meeting in hour-glass shape, the numerous inner whirls partially detached,—the wind rushing in at the edges of the track,—all these features of a real cyclone—ours had them all! Yet the damage to property was very small to what it might have been with a little bend in its course; the injuries to person none.

Something new occurred in the quiet sphere of the Monthly Meeting in making an alteration of one of the answers to the Queries. It was to the effect that too many of the younger portion of the Society passed in their pursuit of pleasure beyond the line of *moderation*, in which alone lies safety. For moderation is the key to true pleasure—"a key to the plan of God." There is no question as to the fact that our young people are becoming more devoted to the pursuit of *pleasure*, than they were in former times. It does not follow they are growing *worse:* only more excited. A whirl not so destructive as the cyclone, but like it, rushing, booming, pushing, has got hold of them; *forward* is the word; but not always onward and *upward!* Like the cyclone, it tends to *uncover the roots.* Hunting the bear and the deer in the glens of the Alleghanies, as was done successfully last fall by some of our young men, who gained health and vigor there, is doubtless gallant sport; but of *that other*—the bag fox business—the least said the soonest mended.

A wise philosopher declares that the fault most prolific of evil among the vices is *sloth.* Philosophers are liable to make mistakes, but it appears to me there is truth in that doctrine. Does not virtue consist in *doing?* All progress certainly does. Now herein lies the excellence of Sandy Spring—such as it is; and in its exemption from sloth consists the freedom from vice—so far as that is wanting.

It is due to facts touching these ethical subjects, that the following record should be made: there came to certain households a visitation of sore disease, attended with deepest affliction. Then were the same young men and maidens who had been foremost in the pursuits of pleasure, now among the first to proffer their kindly services at the bed of pain. While of the manly youth, not one even of those who are most given to sport and fun is ever accused of the excesses that have been the ruin of many flourishing communities.

Scanning impartially the actual condition of our neighborhood, it seems as if the *sanitary* question was now of chief importance. Physical health has so much influence on future prosperity as well as on present comfort that it claims the earnest attention of all who love their race. The best way to get an answer in this concern, to the significant question—"Watchman, what of the night?" is to refer to facts bearing directly upon the situation. Individual cases must here be regarded as impersonal; that is, as concerning us all equally.

The cases mentioned must be taken, as the lawyers use them, to establish their object by employing a supposititious case. They naturally include those belonging to the more delicate half of the race, whose health is undeniably of even more importance to the general welfare than that of the other and more robust half. Inquiring of a mother whose daughter is at present from home, whether the latter would not return to stay during the next year, the reply was—one to be noted—"the social dissipation (using that word in mildest form) prevailing at Sandy Spring is such that I think it would be better for my daughter not to be exposed to the influence, till her *health* is more *consolidated*." The next case relates to a young lady whose health has latterly not been so good as the many friends who love her would ardently desire; having lengthened out a recent visit beyond the appointed period, she gave the reason for it quite seriously, that "she believed it would be better for her health to *rest* awhile from our neighborhood visiting, especially the being out so much and so late at night."

It is difficult to judge how these simple statements will impress those who listen to them; but my feelings in writing them down are something more than *serious*—they are awful! I will spare you further reflections of my own; but entreat most earnestly that you will give the subject the reflection it deserves. You, young men, who must be mainly (not wholly) responsible for the growth of such a social condition as is indicated in cases like the foregoing, your more robust constitutions do not experience so quickly the inevitable results of excess in social pleasures; yet you are, if possible, more interested in the health of those whose soundness of health is to be of such vital consequence to your own welfare and happiness. It is not too much to say that a large portion of the neighborhood's future welfare, growth and prosperity depends on a reform which will bring about the *moderation* demanded alike by good feeling and good sense. Let me here refer to a little book, just published by Dr. Henry Hartshorne, entitled "Home." It contains the counsels of an able physician, and a well-known, highly-esteemed friend.

October was very dry and warm, making the farmers uneasy about their wheat.

November possessed several interesting claims on our attention, as that month usually does. First came the election of our State officers and representatives; in the result of which we were disappointed. Better luck, we hope, next November!

The various Associations flourish. The Benevolent Aid Society holds its Second Annual Meeting, and begins its winter career; the winter proved so extraordinarily mild that the need was small for its charitable ministrations. A general regret was expressed, that the failing health of the President, Caroline H. Miller, compelled her to resign a position which, it is no idle compliment to say, she adorned.

On the 27th of the month a very large gathering of neighbors and friends was received by Roger B. and Caroline M. Farquhar in their new dwelling (before described) near the shores of Rock Creek. It was "Thanksgiving Day," appropriately chosen for the pleasing, ancient ceremony of "House-warming." To the good taste shown in the construction of this fine building was added a greater charm, the *good feeling* that collected so large and so varied a company, filling the house with the warmth of social enjoyment. Chief Judge R. J. Bowie was introduced by his own request to Thomas C. Groomes, the successful architect of the building; and all came away at a seasonable hour, thinking rather better of themselves and of one another.

December was in part enlivened by a wedding on the 16th; followed on the 18th by another entertainment at the Lyceum—the joint production of the Sociable and the Musicale. This mingled æsthetic and useful performance was deserving of the highest praise; being projected and accomplished by the ladies, without any assistance from the other side. It was a full success in all the arrangements, even allowing the audience to get home at a respectable hour of the night. This triumph may be useful in *taking down the vanity* of the other sex, who, in youth, are apt to think *nothing* can be done without *their help.*

In the article forwarded by my younger assistant, full of appropriate material for our history, there is no notice of the "Dickens Calendar" for 1880, a work which has assisted to spread the literary fame of Sandy Spring over a considerable section of the country, and has been acknowledged in England, as something which will be looked for in '81. It was prepared by Mary B. Thomas, with assistance in the ornamental part from Harriet I. Lea.

The year 1880 came in with the remarkable weather which has signalized our Annals. The consequence was a great failure of the now indispensable ice-crop. Not a total failure; some have filled their houses; a number have partly filled; others say they mean to *have ice* some way. Those who have none are encouraged by the old saying, "a warm winter makes a cool summer."

A lady from the north, Amanda Deyo, made a deep impression in the latter part of the winter by her eloquent lectures. The language of Mary B. Thomas is the unvarnished truth, who writes, "If the visit of Mrs. A. Deyo to this community does not bear good fruit in the coming years, it will be the fault of us, who having ears to hear, hear not. Her soul-stirring appeals in favor of peace, of temperance, and of woman suffrage, will long be remembered by those who had the rare pleasure of listening to this truly eloquent and gifted woman. She also delivered several sermons of great power and pathos; and her course of lectures to ladies upon physiology was well attended." Her lecture on woman suffrage was the most able of the four. It may be truly said, the strongest argument presented by Mrs. Deyo in favor of woman's capacity to vote, was the lady herself.

The revival of interest felt in religious questions was not originated by friend Deyo, although well seconded by her eloquent discourses. Several causes were at work. Other ladies from a distance helped to stir up the new life, which gained fresh animation from influences coming from an opposite direction; *opposite* as to modes and forms, and ideas of mediators; the *same*, as looking to the source, centre and end. An indication of new life was shown by numerous meetings of the members of Friends' Society, held for the purpose of revising the Discipline. The changes proposed exhibit a liberal and enlightened sentiment, and if met in other quarters by the same spirit may prove a durable point of reference, perhaps "a new departure," in the progress of the Society.

The allotted space to which the annals of a year are limited, renders it impossible to do justice to the various associations, whose number and quality defy description. Sufficient to say, they have all lived and flourished in lively manner. (The Debating Society was exalted to fame bestowed by the newspaper.) At least two new Societies have entered into existence, if indeed the "Temperance Society" can be termed a new one. Youngest of all is the "Peace Society," which begins already to call for Amanda Deyo; it furnishes however a pleasing, appropriate motto: "Let us have peace!"

As we are nothing with all our societies and lectures if we fail in giving to agriculture the first place in our interests, it would never do to pass without notice the Annual Convention of the Clubs, held now in the 1st month for 7 years (with 8 meetings). The last one exhibited the same lively interest in the great cause as did all the preceding. Farmers coming from a distance formed an acceptable part of the meeting; for, despite the accusation of conceit against Sandy Spring (at which none laugh more heartily than ourselves) we are more than willing to acknowledge our obligations to other farmers, and to own with pleasure the great improvements going on all around. A lively picture of this is given by Mary B. Thomas, one of our historians.

In connection with farming incidents, I note a change made by the venerable "Farmers' Club of Sandy Spring" —the father of all the clubs; having made a new departure in the time of their meetings, so as to have the benefit of moonshine in returning home. The idea was borrowed from the practice of the younger clubs, who must feel great satisfaction in the instruction which they gave their elders.

This year of '79-'80 has been distinguished by the general revival of business over our country. The best evidence which we can offer is found in the annual statement of our Savings Institution. On March 1st, 1880, the amount on hand was $103,088.14, the gain for the year being $14,772.10. The deposits made during the single month of March exceeded in amount the aggregated deposits of any quarter since the Institution was organized. While these results afford a just cause for satisfaction, they impose on our directors a deep sense of responsibility on account of the increased load laid upon them, and a solemn duty to make *safety* the polar star in guiding their future proceedings.

Our other great institution, holding a much higher rank in the business transactions of Sandy Spring, namely "The Mutual Fire Insurance Company, of Montgomery County," has had the opportunity which it has never delayed to embrace, of paying promptly a heavy amount of losses by fire. Yet it is a remarkable circumstance that the losses for the first quarter of the present year, usually running up to about $10,000, have fallen short of $500, owing to the extraordinarily mild winter.

The record showing the three important events of human life alone remains to be put in place. It will be recollected that, in making these statistics, the reference is exclusively to the 85 families—407 individuals heretofore named. Still the interest felt in other neighbors, acquaintances and friends, is too strong to allow an entire omission of events nearly concerning them.

Of marriages are reckoned three.

October 21st, 1879, Charles F. Brooke and Cornelia S. Miller, by the beautiful and dignified ceremony of Friends' Society.

December 16, 1879, Benjamin D. Palmer and Miss Mollie Mackall.

January 15th, 1880, Allan Farquhar and Charlotte H. Pleasants; this marriage being recorded in the clerk's office at Rockville, and the first in the county performed by Friends' ceremony where neither party was a member.

Of deaths there have been but two, within the limit of our neighborhood census.

Ninth month, 15th, 1879. Ann M. Stabler, wife of Caleb Stabler, after a short illness, in the 80th year of her age; a kind and loving spirit, respected by all who knew her, young and old. Her peaceful death was the natural close of a peaceful life. She was laid to rest in the family burying ground at Alloway, in a perfect autumn evening, which seemed typical of her ripe years of usefulness, followed to the grave by children and grandchildren—such as constitute the best "mother's monument."

Twelfth month, 26th. Phebe Farquhar, after a long

and most distressing illness, having nearly reached her 75th year. No children followed her to the tomb; but weeping brothers and sisters, nephews and nieces and sorrowing friends, testified to the high esteem and respect with which she had been long regarded. From her very birth it had been her lot to suffer with complaints of a nervous character; but these, while making life a scene of much distress, had no power to dim the brightness of extraordinary intellect, nor to lower the tone of high, pure moral conduct. Deep thought, strong feelings, yet reserved, and intense admiration of the noble and beautiful in nature and character, were her most impressive qualities.

A wider view taken by our friend Hadassah leads to mention the death of Jonathan D. Barnsley, who died very suddenly by a stroke of apoplexy, on the 29th of January, 1880. And of John Osborne, whose remains were brought from Baltimore to our burying ground; and of Sally Keith, a very meritorious woman.

First month, 23d, 1880. At Philadelphia, in the 52d year of her age, Alice Bentley Stabler. This lovely and lovable woman came in the summer of 1848 from Ohio, where she was born, and resided in the neighborhood of Sandy Spring for a number of years, during which she gained many warm friends. Their interest and affection were manifested in paying the last tribute to her remains when brought back for interment in the private cemetery of Thomas P. Stabler.

Our Statistical Report stands for this year, births 5 (4 boys and 1 girl); marriages 3; deaths 2.

CHAPTER XVIII.

FROM FOURTH MONTH, 5TH, 1880, TO FOURTH MONTH, 4TH, 1881.

Changes, which way ? — Historian's proper business — Evolution — Darwinism — Subjective and Objective — Real Value — (Thermometer 32° on 4th Month, 8th, once 88°) — Peach buds destroyed — Library for Grange — "Local Option Campaign" — Census of Friends — Dr. Scott in Europe — Binders, first employed — Sad, sudden death of Dr. J. W. Magruder, and others — The Farmer's vacation — Improvements at Ashton and elsewhere — Premiums at Rockville Fair — Orthodox Meeting House finished — Gold Mining roused again — "Glorious Victory of Local Option" — Afternoon First-Day Meeting — "Oh, the long and dreary Winter!" — Fast Driving — Farmers' Convention collects 200 — Mrs. Mullan's letter — Judge Bowie's death — S. Ellicott's, Jas. Stone and B. R. Roberts.

The individual who looks back over periods of his past life must recognize the fact that a change has been going on in his inner self; although he may perhaps be unable to satisfy his own mind as to what direction it may have moved. Was it forward or backward, upward or downward? that is the question which the reflecting person naturally asks himself. It must have been one way or the other; and it is scarcely necessary to add that it is a right important matter—*which was the way?*

The interest I have felt in this historical sketch for these last seventeen years has mainly proceeded from the comparison which my mind has been carrying on between the life of the neighborhood and the life of the individual. The conviction has grown and strengthened that there *is a close resemblance;* and I have thought that some profitable reflections might be gathered therefrom.

The proper business of the historian is no doubt chiefly concerned with describing actions and events; what may be called *outward facts:* so that history is properly *objective.* But in a degree it is also *subjective;* for it penetrates into the causes of things; it looks within, to examine the motives from which actions spring.

But human life, whether of the individual or the community, would be imperfectly described if the inquiry be confined either to actions or motives—one or both. Not what we are or have been, but what *we are becoming,* that is, *coming to be,* is the great point. To use the more scientific modern expression, the question to be examined by us is, how does the evolution of the neighborhood proceed?

After having used already the rather hard words "objective and subjective," it may seem severe upon my audience to introduce this formidable term; but there is no advantage in trying to shun such expressions now, especially in a place enjoying the reputation of Sandy Spring for keeping up even with the advanced *literati.* Evolution must be regarded as an established fact. Not necessarily in the way that Darwin speaks of it. As to his theory, which undertakes to describe the beginning and transmigration of all things in the universe, especially of human beings, we may still fairly claim to apply the Scotch verdict—"not proven!"

Still there is no denying the fact, fully established by modern science, that every thing and person, all the faculties of body and mind that go to make up the human being, are always and all the time undergoing the evolving process; and, like "poor Joe," compelled irresistibly "to move on!" This decree of the Creator is established by no Scotch verdict, but the Almighty mind.

Now, just as the individual, be he young or old or of middle age, has been "going on," or "evolving" (which is a better word, because the process is "from within, outward"), so has it been with this neighborhood, viewed as a whole, constantly going through the universal scheme of evolution, ever since it first began to be an organized community by building the meeting house down yonder. It is interesting and not unprofitable, certainly not untrue, to regard that spot, with its change of structure, as the central point where "began, continues, and (may we not say?) will end the life of this Sandy Spring."

My work is now to trace, with the help received from our two valuable auxiliaries, the course of events, and especially such as have most directly contributed to the evolution that has taken place in the neighborhood since the last Annual Record. Of course we shall adhere to the objective mainly, since innermost motives, although the real source of outward actions, are generally too secret and sacred for our pens to intrude. Before commencing the Monthly Records, it seems proper to make the general statement that our people have fairly and fully shared in the obvious acknowledged prosperity of the United States. Yet in setting this claim forward I am forcibly reminded to put the question, What constitutes prosperity? Where the heart is recently torn by grief for the loss of friends who were so near and dear, how insignificant, so far as human happiness is concerned, appear those large crops, big barns, inflated bank investments, and all worldly gains! When some of its best inhabitants are taken away by death, the neighborhood learns to estimate what it is that constitutes real value.

April, 1880. The first event chronicled this month was a fire that occurred near the Patuxent river, among the Johnson family. It was not a large house, but the loss was felt very severely by the sufferers. Such lively efforts were made by our people, living in the vicinity, to provide clothing and other necessaries for their relief, that a portion of the supplies sent from a distance was returned. First came *fire*, then frost; the latter did the most damage. On the 8th of the month the thermometer sunk to 32° (on the same day of the same month, years ago, it rose to 88°). Of course, apprehensions on account of the fruit were generally excited, which were proved by the results to be only too true. Peach buds were destroyed, occasioning serious loss to persons who have been increasing their stock of trees; the few who escaped the damage received corresponding advantage.

The first meeting of the Horticultural Society for the year was held in this month at Olney on the 16th, and was admitted by the large company that attended to be a very interesting affair; but none could tell Charles Farquhar how to save his peaches.

The lovers of amusement, reinforced by a visitor from New York, commenced in this month to gratify their love of sport, by the practice of what is called "Ball Shooting." It is described as an exhibition of wonderful skill; and is certainly very innocent.

An entertainment of quite another sort was had at Olney Grange Hall; it was packed with an animated crowd, that came to enjoy a fine concert and each other's company. The benediction was in the object; the collection of 225 persons producing a considerable sum, to be devoted for the benefit of a library for the use of the members of that worthy Order; and, perhaps, for a number outside.

May. The most important minute of the month's proceedings is found in this notice—"Now begins the Local Option Campaign." The weather was warm last month; but toward the end of this the heat, with the drought, became excessive. The census taken on the first day of this month, of the members of Sandy Spring Monthly Meeting, shows a total of 247—divided as follows: adult males, 76—females, 84—male minors, 45—female minors, 42. This preponderance of boys occasioned some surprise; but it is probably owing to the fact that one party remains under the denomination of minor till he reaches the age of 21, while the girls cease to be so after 18. A singular fact relating to the census is that in each of 20 families there are just 3 children.

June. The first day of this beautiful month was signalized by a large Local Option meeting in the court house at Rockville. A plan of organization was adopted, which worked splendidly, and led to a success beyond the expectations of the most sanguine advocates of the great cause.

Considerable interest was manifested at times during this month and the last, in "cables" from the other side of the Atlantic, telling of feats of skill in shooting at long range, performed by our fellow-neighbor, Dr. Samuel I. Scott. Some pride in the success obtained in the far foreign land by one of our "Sandy Spring boys," was very natural; even for those who prefer to admire the skill manifested in his immediate profession. Still "nothing succeeds in the world like success."

The appointment of our Lyceum President, Benjamin H. Miller, as one of the Maryland delegates to the Presidential Convention in Chicago, was of local interest; his *last vote* being generally approved.

A matter of equal or superior interest, namely the harvest, approached with rapid strides. None earlier is remembered. Considerable excitement was roused in the use of binders, now first successfully employed amongst us. Uncertainty in regard to the yield of the wheat crop continued longer than usual. The correct verdict probably was "somewhat above the average, on the whole, yet varying very much in individual cases." Threshing actually began in this month.

I cannot forbear recording, as a matter of general interest, the return of Eliza N. Bentley to her old home; bringing another charming attraction, beside herself, in books and pictures.

A tragical death occurred on the 14th, caused by kerosene—Mabel Peirce the victim.

July, 1880. Another very sad and sudden death occurred near the Bone Mill; Jane Cuff falling in the night into a well.

It is a time of tragical deaths. In the afternoon of the 13th of this month a large company held the usual monthly meeting of the Olney Grange; and while all were enjoying the entertainment, at which no one assisted so agreeably as Dr. John Willson Magruder, he suddenly dropped on the floor, and by the coming of dawn next morning, his bright, bold spirit had left its splendid earthly tenement a mass of lifeless clay. A void was left there, never since filled.

In this same month occurred, near Rockville, a horrible tragedy, not to be named or described.

An extraordinary rainfall happened on the fifth, which measured five inches, though lasting scarcely two hours. Harvest closed as it began, very early; oats being cut the 4th.

A young officer, Thomas L. Moore, took his place in the "M. F. I. O"—whose services and deportment therein have been wholly satisfactory to those concerned.

In this month, invalids and others not much sick, sought the springs, the mountains, and the ocean shore. I know one who *brought out of the water* a grievous trouble that lasted years. It is a pleasing task to close the record of an awful month with the announcement that the 15th was chosen as their wedding day by Edward N. Bentley and Hallie Chandlee.

August. The farmers' comparatively leisure month—which they are certainly entitled to, for the recreation that best suits them, whether it be travel abroad or enjoyments at home. Tours were taken by Caleb Stabler, B. Rush Roberts, Henry C. Hallowell and others, whose years and character gave assurance that they were not likely to get into mischief, though the line of travel carried some of them near a thousand miles away.

In relation to amusements of the more youthful portion, the remark was made some time in July that it had been so far "a quiet season." It continued so; although the archery games were resumed with lively spirit. Your historian, having a better opportunity of making observations, at a meeting held before his own door, by the large group now constituting the Archery Club, can testify that the players and the game form an animated picture very pleasing to the eye. At the same time, he perceived that there were more and stronger impulses stirred up amongst the players than he had been aware of. All pleasant so far, no doubt; but *capable* of being carried far enough to lead to mischief; "human nature" will exert itself.

Improvements must be noted, as usual, in several

places: buildings at Ashton; a fire-proof at Sandy Spring; the free use of field beans as a fertilizing material; their introduction into this neighborhood being due, I am told, to the enterprising spirit of Henry H. Miller. Corn begins to promise a heavy yield.

September, 1880. This month developed rapidly through its early stages, the assurance that the corn crop was going to be very fine, especially for those who had followed the fashion of *late planting;* the success of a doubtful practice, owing, as seems to me, to unusual amount of rain. The Horticultural Fair held at the Lyceum, near the beginning of the month, was very well attended, but, to use the mild expression of my worthy colleague, "the various articles were not quite as numerous as at some other exhibitions." *Not quite,* indeed. A more *profitable* Fair was looming in the near future; and contributors preferred "to put their productions where they would *do the most good.*" Which they did.

The Fair of the Agricultural Society, at Rockville, again suffered severely from disastrous weather. Great pains had been taken to insure a success, and liberal premiums profusely offered; but no exertions of the worthy President could make up for heavy rain. Contributors from Sandy Spring had not much to complain of; securing over $250 to their portion, out of near $950 offered to the whole county, not including allowance for the races. No doubt those who profited most by the Fair, having merited all they received, will be found ready to assist liberally in relieving the sore need of the Society. Since faith in equinoctials as a reason for changing the time of meeting was not successful, shall we depend on Vennor next time to fix the date?

The wheat seeding began in the latter part of September

more extensively than usual, and the present appearance would favor the practice. A Local Option meeting was held on the 26th, and attended by a large throng. Eloquent speakers, especially Mr. Nye and Dr. Magruder, addressed the meeting, and a boom for Temperance was excited, which will tell at the polls.

The Orthodox Meeting House, built in a very convenient location on a half acre of land, bought of B. Rush Roberts, was finished this month; the first meeting being held and quite numerously attended, in the 11th Month. This being one of the subjects affecting the interests of the neighborhood, a few remarks may not be out of place here. I think the general impression is one favorable to the influence of the new church. Some stir was produced among us at first, and that may do good in a community for the most part so well satisfied and comfortable as to be in some danger of growing too indifferent and quiet. The moderate degree of excitement thus awakened being controlled by the spirit of charity, which, I verily believe, prevails throughout this section, can only tend to freshen up the interest of our members in the principles inherited from a long line of faithful ancestors; while it must confirm their regard for the *old spot* where the forefathers began to assemble a century and a half ago, and where their remains rest in peace.

October, 1880. A month dry and very dry, but drilling in the wheat goes on lively. Gold mining, or rather the spirit of it, is roused again near the old spot, at Brooke Meadow. Digging has also been done in the land of James S. Hallowell, but so far without practical result. Many wells have given out that failed to be restored until far into the winter. My colleague writes that she has nothing to note during the month. The politicians would not agree with her. One thing does deserve to be noted, for it was indeed "a thing of beauty," namely, the more than usual brilliancy of the autumn foliage.

November. No scarcity of subjects now. The great event of the second being the election of the President, for whom the larger number of us voted, attended with the still finer victory of "Local Option"; these taken together produced more pleasing excitement than I ever knew at any previous election. The best part of the triumph is the moral one: every district in our county giving a majority, in all amounting to 1530, against "free liquor." The coming May will see it put into action, unless those who won the victory shall suffer its fruits to be lost.

The day thus made so bright and glorious was followed by one that filled with sincere mourning the many friends of Samuel Ellicott, who departed this life the third of November, 1880.

It was in this eleventh month that one of the concerned female friends made the proposition to have an afternoon meeting on First-Day, with a special object to interest the young friends in the principles of the Society. The suggestion (of Patty T. Farquhar) met with approval, for it was thought that some explanation might be given of Friends' doctrines that would be new to many and profitable to all. The first gatherings were in considerable numbers, and they have continued, although diminishing in degree, and designed to be kept up on every alternate First-day. It was to be anticipated that an undertaking of this kind, so new in its character, would meet with doubtful support, if not direct opposition from some of our members. The purpose was not fully understood; and as it came to be explained by those who differed in their views, it was natural that some confusion might result. One of the chief objects of the undertaking was to impart to children clearer views of the principles of the Society to which they belong. Probably this purpose has not been fully accomplished as yet; but it may well be regarded as within the reach of diligent, devoted effort, even though there are difficulties connected with it. The alternate evening gatherings to hear expositions of Scripture, and consult on other religious subjects, still go on. It may be justly claimed that the evidences afforded during the year now closing of increasing interest in religious questions cannot be doubted; which ought to encourage all who feel that such interest is essential to true, real progress.

During the early part of November a sufficient quantity of rain fell to give the wheat a fine start. Also a violent wind-storm came on the 6th, about 11 P. M., doing considerable damage to the trees at Rockland, and to sheds and stacks elsewhere, performing some very remarkable feats, resembling a cyclone.

On the night of the 28th, at a point of time very near the coming of a new day, Benjamin Rush Roberts passed from works to rewards.

December. The new month came in with his funeral; and the long train of friends that followed his remains to the grave, showed, though imperfectly, the high respect felt for the departed.

On the morning of the 8th, James H. Stone passed away very quietly, after a long illness of nearly two years. He was last to go of the three whose death made such a serious break in the long list, hitherto unbroken by death, of the old "Farmers' Club of Sandy Spring."

Until the 20th of this month the weather had been variable, though rather cold; now, the winter is on and before us—the memorable winter of '80-'81, the most severe for a quarter of a century. "Oh, the long and dreary winter! Oh, the cold and cruel winter!" was the cry of many, in sympathy with Hiawatha. Yet few were much hurt. The impressions produced on our minds by the sad losses of friends at the beginning of the season, had, doubtless, much influence in casting an aspect of gloom over the period that followed.

Among the events of the season the writer must not forget to refer to the long period of sleighing, lasting nearly eight weeks; and in perfection of quality probably never surpassed. How much pleasure attended it and what interesting combinations are yet to result from the numerous merry rides taken by our youths and maidens, I am quite unequal to describe or foretell,—but must speak a word for an important party in the jolly concern. Fortunately for the riders and the beasts that drew them, the epizootic of the previous autumn had borne lightly on the health and strength of the horses; else the immediate *sequelæ* of the sleighing frolics might have been less agreeable. It is a scientific conclusion susceptible of proof, that a considerable portion of vigor and power was drawn out of the beasts by the continued rapid movement which was unavoidable. It is not to be supposed that many of the horses which flourished in the winter of '80-'81 will ever reach the 25, 28 and 35 years that were attained by three at Clifton. In those earlier times, the average speed in lively driving was not over five miles an hour; now it could not be put below seven. Probably the period in which the owners of horses will enjoy their use will be found in the same proportion; that is, as 5 to 7. This makes a great difference in actual value of the noblest of beasts. Does the comparative satisfaction hold the same?

In agricultural communities, the treatment and condition of horses are justly considered next in importance to that of human beings. It is an undeniable fact that horses are being driven fast and faster; in one sense I suppose this is progress. But I could not forbear an earnest effort to invite attention to a subject that does really come near to "the business and bosoms of the people."

If prose fails to convince, pray listen to a few lines of genuine poetry. While riding the other day behind a horse, once very sleek, but now looking rather forlorn, the idea rose to put a question to the animal—"What do *you* think about this fast driving, which I well know you have experienced?" and the answer came:

"The only art my shame to cover,
To hide my ribs from every eye,
To bring repentance to my lover
And pinch his pocket—is to die!"

and die he did—or soon will.

January, 1881. The new year being that of which so many disastrous prophecies have been made, came in with thermometer at 10° to 28° (minus), the latter being the lowest figure ever reached in this neighborhood; and was at or near the banks of "Hawlings River."

The first business affair, as usual, was the Annual Meeting of the stockholders, or rather members of the Mutual Fire Insurance Company of Montgomery County. It was attended by a larger number of persons than usual, on account of the interest felt in the election of a director to supply the place of B. Rush Roberts, who had been for many years one of the most active and useful members of the board. The choice of Charles G. Porter gave general satisfaction. This large institution, having now property insured to the amount of $13,750,000, with premium notes over $930,000, has paid during the year losses by fire over $22,000 (which is less than the average of late times).

The Farmers' Convention was worthy of a fuller account than I have time or space to give; but the published notices of the proceedings amply supply deficiencies here. The number coming from a wide sweep of country was estimated at 200. A new feature was introduced which proved very popular. The meeting beginning now at 10, the ladies came in at 12, bringing us a luxurious dinner, and went like a flash of light. The president's introductory remarks were excellent, and two essays read by Dr. Frank Thomas and Charles F. Kirk were far above the common sort. The new feed called ensilage was exhibited, and well explained and recommended by Robert F. Roberts, of Alexandria, Va. The County Grange held a delightful quarterly meeting at Brighton. Lea's mill changed hands, Henry T. Lea coming to the steam mill, and George L. Stabler taking the one he left.

A newspaper article appeared in the "Baltimore American," written by a lady, Virginia Mullan, giving to our beloved neighborhood, so far as she became acquainted with it, such admiring appreciation as would no doubt be almost too much for our well-known modesty to allow of my copying it in this place. It shall be filed away for future reference. What a loss that the lady did not get to see the whole of the neighborhood, when she manifested such true perception of a part!

In this month of January, on the 22d, Wm. Henry Farquhar, Jr., was married to Isabella Robbins, of New York.

February, 1881. About the middle of this month the

snow and sleighing left us, and we saw with great satisfaction the bare ground once more: wheels took the place which runners had usurped so long. Even the young men acknowledged for once they were tired of sleighing; but it would appear that a young woman tired of sleighing is a phenomenon yet to be seen. On the 22d of this month three persons went from the neighborhood to attend a "Centennial of a Friends' Meeting House," in Baltimore, the oldest place of worship in the city. The house is kept in beautiful order.

As usual, February is not an exciting month. Excitement waited for

March. The inauguration of President Garfield was a grand affair, more fully attended and more interesting than usual. The only drawback was the dismal weather. No President has taken his seat with so many favorable omens for very many years. But troubles must come. (!) The world is in such a state of universal excitement, the booming elements so far from a condition of harmonious operation, and yet all the nations drawn by recent discoveries and inventions so much more nearly together than ever before, that a clashing in some point is surely unavoidable; and when it comes, history will have to record other scenes than those which happen in our peaceful neighborhood.

Peaceful as we are, we cannot all *think* alike. The spirit of compromise is, however, always at hand to settle such differences as may occur. So it proved at the annual meeting on the 10th of this month, of the "Sandy Spring Savings Institution." The new treasurer, Joseph T. Moore, who has certainly found the place he was designed for, produced a report which was very flattering: it shows amount now on hand, $136,698, paying to depositors an interest of $6278.56, leaving a surplus owned by that mysterious body called "the Institution," of $2320.59. It also exhibits a list of moneyed investments now worth $7000 more than they cost. The question arose, shall the interest now allowed be 4 or 5 per cent.? That blessed spirit of compromise decided on 4½, to the general satisfaction.

How varied the incidents that affect the feelings of mankind! At the usual First-day meeting, held on the 13th, after listening with rapt attention to a moving discourse delivered by Caroline H. Miller, with that clearness, beauty, and impressiveness which characterize her addresses, we were startled and shocked by the announcement from Roger B. Farquhar, of the death of Judge Richard J. Bowie, about the middle of the preceding night. If it is ever proper to include the name of one not a resident in our local mortuary record, Judge Bowie had the fullest unquestionable claim to this tribute of our respect and love. He had always manifested these feelings towards us in a remarkable degree. At a time when Sandy Spring was far from receiving the testimonies of regard ordinarily shown by neighboring communities toward each other, we could look to Judge Bowie as a fast friend, I might almost say as a protector in those troubled days. Thus was our mutual regard cemented by ties that only death could sever. So much has been well, truly, and beautifully written and spoken of this departed ornament and stay of our county and State, that it is needless for me to enter into further delineation of his spotless character, or to repeat in this place the praise profusely and justly lavished on Judge Bowie by the many writers and speakers who were prompt to undertake the ready task. Measured by my feelings, it is a relief to express the opinion that he who praised highest came nearest the full truth. Such a union of purity and mental power, of firmness and gentleness, of courtesy and dignity, of those excellences of mind, soul and person "that give the world assurance of a man," is indeed rarely found.

We hear nothing but favorable accounts from our various societies, social and literary; Olney Grange with its new library in the number. The Lyceum proceedings are rather stagnant; the suggestion being made that its bright spirit has moved to the village of Mechanicsville, which is "all right!"

Special mention is due to the Benevolent Aid Society, which began its work on its regular day, the first Tuesday in November, and continued its semi-monthly meetings till the 29th of this month. Although the demands for assistance during this most inclement season might have been expected to increase over the past year, such was not the case. Of the $50 received from subscriptions and donations, there remain at the winding up $15, which can be usefully employed in the summer. Does this look like a justification of thoughtless remarks predicting that the alarming influence of these charities would be to increase the number of worthless idlers? No; it is very safe to *give* to such distributors as this Association—just try it freely—"and don't you forget!"

William John Thomas, after a very busy life as a farmer, last autumn relinquished the occupation to his son, who bears the name of the old-time original builder of the house—John Thomas—a brother of his great-grandfather. This is the third case of the kind happening in this neighborhood within a year; wherein the venerable sire, having done his share of the world's work, leaves his son to do the same. May he, in each case, do as well, or better!

Your historian, having already prepared in writing several tributes to the memory of our three friends who departed this life near the close of the year 1880, has received with much satisfaction the following obituaries from the pen of his two colleagues.

Samuel Ellicott died 11th month, 3d, after a long and suffering illness. He was a very remarkable man. Though deprived of sight in his boyhood, he became one among our best farmers; loved and respected by all his friends. He was the first member of the old club "to cross the river and enter the Beautiful Land"—

"The Land—by the spoiler untrod,
Unpolluted by sorrow or care;
It is lighted alone by the presence of God,
Whose throne and whose temple are there:
Its crystalline streams, with a murmurous flow,
Meander through valleys of green,
And its mountains of jasper are bright in the glow
Of a splendor no mortal hath seen."

Died, 12th month, 8th, James H. Stone, passing away quietly, after a very long and depressing illness; fully prepared for "the happy change"—so far as one human being can judge the condition of another. He was faithful and industrious in the work which occupied his time. A farmer of the sort so much needed in our neighborhood, distinguishing himself by a steady course of improvement; so that he left a flourishing, productive, inviting tract, where he found one little better than a barren waste; and to do this is to perform one of the cardinal duties of country life. He was a true friend and kindly neighbor, always ready to lend and to help.

Benjamin Rush Roberts was born in Chester county, Pennsylvania, in the year 1810. His father dying prematurely, the young lad was thrown on his own resources at a tender age, but he took with him out into the busy world the priceless riches of truth, honesty, perseverance and a good heart. He came to Baltimore to live, apprenticed himself to an apothecary, and after some years of close application, he entered into the drug business on his own account, and was, almost from the first, very successful. He once told the writer he was convinced that any one, working steadily and honestly at *whatever* he could *do best*, might secure a competency for old age. He married the eldest daughter of John Needles of Baltimore, and they lived together nearly 44 years, a happy, united couple.

The druggist is almost proverbially short-lived. B. Rush Roberts, preferring health to wealth, relinquished his occupation when in the full tide of prosperity; and moving to Sandy Spring in 1851, he took his place among us as a practical farmer, and was ever foremost in advocating agricultural reforms. It will be within the bounds of truth to state that there was not a single public effort here aiming at good results in which he did not join heartily, identifying himself completely with his new home. With no children of his own to provide for, the boys and girls whom he wisely aided to become self-supporting are scattered from the Delaware to the Mississippi. Who can estimate the future harvest of good deeds which may spring up from this good seed? His house was ever open to any who needed shelter; he constantly put in practice the truth that "when you *trust* a man you place him under the wholesome restraint of public opinion"; and although he gave the meanest tramp shelter, his hospitality, so far as we know, was never abused. A servant who lived at his home of "Sherwood," said that "if people were not *nice* when they *came* there, they got so before they left." During the war Miss Dix was quietly informed that she might select a number of hospital nurses who needed recreation and send them to Sherwood for a fortnight each; they came by twos and threes, and returned cheered and strengthened.

His offices of trust were many and varied, and the duties of each were discharged with energy and fidelity. While he was no man's enemy, he was not afraid of any man; and in small things as in great he dared to do what he believed to be right. His cheerful disposition, his charity of thought no less than of deed, his kindly greeting to young and old, combine to make his memory precious, and we believe that all who knew him will agree that Sandy Spring is the better for his sojourn amongst us.

While a noble and correct life enabled him to meet death without fear, still the complete and orderly arrangement of his temporal affairs had much to do with the serenity of his last days on earth. His sufferings were great, yet his patience and sweetness of disposition never failed, and his childlike faith never wavered. Not long before he died he said: "It has always seemed to me that religion was a simple thing, and I have thought it consists in doing each day what we believe to be right." He quietly passed away during the night of the 28th of November, and was laid to rest on the first of December, 1880, while the flood of the sun's setting rays seemed typical of the glory into which he had surely entered.

Statistics of our neighborhood for the year, as before stated: Births, 4 (2 of each sex); Marriages, 2; Deaths, 3.

CHAPTER XIX.

FROM FOURTH MONTH, 4TH, 1881, TO FOURTH MONTH, 3D, 1882.

Transfer of the "Early History" to "The Introductory"—The Woman Board of Directors—Fund for benefit of Library—Close of the long, cold winter of 1880-1881—Three little boys and a girl, great comfort to Grandparents—Death of President Garfield—Excursions to a distance—Successful use of Ensilage—Double Tin Wedding—Schools looking up—Aid to sufferers by Michigan fires—Election of a Friend, Joseph T. Moore, as Senator of Montgomery County—Engineers come and go—New arrangements in Friends' Graveyard—F. D. S.—Exhortations to the Young—Diphtheria.

[In the manuscript book where these Annual Reports were originally entered, this Chapter was made to consist chiefly of the "Early History of Sandy Spring." The publication of the book has rendered it appropriate to transfer that section to the beginning, where, with the aid of a more careful research, it may occupy its place as an Introductory.]

The usual amount of space and time being thus fully employed, the historian will be excused for giving a very condensed account of the incidents of the last twelve months. In order not to neglect any important events, we take them as usual in monthly order.

April, 1881. The first entry of my esteemed and respected colleague describes the death of her niece, Sarah F. Townsend, in language so appropriate and beautiful that it will (as it should) be carefully preserved. It occurred at Dresden, Germany, 4th month, 11th, 1881.

My younger colleague makes the statement, very properly inserted here, that "for the first time a Board of Directors composed entirely of women was elected at the Annual

Meeting of the Lyceum Company." Also, that "a delightful Concert at Grange Hall was given for the benefit of the Library; amount collected being nearly $50." The latter part of this month was rendered pleasantly memorable by the change of weather, closing up at last the long, severe winter.

May. Only the sad record of the birth and death in the same day of a son to Edward N. and Hallie Bentley, is furnished this month. The little one, who is without a name from either of my associates, finds here, at least, a slight memorial. (Grandma finds a name—Herbert.)

June, 1881. This is one of the months that shall be called "wonderful," and none can dispute the name.

On the 10th, a little boy, at Charles F. Brooke's, name "Warwick"—their firstborn.

On the 13th, Helen Lea presented her husband with twins—"John" and "Henry."

On the 16th, a little girl, at the "Cedars," name "Marion." Quite a time of rejoicing; granddaughters being scarce in that family circle!

The Seventh month (July) opened with an event of the saddest nature and of universal interest. The tragical murder and death of President Garfield was felt as keenly at Sandy Spring as everywhere over the world.

One of the many expressions of the general grief is preserved here, as too feeling and comprehensive to be forgotten:

"The emblems of mourning which arrest the eye on every hand, and also in remote and unfrequented places, attest in the most touching manner the extent and depth of the public grief over the death of our late President. It is expected on such occasions that public buildings and tall edifices will be hung with the symbols of sorrow, and such manifestations are taken very much as matters of course. But when private dwellings, including those of the poor and humble, in city and country, the shop of the artisan, the secluded farmhouse, the country blacksmith's shop, the sleeve of the errand boy, are alike decorated with something which tells that a human heart is sore because our President is dead, we feel that a great wave of human love and sympathy has swept over the land. And not over our land alone. The echo of our lament has come back to us from the other side of the water—first in the noble and womanly message from the Queen of England, herself a widow, to the widow of our unburied President; then in the tolling bells and draped flags of that stern old country, whose sorrow is never counterfeited, and whose sympathy has seldom, if ever, been so greatly stirred by a calamity happening beyond her own borders. Never has there been an affection so nearly universal among all civilized nations. Nobody can stand in its presence without gaining a grander view of human nature and feeling a closer kinship to his fellow-man. It has been the lot of President Garfield to fill great places in the world, but the greatest by far is that which he now holds, unchangeable by events and incorruptible by time, in the hearts which far and near follow him to the grave."

Eighth month. Month of vacation for farmers, who *use* it in that way. As usual, many strangers and boarders in the neighborhood, and a receding wave from Sandy Spring. Boston, White Mountains, Mount Desert and New Mexico, with excursions to "the Springs" and the Ocean, also the new, increasing attraction of Luray Cave, were the chosen spots for the summer. Drought begins.

Ninth month. Drought continues and becomes severe. The experiment with Ensilage was tried by Edward P. Thomas with complete success. Whatever helps the dairyman is bound to be a success.

A very interesting tin wedding was celebrated by Alban G. Thomas and his wife, which was conveniently made to include, at the same time and place, a similar celebration for Roger Brooke and his wife. The next entry I see and copy with regret is simply "rowdy games." When, where, or by whom played is no way mentioned; certainly they had no connection with the preceding celebrations.

The death of President Garfield prevents the Horticultural Fair. On this sad theme Caroline H. Miller delivered an eloquent address in the Meeting House, which was highly acceptable both to those who heard and those who afterward read it.

Rockland School opens its fourth session with a large number of very interesting pupils. Other schools resume their duties; among which that of J. Llewellyn Massie deserves respectful notice.

Tenth month begins with a very high temperature; but on the 6th frost comes, with thermometer 32°. The ladies form a Literary Society, conducted in a way that does them much honor. A larger group of the same active, benevolent, refined portion of the human race make a highly successful effort to aid the sufferers by the Michigan fires. A full narrative from the pen of the Chairman of the Committee, Sarah T. Miller, is appended to this record, by request of the Benevolent Aid Society.

Eleventh Month, 1881. The most exciting event of this month was the State and county election, at which one of the Friends of Sandy Spring, Joseph T. Moore, was chosen Senator for Montgomery County.

The engineers for a new railroad appeared on the old ground; they did not fool us much this time!

A proposition was made in the Monthly Meeting, which

was afterwards approved, to have family lots in the graveyard.

The First-Day School was removed to the Lyceum; where some 40 girls and boys attend with profit.

Caroline H. Miller gives another excellent address in meeting, being an exhortation to the young people to devote themselves to pursuits of a more improving character than the pleasures for which there is a growing attraction.

A little girl arrives at Granville Farquhar's; her name is "Faith."

Twelfth Month, 1881. A general aspect of green over the face of nature, rather peculiar for the commencement of winter.

The sympathies of the whole neighborhood were greatly moved by the ravages of diphtheria in the family of a highly-respected neighbor, John Brady. Within less than a week four of his children, all grown, were carried to our graveyard. Notwithstanding the danger of infection, two of our young friends, Lucy Fawcett and Hannah B. Brooke, went to the fearful dwelling to assist the suffering ones—the former remaining two months.

On the 26th of this month, Cleorah Palmer, the widow of our old family physician, passed away to "the Spirit Land," after being afflicted with delicate health for several months; a truly kind and thoughtful friend and neighbor.

First Month, 1882. A new director, Henry M. Murray, of Anne Arundel County, was elected to our Fire Insurance Company.

No ice came for a long time; but about the 25th we got a fair abundance. It is worth while to state the fact that several of our ice-houses have had a supply of this now essential article for every year of the past thirty.

At the Farmers' Convention, on the 12th, 150 men

collected and discussed the interesting subjects of their business. This institution is no longer confined to the reports of our Clubs.

Second Month. Henry C. Hallowell delivered a lecture on Health, being the first of the Lyceum course this winter. It is pleasant to see the literary hall again in use; and upon a subject which is at last discovered to be one worthy the attention of the people.

Third Month. In the absence of other material for this last month of the year, I have to record a list kept by one of our lady friends, of the number of "Visitors to Sandy Spring" within the past twelve months. She reports the number at 750—coming from ten States and England.

Year's Statistical Report: Births, boys, 7; girls, 3; total 10; deaths, 8; marriages, 0.

CHAPTER XX.

FROM FOURTH MONTH, 3D, 1882, TO FOURTH MONTH, 2D, 1883.

Conclusions of the Lyceum Company to print the "Annals"—The Last always melancholy—Gibbon's Decline and Fall—Metamorphoses from the War, its epithets "scattered to the wind"—Difficulties of the Historian—Cold May—Close of F. D. S.—The army worm—Pleuro-pneumonia—Infants' party—The three weddings at Rockland—Great crops of corn—Fruit scarce—Telephone makes slow progress—Horticultural Exhibition at its best—Potato rot—"Benevolent Aid Society"—"Heat is life, and cold is death!"—Higher grade school at "Sherwood"—Rise of the farmers—The R. R. look to the "Narrow Gauge"—The "Bank" and "F. I. Co."—Obituaries—Last tribute by C. H. M. to Garfield.

The proceedings of our last Annual Meeting are brought up afresh in your memories by the report of the Secretary, and the decision in regard to printing the "Annals of

Twenty Years" must now be made. Whatsoever be the conclusion at which we arrive, it is certain that the Historical Sketch here laid before you by the present writer will be the *last*. This word, however or whenever it is used, has a pathos of its own which I am confident you have all experienced. The readers of Walter Scott's finest poem—and who has *not* read "the Lady of the Lake"?—must remember the lines—

> "It is the last time—'tis the last,"
> He muttered thrice—"the last time e'er
> That angel voice shall Roderick hear."

The pathos of this oft-repeated word is naturally much more deeply felt on this occasion by the writer than by any who listen to him. In the same spirit he cannot forbear quoting a few celebrated lines—in form *prose*, but truly poetic in dignity of style. They are the author's leavetaking of "Gibbon's Rome"; and thus rather more appropriate *now* than was Roderick's sigh of love. Gibbon describes what he calls his "final deliverance" after twenty years' devotion to his great History.

He writes: "It was on the day, or rather night, of the 27th of June, 1787, between the hours of eleven and twelve, that I wrote the last lines of the last page, in a summer-house in my garden. After laying down my pen I took several turns in a 'berceau,' or covered walk of acacias, which commands a prospect of the country, the lake and the mountains. The air was temperate, the sky was serene, the silver orb of the moon was reflected from the waters, and all nature was silent. I will not dissemble first emotions of joy on the recovery of my freedom and, perhaps, the establishment of my fame. But my pride was soon humbled, and a sober melancholy was spread over my mind by the idea that I had taken an everlasting leave of an old and agreeable companion; and that whatsoever might be the future date of my History, the life of the historian must be short and precarious."

There have been few writers of history who would venture to institute any sort of comparison between their works and "the Decline and Fall of the Roman Empire." It is quite needless to say that I have done nothing of the kind. But there has long been a particular attraction that drew my thoughts in writing the latter chapters of these Annals, to the melancholy view of Gibbon's great work; and the recent revision of those chapters has served somewhat to deepen the mournful impression. Not that I perceive such decided indications of decline among us as would justify the fancy even, that the evident progress in our special business, in our growing institutions, and in other improvements of high character—all which are to be described without exaggeration further on in this chapter—that these *last* are to be *doubted* as *more* than overshadowing all gloomy prospects, not even *fancy* will allow. You will naturally be quite ready to attribute the sombre coloring spread over some parts of the present narrative, if any such there should be, to the difference which is unavoidable between the eyes that look out upon objects at the age of fifty and those which are dimmed by gazing around for seventy years. Having nearly attained the latter era, your once lively historian has reached the experience of the solid Frenchman, who declared that indeed "this world would be a very happy place to live in if it were not for its *pleasures*."

Looking back over the long period since these Annals commenced, and reflecting upon the various changes which are presented to the mind, one can hardly fail to perceive that the Sandy Spring of 1863 has been passing through certain metamorphoses indispensably required by the active movements of the busy world. During the first two years we were necessarily in the midst of a tremendous war. This experience, so strange and uncongenial to the principles and habits of the larger portion of our people, must have given a certain twist to the neighborhood which it would probably never wholly lose. War is a tremendously stirring influence; while its natural tendency would seem to be separation, it sometimes serves to unite. The latter effect was produced in this region; and to such extent that it pains the writer to read now the expression of "rebel," which he freely used in the earlier pages of this history. All feelings of a hostile character are scattered to the winds; bitter enemies in those days are warm friends in these. In this spirit our neighborhood has moved on; losing in the natural order some of its valuable members by death, receiving other valuable accessions from new settlers and from the growing strength of our own energetic youth; extending our borders by closer acquaintance with pleasant neighbors; increasing the profits of our regular business by improving the soil, by new machinery, new stock and new material for feeding them, by new ways of operating with greater profit on the same old articles.

From year to year it has been the aim of these annals to sketch the changes, and, especially, the *progress* of things and people in and around Sandy Spring. A great difficulty has occurred in drawing the lines that bound the neighborhood. So cordial are the social feelings of our people generally, that the effort once made to produce a map of the neighborhood, which failed at that time from certain causes, appears now to be almost impracticable. The roads and the streams can be laid down with sufficient accuracy, but where will you find *two* of our own people who would fill the statistic column with the same names? Several attempts at forming a census are exhibited in the annals, showing an increasing population; but the increase evidently exceeds the natural order, and must be owing, as it ought, to the growth of *social influences.* Neither sect, nor politics, nor aristocracy, not even *county lines*, define the limits of the neighborhood of Sandy Spring. The last attempt at a census was made for the first of the Fourth Month, 1879; when the number of persons was stated at 407—the families 85.

The year closing on this day has been a stirring period; events being made the more exciting by their more than usually opposite characters of grief and joy. These incidents of human life have both come with features so strongly marked as to produce a deep impression upon us all. Leaving each event to its proper place in the record, we will go on with the usual monthly calendar.

Fourth Month (April), 1882—(to commence with the first act of the year). It was concluded at the Annual Meeting of the Lyceum that the historian should continue his official work another year, with a view to possible publication.

The first note made by our respected friend who has been so important an adjunct in preserving the emotional statistics of these annals, is, as she says, "a sad one: Again the angel of death has passed over our neighborhood; and Eliza Brooke, wife of George E. Brooke, has left us for 'the Beautiful Land'; loved and respected in a wide circle, she will long be missed, not only by her family and relations, but by her many friends. She was brought to

Brooke Grove a bride in the springtime of the year 1840; and at the same season her loving eyes were closed forever —having been married just 42 years and one week."

On the morning of the 26th, Cornelia, wife of Philip T. Stabler, presented him with twins—two little girls. Certainly our neighborhood is in a very flourishing condition; two sets of twins having been born in less than a year.

Fifth Month (May). Ann R. Stabler, wife of Edward Stabler, died on the morning of the 3d of this month, having reached the age of 84 years. A kind and loving spirit passed away to its heavenly home; after having lived more than 58 years in the same house. Therein all her children—ten in number—were born, all are living still. She was grandmother to the twins above spoken of, but had never seen them. A sketch of her life was printed by her husband and sent to many of her friends.

The weather of May was not very May-like. At its commencement the Benevolent Aid Society appointed a meeting to provide clothing; the thermometer starting at 44°, with ice in the night. On the afternoon of the 2d, a very pleasant and large horticultural meeting was held at Falling Green, though the weather was rather uncongenial for commencing the rosy spectacle. Indeed, roses suffered that night, where exposed to a temperature of 34°. The gardens were faithfully attended to, so far as wet grounds permitted.

The prettiest and most charming event of this May month was exhibited on the 21st, in the women's side of the meeting house, it being the closing scene of the First-day school. A large collection of girls, with a smaller number of boys, who had attended faithfully through the season at their profitable morning exercises, listened to short speeches, and received the prizes they had merited. The same afternoon, at a few steps' distance, occurred the funeral of Richard Tucker, an old resident of the vicinity. Another old resident, T. Jefferson Higgins, died on the 18th of the 12th month. He had won the sincere regard of our people.

Sixth month (June). Our Quarterly Meeting has naturally received from our friend the first notice of events in this month, claiming that "it was a very good one; unusually quiet and orderly on the porches and around the house; the committee appointed by the meeting to keep order did their part very faithfully."

For the first event of June, another hand writes: "Two formidable visitations break suddenly upon the neighborhood; the army worm and the pleuro-pneumonia. The first was an entire novelty to all of us under 50 years old. The earliest conversation on the subject which I heard from was on the 18th of this month, at Edward P. Thomas's, and so uncertain its character at first as to use the expression 'pseudo-army worm.' The mischief was considerable in a few places, chiefly on the grass and oats, while neither wheat nor corn appeared to suffer seriously. The stay of the unlovely worm was brief." Pleuro-pneumonia on one farm, that of Wm. W. Moore, proved quite a serious affair. The official gentleman, Mr. Le May, paid two or three visits, but the legal arrangements intended to bear upon losses by this much dreaded disease appear to be less satisfactory than is desirable. This month gave us a considerable amount of cool weather. Of the 6th there is this record, "An unusual day; thermometer 51°, but no frost, which was actually feared."

The most lively incident of the whole month was the "Infants' party," on the 16th. It was given, we may say, by Marion Farquhar, who was just one year old. The infants present were seven, with five other little children, and divers connections, including grandparents of course.

Rockland School closed in a very interesting and pleasing manner to all concerned, including the girls themselves. On the 28th Samuel Wetherald and Florence Sullivan were married, in Ashton Church.

7th month (July). The most pleasant peculiarity of the weather this hottest of all months of the year, was this time an unusual coolness. This did not produce an unusual degree of healthfulness, but had rather a contrary tendency. The physicians were very busy, and in the end had the great satisfaction of seeing their patients restored.

There was a lively and memorable portion of the month, on which my respectable colleague comments in these words: "The three beautiful weddings at Rockland! how can I write about them? I will leave the full particulars to another hand, for it was an occasion long to be remembered, especially by the very many who were present there." The peculiar interest of the celebration consisted in this: the most important periods in the life of six individuals were singularly (and very conveniently) joined in one. The marriage of the two young people, John C. Bentley and Cornelia Hallowell, taking place on the green sward and under the shady trees, was, of course, an event of the most consequence; while the "silver weddings" of the bride's parents, and of her mother's sister, added to the presence of a hundred near relatives, of whom a large number had come from beyond the Mississippi to congratulate the happy parties, rendered the ceremony unique, as well as highly interesting; and when in the evening, the lawn lit with lanterns, and the dwelling with liveliest lamps, were filled by an added crowd of friends and neighbors near 300 strong, the happy event was complete to the satisfaction of all.

It is pleasant to remember that the month was closed by a successful exhibition at the Grange Hall, which was got up in the cause of benevolence.

8th month (August). On the 4th of this month the twins of P. T. and Cornelia Stabler were buried in the same coffin, having died about twelve hours apart, but not in this neighborhood.

Rains fall of the sort very congenial to corn, which now shows how great the crop is to be. The grasses are similarly favored, so that agriculture may be said to be *up*. The value of ensilage is coming to be fully appreciated, and suitable preparations made to provide properly for one of the greatest agricultural discoveries of modern times.

Fruits, especially apples, are very scarce; peaches, partially distributed among a favored few.

The scheme for a telephone was again vigorously started. It does not seem to make progress, except in the hands of James P. Stabler, whose inventive genius promises to be an honor to his name and neighborhood.

Ninth month (September). The tribute due to a dear old friend, who died in this month, will be rendered hereafter from the expressive sketch of Caroline H. Miller.

The continuance of the rains kept the corn too green to be cut at the usual period, and caused delay to seeding. Malarious influences still prevail. The Horticultural Fair was pronounced the most successful during the whole seventeen years. The President, who had been the life of it, showed his energy in another form by erecting buildings for the benefit and improvement of his prosperous school at Rockland. Two other very appropriate buildings were put up by Charles Stabler and Samuel P. Thomas.

Tenth month (October). Our friend mentions, as her only record in this month, a wedding on the 5th which she denominates "a very pleasant one, that passed off very nicely in every respect,"—the parties being Wm. C. Riggs and Annie S. Hallowell.

The three events in which our own business was concerned are the facts that corn was cut in this month, scarcely ever so late before; that no frost came worthy of notice; lastly, that the rot in potatoes is found to be a very serious infliction; this loss has not been so heavy for a number of years—owing, no doubt, to the rains.

Eleventh month (November). My senior associate "does not remember anything of extra note occurring in this month." The Clubs and other Associations took place as usual, also a revival of a precious, rational, improving "Reading Circle." But there is a portion of our citizens who found the early part of the month more interesting than agreeable. I refer to the politicians; many of whom were disappointed by the election; and yet not so *badly "disappointed."* Several of us thought that *good* may come of it.

The Benevolent Aid Society resumed its hallowed mission; that is to say, the ladies did; the men rather avoided conspicuous position; they *allow* women to be conspicuous in some matters, I should say, "in their sphere."

Winter came on as it always does. The weather, which is the presentation of its leading phenomena, is the proper theme of your meteorologist; and he doubtless treats of the degrees of the thermometer, of the snow that shelters the wheat and troubles the old, and the sleighing that charms the young. How different the impression made on us at the two periods of life! The explanation was made half a century ago by one of those self-taught men of genius that come occasionally to give a shock to the learned, who, while affecting to despise the rustic, are not ashamed to borrow and profit by his discoveries. It was Samuel Thompson that was the author of the great maxim "Heat is life, and cold is death." No wonder that we who are nearing life's *upper* border, should regard winter in rather a different light from that which shines on and warms the young.

Although the temperature of the winter of '82-'83 has been far from the severity of several seasons fixed in our memories, it is certain the season was not a genial one; neither in the heart of winter nor the month that foretells, without bringing on, the spring. As I write—on the 24th of March—my eyes are dazzled with the snow spread widely over the fields, and I have just exchanged salutes (not congratulations) with a company that came in the sleigh. Without indulging in complainings that are wrong and useless, we may be allowed—we cannot *avoid* grieving for sickness and death. Both have been with us to an extent beyond common experience.

Before giving expression to the natural emotions excited by our sad loss, it seems only proper and right to refer to the pleasant topics and the earnest efforts toward improvement of the people which have also characterized the cruel portion of the year. Toward the beginning of the monthly records, allusion was made to the charming close of last year's First-Day School. The resumption of last fall was rather later than usual; but since it began and got fairly under way it may be said to have proceeded with more satisfaction than ever. The voluntary coming of 40 or 50 little girls and boys into a school devoted wholly to their improvement in that learning and those qualities that are the *best* for the life on which they have just entered, cannot fail of receiving the approbation of all.

Perhaps the gratifying success of this juvenile moral school has assisted to arouse the whole community of Sandy Spring, including some who are no longer residents, to a vigorous exertion of their best efforts to procure a school of higher grade, composed of both sexes, than any we have ever had. Help has come from nearly all directions. Our friend Mary Roberts at once made the generous bequest of the land, which her husband, no longer with us, would so freely have bestowed. The essential pecuniary means is now secured, and there remains to be obtained only the one most important figure of all,—a well qualified teacher, to take the most useful post in human society. Next in importance to these promising improvements of an intellectual character, showing that our people are resolved not to neglect their progress in mental pursuits, there has been strong evidence that the main business of our lives has lost nothing of its interest. Agricultural improvements abound everywhere in the variety of machinery procured regardless of cost, in new stock of pure breed, and in substituting one farm product for another less profitable. The use of ensilage, lately pronounced by high authority to be the greatest discovery of modern times, is an encouraging proof that farmers deserve the disrespectful epithet of "old fogies" no longer. The spirit of improvement has spread all around the once neglected and forlorn fields of old Montgomery. A pleasant and lively evidence of this fresh spirit was exhibited at the last meeting of the Farmers' Convention in this hall, where a gathering of nearly two hundred practical agriculturists manifested the interest which they felt in actual improvements, and the determination that they should go on and prosper. Depend upon it, a force almost electric is being aroused over the whole land, to raise not only the *soil* but also the *men* who cultivate it, up to the elevated position which is their rightful place in a world that depends wholly upon them for existence.

It is with great pleasure that the last chapter of the Annals which contains so many disappointed hopes of getting a railroad for Sandy Spring, shall not be left by the old writer without some reference to future possibilities that the object so long desired may yet be attained. The scheme is *possible* now, because it looks no longer to *other* selfish corporations, but to its own energies. The practicability of "narrow gauge roads" being fully established, and the cost being thus brought within our reach, what shall hinder?

The railroad is one of the very desirable improvements for Sandy Spring that is *in anticipation*,—it may be "long a coming," but there are two *accomplished facts*, the Fire Insurance Company, and the "Savings Institution," that have actually *reached* an elevated position, the statement of which is restful and reviving to the weary hand of your old historian.

The Mutual Fire Insurance Company of Montgomery County will, in another month, have been in successful operation just thirty-five years; Edward Stabler being continuous President, and Robert R. Moore, Secretary, with the office at Sandy Spring. It has had property insured in every county of the State, to the total amount, January 1, 1883, of over fourteen and a half millions of dollars, and holding premium notes over a million. The losses by fire on these notes annually have been a little over three per cent.; the payments having been promptly made, and with the least possible dispute. Estimated assets are $130,500.

The "Savings Institution of Sandy Spring" has been in existence over fifteen years, commencing in a very humble way (as set down in former pages), and reaching March 1, 1883, the condition as follows:

"Amount on hand,		$173,061 54.
Investment in bonds,	$79,364 05	
In mortgages,	73,325 00	
Sundries,	20,372 49	

The year ending March 1, 1883, has been a very prosperous one in every respect; the business large, with no known bad debts; every demand promptly paid over the counter, without a second notice.

[Extracted.] JOSEPH T. MOORE, Treasurer."

It now only remains to pay our sorrowing tributes to our friends who have gone before. The number is largely in excess of previous average losses by death. Of the two who left us in the spring, a feeling mention is made at the time of their departure by my associate; who, in the present writing, takes her leave also of this record. In the next obituary you will easily recognize the words of Caroline H. Miller.

Ninth month, 4th, died Edward Thomas, aged 72. Some thoughts of the dear friend, whose once familiar face must henceforth be but a pleasant memory, dwell so earnestly with me, that I trust their expression may not seem inappropriate. With him another link has fallen from the chain of goodly, I may say, of godly brothers and sisters; a chain which they have kept strong and bright through many years by love and truth.

Another life has been laid down—that had indeed grown heavy through burdens of the flesh too grievous to be borne. Another faithful and loving wife has been left, to bear for a few years the saddest of all titles and loneliest of all lots! We have parted with our loved friend forever to the outward vision; but it will be long ere he is forgotten! Though "he had known sorrow and was well acquainted with grief"—whom did he ever oppress with his murmurings? None! for true hero that he was, he wore his sackcloth *underneath;* his greeting always bright and pleasant; his words glowing with innocent mirth or sparkling with harmless wit—when can we forget him? Never! His memory will still be green in the hearts of his children's children when their fair young heads shall be whitened by the snows of time. Cheerful, patient, enduring man! *Strong* in all that was good and true! Such deaths are a real bereavement. We mourn him with sincere sorrow; while we fervently exclaim—"Let me, too, die the death of the righteous, and let my last end be like his!"

Twelfth month, 8th, died Carrie M. Stabler, aged 9 years, nearly. Our three friends whose departure has been recorded had reached an age that averaged over 75 years. Highly as they were esteemed, and deeply as they were lamented, the loss had nothing *unnatural* about it. In the regular course of things their time had come to depart. The ripe apple falls easily to the ground. But for this dear, bright child, just come to an age when life begins to gather its sweetest fruits, and the *power* comes with it to distribute of them—oh, so much!—and most to those who are most near—how strange and mysterious are the laws that bring about these cruel ends! Vain, indeed, is any attempt to fathom or explain. Perhaps it is something worse than useless to try. I know that the little pet of our First-Day School will never return to join the companions she loved; never *fill out and perfect in this* life the bright qualities of the true woman which her early years seemed to promise. This thought, in my own experience, under a similar affliction—this sorrowful thought that the gifted child could never *unfold* its gifts, was saddest of all. But another and holier thought also came: "Could such hopeless things be? Could that which was best and most precious and most promising of all that we see or know, or have to do with, in our whole experience of this life, can it pass as if it had never an existence, wholly away? This universe exhibits no such wasteful management. And once assured that our little lamb is safe folded in the arms of the Good Shepherd, it is not so long to wait!"

Twelfth month, 12th, died Mary B. Kirk. The writer of these tributes of affection to long-tried friends, thus rendered to him a "labor of love," has always been a warm advocate of marriage. But in contemplating a life such as hers, whose name is above written, one may justly feel a degree of uncertainty, at least as to the duty or necessity resting upon every woman to enter into wedlock. I have known Mary intimately ever since I was a boy; and was acquainted, for the most part, with her manner of life. While sitting with the solemnized gathering of friends, assembled to follow her remains to the grave, within the room where she had dwelt during the chief portion of her life, a deep impression came over me. I seemed to see, and followed in thought, that life of hers spread out before me. And one clear figure marked the whole, forming into words substantially such as these: "The labors of her active life were directed to efforts, generally *successful*, to make *other people* more comfortable," always seeming ready to help everybody. Yet her life, especially the early part of it, was one of great, continued suffering; as the victims of the demon, dyspepsia, alone can rightly understand. Fortunately for her, and for so many others, she succeeded almost in throwing off the scourge. Then her devoted spirit was able to manifest itself; with results which tempted me to the suggestion that perhaps the world was the better for her life to have been one of single blessedness.

2d month, 22d, 1883, died Wm. Henry Stabler, aged 81. Again the hand of death, so busy this cruel year, struck upon the old. But it fell with gentle force upon one well prepared for the stroke. For the period of a few years the strong life current which had marked his active, decided nature had somewhat failed, but long before his departure it returned calm and refreshed. Wm. Henry Stabler was a man so long and widely known, his death forms an historical event in our annals. On a former page there is a brief obituary notice of his son William, and a line describing him reads—"His industry, honesty and solid sense distinguished him as one to be relied upon." The father and son were much alike. As the phrase is often used, "He was a man who had very little nonsense about him." Steady and straightforward in his business, he asked and expected of others to do only what in similar circumstances he would do himself. While attending closely and with success to his own affairs, he was by no means deficient in active efforts to promote the general welfare. One example of this I cannot refrain from placing on this record. It is some years now since the landowners of Sandy Spring were relieved from a nuisance both onerous and expensive. Probably there are many who forget the times when hogs and cattle roamed freely through our woods, compelling every one to keep his gates shut; *more still* who forget the man most active to get the nuisance abated. That man was Wm. Henry Stabler. He was not the only actor in the case, but it is my distinct recollection he was decidedly the most efficient. Another and yet more important change in our neighborhood is due to the same source. But enough has been written; of all the men among us he cared the least for praise; only *substantial* qualities attach to his memory and name.

It is by a strange coincidence that your historian's last "labor of love" in this way should be directed as it has been. The last similar contribution of the friend whose care and accurate observation have added so much of real value to our sketches is "to mention with expressions of deep sympathy" the death in Alexandria of one of the "Rockland scholars" from Bermuda. She remarks that it spread a gloom over our pleasant neighborhood; softened somewhat by the tokens of lovely Christian resignation manifested by the stricken mother in the island far away.

The record of our sincere tributes of sympathetic feeling toward valued friends would be quite imperfect without referring to the afflictions which now for three months have prevailed in the household of Washington B. Chichester. While it has been the lot of the distressed family to suffer in nearly all its members, the chief anxiety centred during this long period in one who was the especial darling of her many friends. Hope of her recovery is now growing stronger from day to day.

Twice before in the course of these annual records, which have ventured to come together and call themselves a history, the writer has made an unsuccessful attempt to bid "good-bye" to *you*, the constituents and proprietors of

Sandy Spring Lyceum, and now and here the leavetaking is final. This hall may be truly called the centre of the intellectual movement of the neighborhood. Pass your thoughts over the twenty-four years since its construction. What a variety of uses it has subserved! Perhaps it has never witnessed a brighter succession of rational entertainments than during the last year. This speaks well for its present managers and its future prospects. Our latest entertainment (though entitled by its high object to a more exalted name) was signalized among the many successful exhibitions by its large audience, by the nobility of its purpose, by the charm and excellence of the performance, above all by the earnestness, dignity and eloquence of her who instituted the brilliant scene. Francis Miller in this hall, just twenty years ago, made the suggestion which led to these historic records. How proper and agreeable then is it that the long narrative should close by referring to the success of his wife, Caroline H. Miller, in securing to the Lyceum Company a delightful entertainment, while furnishing a profitable contribution for the benefit of a hospital to be erected in honor of the lamented Garfield.

The following sketch of Sandy Spring at an early period in its history, drawn up by Thomas McCormick, when nearly 90 years of age, was, at the request of Caleb Stabler, inserted in the Annals.

My earliest recollections of this most delightful locality date back nearly 80 years. In 1797 it fell to my lot to become a member of the family of my uncle, Thomas Moore, of precious memory, after whom I was named. He was then living on his farm, known as "Retreat," near Brookeville. Being only about six years old, I had been but little at school; the only instruction I had received in that line was from drunken Irish wandering teachers, who knew but little themselves, and did not know how to teach children even when sober, much less when drunk. Such for the most part were the teachers we had at that time in Loudoun county, Virginia. Soon after I came to live with my uncle I was entered as a scholar in an excellent school that had recently been opened under the care and management of Isaac Briggs, a member of the Society of Friends. The school building was a very neat log structure, situated on the road leading to the Sandy Spring Meeting House, and near the residence of Basil Brooke. This school was patronized not only by the immediate neighborhood, but from the adjoining counties and from other States and cities. It may be interesting to the few that still survive to see a list of their former schoolmates. I believe I can give them nearly all from memory.

1st. From the neighborhood, viz.: Thomas P. and Edward Stabler, Richard and John Brooke, Mahlon Chandlee, Francis and James Hance, Richard Holmes, Samuel and Remus Riggs, Samuel White, Sarah, Elizabeth and Ann Gilpin, Anna and Mary Briggs.

2d. From adjoining counties: Richard P. and Gerard Snowden, Nicholas Snowden, Joseph Harrison (West River), John and Samuel Ellicott (from Ellicott's Mills).

3d. From Baltimore: John and Samuel Carey, Samuel Patrick, Isaac and Thomas Tyson, John Brown, Isaac and Wm. Trimble, Jonathan Balderston.

4th. From Philadelphia: Three brothers of the Garriguez family, two Miss Thompsons, from Loudoun, Va., and three young Frenchmen, who came to learn the English language: their names were Derazon, John Batter and Dugravia Shaulattle.

From these young Frenchmen we boys learned all the French we ever knew; and that was, how to ask permission to go out; and would receive our answers in the same language. I would put it down here, but fear I shall be criticized by the *learned boys* of these times; now look out—but don't laugh! "*Plait-il de me laisser sortir?*"—"*Oui, on peut sortir,*"—and out we go.

Now if any boy of our then age can give us better French, let him speak out!

All the scholars from a distance boarded among the neighbors; the teacher taking a full share. There was no corporeal punishment used in the school; "the dunce bench" and "dunce station" were often in requisition, until some lazy fellow thought one place about as good as another, and they were content. It so happened that several of these delinquents boarded with the teacher; and in the woods between the school and home there were some fine *birch trees*, with long, slender switches, and you may guess the rest! Our beloved teacher was a good, kind-hearted man, was as fond of a little exercise on the playground as any of us, and often either brought his dinner with him, or would hurry back after dining at home, to have a race in the woods. Though rather a stout man, he was active on the foot, could run very fast for a moderate distance, enjoying it very much when time would admit.

On one occasion, I well remember, when he was pursuing or being pursued, he stumbled, fell, and broke his collar-bone. This was a sad accident for him, and while we sympathized with him in his affliction, we (bad fellows) thought we saw in it the prospect of a few weeks' release from school duties; but, alas! this hope was soon cut off. William Stabler came forward fully equal to the occasion, took the professor's chair, and we well knew that meant *business*—no holiday, no play now. "Come to books!" sounded from the door next morning.

Here I pause a moment to think of William Stabler. I remember him well; saw him in his last illness, being often sent by my anxious uncle and aunt to inquire after him; and his most excellent companion, Deborah Stabler—who ever knew her, but to love her? She was a dear friend of my mother, their acquaintance having commenced before either was married. She lived and labored for her Divine Master, preached His word to many, and was taken to her reward in the mansion prepared for her. It was the custom of our teacher, on each and every 4th day, to take the whole school to the meeting house for worship, which practice was right and profitable.

Having noticed the school and teacher, I will now mention the families that then composed the Society of Sandy Spring Meeting. I begin with Evan Thomas and Mary Brooke, who sat at the head of the meeting, regular in their attendance, and seldom allowing a meeting to pass without having a message to deliver. Here I will take the liberty of saying for myself that some of my earliest religious impressions were made under the ministry of these dear ministers of Christ.

Then follow, John Thomas and wife, Richard Thomas, Sr., and Richard Thomas, Jr., Basil Brooke, Gerard Brooke, James Brooke, Samuel Brooke, Thomas Moore, Bernard Gilpin, Caleb Bentley, George Chandlee, Samuel Hance, and some others I might mention. How few of that large company of Christian believers remain! Only about three or four now; and very soon *all* will have passed away. But it is a pleasant reflection that nearly all of them have left representatives in children, grand and great-grandchildren. Some have already, and we hope *all may*, prove worthy representatives of such a parentage; not in membership only, but in spirituality also. But who out of all these families are now laboring in the ministry? Can a church long continue to live and prosper without a living ministry? Look to this, my young friends! There is work for you.

I hope I shall not be thought officious in thus giving counsel when it has not been asked. No, no! what I have written is dictated by the kindly feeling I have for the place and people, among whom I have spent so many happy days; first in my boyhood, then in middle life; and *now*, when I am old and gray-headed, I delight to visit and enjoy the society of the few of my early companions that are left, and of their immediate descendants. And if it should be decided by my Heavenly Father that I may not see you again, I leave this testimony of the love I still bear to my dear friends of Sandy Spring.

August 17th, 1876. THOMAS McCORMICK.

If the foregoing hastily-prepared sketch, after examination by my friends of Sandy Spring, and particularly by my ministerial brother, Benjamin Hallowell, it may be copied for future reference, with any alterations or additions that may be suggested. T. McC.

Note.—Of the 45 persons herein named, six are living.

A letter from Hon. A. B. Davis, furnishing, by request, his recollections regarding the origin of "The Mutual Fire Insurance Company of Montgomery County."

GREENWOOD, Oct. 8th, 1883.

Wm. Henry Farquhar, Esq., Sandy Spring.

My Dear Friend:—Your esteemed favor of the 6th inst. informing me that you were about to write a sketch of the history of the Montgomery Fire Insurance Company, and asking my recollection and co-operation in the first effort in that direction in 1842, in which your brother, Dr. Charles Farquhar, Benjamin Hallowell and others were prominent, is received. Allow me to express my gratification that you have undertaken so important and interesting a task. Your knowledge and experience is well known, and affords a guarantee that the work will be well and faithfully performed, and the rise and progress of an institution which has been so successful, and has relieved and assisted the unfortunate sufferers by fire in so many instances, ought to be perpetuated and made known to the whole community.

With regard to the meeting to which you refer, I cannot remember whether my name was attached to the call, but I have a distinct recollection of being present; and that the meeting took place in the old Academy building in Brookeville, with a goodly attendance from the neighborhood of Sandy Spring and Brookeville, at which your brother, Dr. Charles Farquhar, was the chief speaker. He held in his hand and read from a pamphlet the plan and working of a Fire Insurance Society, gotten up especially for the benefit and protection of farmers. No society, however, was formed, as the result of that meeting; for the reason, doubtless, which you suggest, viz., that "the community was not ripe yet for so useful an organization." Success was reserved for a later day, under the leadership of the late Edward Stabler, who had obtained a copy of the Lycoming plan, a cheaper and more liberal one for an agricultural community. This he espoused with great ardor and zeal, and pressed with success upon our people.

But the first meeting to which you refer, at which your brother and the late Benjamin Hallowell took the leading part, must have made a strong and favorable impression upon me; for I find that subsequently thereto, and before the organization of the present company, I had for the first time effected an insurance upon my dwelling-house, in the Frederick County Mutual Fire Insurance Company. At this time, as one of the State agents, I was a frequent visitor to the City of Frederick, on behalf of the then prostrate and unfinished Chesapeake and Ohio Canal; and thus had an opportunity to learn something of the working of the Frederick Insurance Company.

Soon after the organization of the present company, Mr. Stabler, by letter and by personal visits, urged me to become a member and director of the Montgomery company. He appeared anxious to have both myself and my friend and neighbor, Mr. Remus Briggs, in the Board of Directors.

This service as a director (having withdrawn from the Frederick company to become a member of the Montgomery company) enabled me to witness the intelligent zeal and devotion of Mr. Stabler, as President of the Company, of which he was justly entitled to be called the founder; also the invaluable services of another officer of the company, Robert R. Moore, its faithful, efficient and devoted Secretary and Treasurer; who, in my judgment, and without in the least disparaging any other officer, is entitled to share the honor of the success of our insurance company.

When this company was organizing, and in the first years of its comparatively slow growth, I met in my visits to Frederick, about the Canal Company, the Hon. John Davis, of Massachusetts, "Honest John," as he was familiarly called. I learned from him that he had organized a similar company in Massachusetts, and it had met with wonderful success, more than double ours, in the same time. I asked him the cause of his success; he replied that "under the mutual plan, insurance was so cheap that a farmer who neglected it and met with a loss, got no sympathy or assistance; and that this absence of sympathy forced every one into the Insurance Company—hence their success!"

Another important lesson I learned from my interviews with these gentlemen, Messrs. Davis and Hale, and Capt. Swift, a distinguished civil engineer. I asked the latter gentleman how it was that with their turnpikes, railroads and manufacturing companies they succeeded much better than we did at the South. His reply was—"In Boston it had gone into a proverb that every company, managed by a Board of Directors, was a *failure.* Now, when a company was organized, their first act was to look for a person acquainted with the business and qualified to manage it, and with a salary sufficient to secure his whole time and services, to give him full control, and fix upon him the responsibility of success." There can be no doubt of the wisdom of this course of management. I have had several occasions to observe and test it.

I shall look forward with interest to the forthcoming of your history, and wish you success.

Very truly, your friend,

A. B. DAVIS.

STATISTICS OF

Year ending April.	Births.	Deaths.	Marriages.
1864	10	5	1
1865	8	9	3
1866	7	7	6
1867	8	6	1
1868	8	1	4
5 years (average $8\frac{1}{5}$)	41 (average $5\frac{3}{5}$)	28 (average 3)	15
1869	7	0	1
1870	8	4	0
1871	7	0	3
1872	5	4	4
1873	11	4	2
5 years (average $7\frac{3}{5}$)	38 (average $2\frac{2}{5}$)	12 (average 2)	10
1874	9	2	0
1875	8	2	3
1876	5	6	1
1877	8	7	1
1878	3	4	3
5 years (average $6\frac{3}{5}$)	33 (average $4\frac{1}{5}$)	21 (average $1\frac{3}{5}$)	8
1879	14	1	2
1880	5	2	3
1881	4	3	2
1882	10	3	0
1883	3	8	3
5 years (average $7\frac{1}{5}$)	36 (average $3\frac{2}{5}$)	17 (average 2)	10
(Total 20 yrs. av. $7\frac{2}{5}$)	148 (ave'g $3\frac{9}{10}$)	78 (average $2\frac{3}{5}$)	43

In 20 years there were 43 marriages; divorces, none.

STATISTICS FROM POSTOFFICE AT SANDY SPRING, MD.

Amount of stamps cancelled for quarter ending March 31st, 1881, (equal to 25,876 letters @ 3 cts. each)..	$776 29
Amount of same for 1871, 10 years ago......	638 64
Excess this year..............	$137 65
Amount of money orders issued for year ending March 31st, 1881............................	$3,517 00
Amount of money orders issued for year ending March 31st, 1871............................	2,461 00
Excess this year..............	$1,056 00
Amount of money orders paid to persons here to March 31st, 1881, one year..............	$1,783 00
Amount of money orders paid to persons here to March 31st, 1871, one year..............	724 00
Excess this year..............	$1,059 00

It seems there is $1734 more sent out of the neighborhood this year by money orders than received by same, just about double.

EDWARD STABLER, *Postmaster*,
S. BOND, *Assistant Postmaster*.

1868.

Last snow in 1866-67 was..................................May 3d.
First snow in 1867-68 was....................November 12th.

On the 14th of February, 1865, there was a remarkable variation in the thermometers of the neighborhood, the observations having been made about 7 A. M., viz.:

Highest, 11°, at Stanmore and William J. Scofield's.
Lowest, 4°, at Riverside.
Range 15°.

On the 8th of January, 1866, at twelve central places in the neighborhood, the thermometer ranged from 4° to 8°.

1869.

Last snow in 1867-68 was.....................April 12th.
First snow in 1868-69 was on ....November 20th.

On April 12th, 1868, there was a remarkable fall of the thermometer, viz.:

On April 12th, at 12 o'clock M.............. 72°
" " " " 10½ " P. M.............. 27°
" " 13th " 7 " A. M.............. 22°
Being a fall in 19 hours of...................... 50°
or more than 2½° per hour.
On April 23d, at 4 o'clock P. M............ 76°
" " 24th, " 7 " A. M............ 30°
Being a fall in 15 hours of...................... 46°
or more than 3° per hour.

Snow on only one day in January. No sleighing during the entire winter of 1868-69. Thunder heard in February.

On the 24th of the 7th month there was a terrific flood on the Patapsco, Patuxent, and some other streams in Baltimore, Howard and Montgomery counties. Bridges, dwellings, mills and factories were washed away, many lives and much property were destroyed; some, who escaped unharmed as to person, losing everything they possessed in the world. The scene of devastation and ruin at Ellicott City beggars all power of description. A sudden and tremendous rain fell in the section of country near the head-waters of the streams, and the water being checked in its very sudden rise and flow by bridges and dams, either swept them away or flooded the adjacent country. In Baltimore the water was up to the top of the lamp-posts in certain streets.

Seventeen year Locusts (*Cicada septemdecem*).—The locusts were first noticed ascending the trees at night in great numbers on the 30th of May. In the morning early they came out of their shells, and after being warmed and turned black by the sun, flew away. For about two weeks they came up in great numbers. They then filled the air with their harsh noise, and in about two weeks more had pierced the limbs of bushes and tender trees, particularly the chestnuts. They did *not* seem to pierce the locust tree. They then began to die off rapidly, and by the last of June but few were seen or heard. The damage done was slight compared with their countless number. A few young peach orchards were injured or destroyed. Their noise was at its height about the middle of June. The male only makes the noise, by means of a tight parchment-like membrane under the wing, moved by internal fibres or muscles. The eggs are deposited side by side in the slits or punctures made in the limbs, about a dozen in each place, and each female laying about one hundred eggs. Their empty shells or jackets are left sticking to the bark and limbs of the trees. The chickens and hogs fattened on them. They are *not* poisonous to beast or human. But few crows were seen while they were abundant, and corn was undisturbed, the crows finding plenty of food near their nests in the fat grub and winged locust. They do no damage to vegetation except by piercing the young twigs, which generally die and break off. The little grub, about $\frac{1}{16}$ of an inch in length, hatches out about the first of August, falls to the ground, finds its way into the earth to a depth of about four feet, and emerges at the end of seventeen years, piercing the ground with myriads of holes.

1870.

Last snow in 1868-69 was....................April 11th.
First " 1869-70 " ....November 13th.

Haze.—In July there was a haze for five days, during which the sun had the red appearance usual in "Indian Summer."

Drought.—There was no rain to wet the ground from July 29th to August 28th, and then not enough for plowing. It lasted until Sept. 26th, nearly two months. Corn and potatoes were affected by it. It extended through the Southern and Middle States, much of the corn fodder in Virginia being left uncut. In the West, on the contrary, the crops were shortened by excessive rains. Large fields of grain were lost because the ground was too soft to allow the machines to work, and there were no "cradles" to cut with.

Flood.—On Oct. 3d there was a heavy rain, flooding the streams and doing much damage in some places.

Mild Winter.—Winter was very mild. Most farmers plowed both for corn and oats. The birds were frequently heard singing, a number not having migrated. It was with difficulty that ice was stored, some not filling their houses. Jan. 10th and 11th it was gathered four inches thick. On Feb. 8th and 9th we had the only sleighing for this winter, and the first since the winter of 1867-68.

Eclipse.—The great phenomenon of the year was the eclipse of the Sun on the 7th of August,—nearly total here, and entirely so in portions of the United States. An audience so intelligent as this has doubtless read many and accurate descriptions of this wonder of wonders which in grandeur and interest stands unrivalled.

1871.

Last snow in 1869-70 was......................April 5th.
First " 1870-71 " ....December 17th.

Haze.—In August there were five days during which the sun presented a red appearance, and was partially obscured by a haze caused by destructive fires in Canada.

Hailstorm.—On May 10th a hailstorm did some little damage, but less than might have been, being unaccompanied by wind. In Philadelphia and New Jersey there were violent hailstorms which did very great damage to crops and to property.

Wet weather.—The early part of June was so wet as to prevent the proper cultivation of gardens and crops.

Heat.—July was remarkable for intense and long-continued heat. The thermometer at 1 o'clock on the 16th was 91°; 17th 94°; 25th 93°; 26th 91°; 28th 90°. In the cities there were many deaths from sunstroke, and the mortality was greatly increased.

Auroras.—There was a brilliant aurora on Aug. 19th. Fine auroral displays were noticed in October and other months.

1872.

Last snow in 1870-71 was ....March 4th.
First " 1871-72 " ....November 28th.

April was unusually dry, garden seeds not sprouting from lack of moisture. The early part of the month was very warm, viz.: Thermometer at 1 P. M. on the 8th was 86°; 9th 82°; 10th 80°, etc. The average for the month was 50°, which was from 3° to 7° higher than for a number of years past.

There was frost on the 11th of May. The latter part of the month was dry and dusty, the dust flying after harrows and carriages in clouds.

A most remarkable and almost appalling evidence of the force of electricity was manifested on the 28th of April, about 8 o'clock P. M., upon the farm of Elizabeth E. Tyson. Two trees standing nearly 30 feet apart were struck, one being about 1½ feet in diameter, the other 2 feet. One was cut off 12 feet above the ground, the other 8 feet above the ground, the pieces being scattered over a space of 4 acres. Some of them were as large as sticks of cord-wood. One piece 6 feet long and 6 inches in diameter was thrown 70 yards from the tree, and another 12 inches in diameter and 8 feet long was thrown 20 feet. Long strips were lodged in branches of trees 30 feet from the ground and 40 yards from the point of departure. The electricity followed a root from the largest tree, plowing out a ditch 40 feet long, 4 feet wide at the top, and 3 feet deep near the tree, and running out to a mere mark at the end. Some of the dirt thrown out was seen sticking to the bark of the surrounding trees, 6 or 8 feet from the ground.

In July there were many thunderstorms and heavy rains. On the 7th a tornado, limited in extent, blew down fences and overturned and twisted off a venerable locust tree, 73 feet in height, in front of the house at Rockland.

September was dry; wells and springs failing.

On the 12th of October the atmosphere was filled with smoke from the great fire in Chicago. The smell of ashes was perceptible. Persons in Maryland, Pennsylvania, New York, and other widely-separated places, were aroused in the night, thinking their own premises were on fire. It was an admirable illustration of the divisibility of matter.

December was remarkable for high winds. On the 21st

the thermometer was —3° at 7 A. M., 6° at 1 P. M., and 4° at 9 P. M., making the average of the day 1¾°. The old Washingtonian saying that if we have ice thick enough for gathering before Christmas we will not have after, though often true, was falsified this season. Ice 6 inches thick was stored on the 16th of December, and on the 21st of March there was skating upon ice 6 inches thick.

March was remarkable for its low temperature. On the 5th the thermometer was 4°. On the 21st it was 16°. The average for the month was 28.4°, being nearly 13° colder than the year before. But little spring work has been done, the ground being frozen the greater part of the month.

The ground was not without patches of snow from November to about the 20th of March.

The most striking point in connection with the meteorology of the year is the small rainfall in this latitude. The amount of rain and melted snow that fell in the State of Maryland as compiled from reports of 5 or 6 stations, was for 1871, 38.88 in. Average for 6 preceding years, 50.41 in.

The past winter has been one of unprecedented severity, and heartrending accounts have reached us of terrible suffering in the West and Northwest. On one railroad 9 passenger trains and 1000 cars of freight were detained, entailing a risk of life and a heavy loss of property.

A great advance has been made in meteorological knowledge, and the public are beginning to reap some advantage from the long-continued labors of scientific men, commencing with Franklin, and ably seconded in latter days by Prof. Espy. By attentively watching the phenomena connected with rain, currents of air, changes in the height of the barometer, and other things, and by laboriously collating the results, a law of storms has been developed which by the aid of the telegraph in announcing the changes as they occur over the country, enables the central observer to give us the daily "probabilities" that have proved so wonderfully accurate even thus early in the experiment. By cautionary signals on the lakes and on the coast many lives and much property have been saved. When experience adds to the knowledge already gained, it is proposed to have a system of signals by cannon from various points for the benefit of farmers and others. We are as yet in the infancy of meteorology as a science, great as have been the advances made in recent times. The day will no doubt come when we shall know the "probable" weather of the coming 24 hours with almost the same certainty with which we now foretell an eclipse.

HENRY C. HALLOWELL.

APRIL 7th, 1873.

Last snow in 1871-72 was....................April 15th.
First snow in 1872-73 was..................November 16th.

On the 26th of April (1872) the thermometer at 2 P. M. was 90°, and at 11 P. M. it was 70°.

May was almost without rain; small garden seeds in many places not germinating.

June was exceedingly dry. July was hot and dry. On the 1st the thermometer was 94°; on the 2d, 97°; on the 3d, 98°; on the 4th it was 91° at 10 A. M. There were many deaths in the cities from heat. Streams were low, many springs and wells were dry, and some mills were unable to grind. In some cases cattle had to be driven a considerable distance for water.

August was warm and oppressive. There were many auroras. Part of September was oppressively warm.

A long, cold and hard winter began in December. On the 22d the thermometer was 0° at 7 A. M., 6° at 1 P. M., the average for the day being 4°. On the 26th there was a snow 6 inches deep, and great snowstorms were reported all over the Northwestern and Middle States.

On the 30th of January the thermometer through the neighborhood ranged from zero to 26° below, the greatest cold ever recorded in this latitude. On the 27th a snow 9 inches deep fell, and, being followed by cold weather, was packed into fine sleighing.

February was cold and wintry, the thermometer being —1° on the 24th at 7 A. M.

March began cold, the thermometer on the 4th being 2°. There were great discomfort and suffering amongst the vast multitudes attending the 2d inauguration of President Grant. By the middle of March the hard grasp of the Frost King began to relax, and the swelling buds, the notes of the robin and blue-bird, and the smell of the freshly-turned sod gave unmistakable evidence that the earth would be once more clothed in the countless glories of another spring. The invalids began to revive under the bright anticipation, the aged to enjoy once more their accustomed walks and drives, and all to prepare for the busy pleasures of a country life. Some gardens were plowed, and early seeds were planted on the 19th, and although there was some cold and blustering weather afterwards, this glimpse of a warm season served to keep our spirits from drooping when winter gave us a parting blast.

The rainfall for the year was considerably below the average, the record at Washington, D. C., showing a total of only 38 inches, while the average for the first 4 months (April, May, June and July) was but 1.7 inches per month.

HENRY C. HALLOWELL.

APRIL 6th, 1874.

Thermometer at 7 A. M.

Year.	Highest.	Lowest.	Range.	Average.
1866-67	84°	4°	80°	48.8°
1867-68	79	1	80	47.8
1868-69	83	8	75	48.9
1869-70	81	8	73	48.1
1870-71	84	4	80	49.9
1871-72	78	— 3	81	47.4
1872-73	82	—12	94	47.9
1873-74	79	8	71	49.9
Average for 8 yrs.	81.2½	2	79.2½	48.6

Last snow in 1872-73 was........................March 26th.
First snow in 1873-74 was..................November 12th.

Thermometer Averages at 7 A. M.

	Jan.	Feb.	Mar.	Winter. Nov., Dec., Jan.,	Feb. & Mar.
1865	22.°	27.°	41.°	1864-65	31.68°
1866	26.9	27.4	35.4	1865-66	32.86
1867	19.6	34.4	33.	1866-67	31.96
1868	24.5	21.6	36.8	1867-68	30.96
1869	34.	33.8	32.6	1868-69	33.50
1870	35.	29.	32.7	1869-70	32.82
1871	27.4	30.5	41.2	1870-71	33.70
1872	26.5	27.3	28.4	1871-72	29.4
1873	24.7	27.3	32.8	1872-73	28.9
1874	34.2	30.2	37.	1873-74	34.4
Av. for 10 yrs.	27.5	28.8	35.1		32.02

April 9th the thermometer was 85° at 2 P. M. The first 15 days averaged 7¾° higher than the last 15 days. In the first 15 days there were only two days that the thermometer did not get above 62°; in the last 15 days there was only one day on which it reached 62°.

July. Dry. On the 3d, thermometer was 94°; on the 14th, 95°. On the 15th, an appearance similar to a rainbow was observed in the west in the afternoon.

August. Violent thunderstorm on the morning of the 12th; many telegraph poles near Hermon and Olney being shattered by lightning. On the 13th very heavy rain, amounting to 7 inches, and carrying away the Brooke Grove dam. From the 12th to 21st some rain fell every day; 9.42 inches in 10 days. In many localities there were terrible and destructive storms. In Moorestown, N. J., the hailstones were 7½ inches in circumference, and on a plate looked like apple dumplings. The devastation was proportionate.

October. On the 30th the thermometer was 24° at 7 A. M.

November. Winter set in early. On the 17th the deepest snow of late years fell and lay for a week.

December. On the fourth the thermometer reached 69°; on the 12th, 71°. On the 24th a magnificent meteor was observed, which was fully described in the papers of the succeeding week. It has rarely been the fortune of any one to see so grand and beautiful a sight. (See extract from *Scientific American* of Feb. 7, 1874, on file with original Met. Reports.)

January. On the 4th the thermometer was 67°. On the 23d, 62° at 7 A. M.; the next morning 29°, a change of 33° in 24 hours. Month remarkably warm; farmers at their spring work; grass growing, buds swelling. Frogs heard on the 29th.

February. On the 6th a very fine sleighing snow.

Average of thermometer on the 22d was 63⅜°. Flocks of blackbirds seen. Fires went out in many houses during the day. On the 23d the thermometer reached 76½°, being the warmest noon since September. On the 23d the thermometer averaged 62⅝°; on the 24th it averaged 33⅓°, a difference of 29⅓°. On the 25th fell the next deepest snow of the winter.

March. On the morning of the 4th the thermometer was 51° milder than on the same day one year before. A remarkably high wind was blowing uninterruptedly for 7 days from the 8th to the 14th.

APRIL 5th, 1875.

Year.	Clear.	Cloudy.	Rain.	Snow.	Falling Weather.
1866-67	181 days.	71 days.	97 days.	16 days.	113 days.
1867-68	186	71	85	24	109
1868-69	189	70	90	17	107
1869-70	209	50	90	11	101
1870-71	213	48	85	14	99
1871-72	220	59	69	18	87
1872-73	228	55	64	18	82
1873-74	197	77	73	18	91
1874-75	202	64	84	15	99
Av. for 9 yrs.	203	63	82	17	99

Last snow in 1873-74 was........................April 29th.
First snow in 1874-75 was.............. ....December 1st.

April. Very cold and disagreeable. The highest noon temperature was 67°, although it reached 76° the preceding February. Thermometer was 25° at 7 A. M. three days in the month. 28th, first sign of asparagus. 29th, a furious snowstorm, 4 inches deep. The contrast of the snow with deep green grass and wheat was peculiar; pear blossoms looked dark in comparison with the snow. The whole day was remarkably cold (average 36⅓°), and ground crusted at night. Far the coldest April on record, being 7½° below the average for 7 years previous.

May. Apple in bloom on the 1st; peach came out March 19th. A warm spell from the 10th to the 15th caused an unusually rapid transformation in the forests. The coldest spring on record.

June was the warmest on record. Thermometer above 90° from the 7th to 10th at noon; 99° on the 29th, the warmest day for 6 years. Comet first observed on the 21st.

July. A violent storm on the 4th demolished a church in Beltsville, buildings in Washington, etc. Lightning struck and shivered a post on the Brook Grove farm, partially melting a nail. Comet disappeared on the 15th.

August. 20th, thermometer 98°; 21st, 96°. Yet it was the coldest August on our record (8 years). Drought injured pastures and the corn crop.

September. Nearly 5½ inches of rain fell from the 15th to 17th.

October was wonderfully dry; there were but 2 or 3 sprinkles fell in the whole month. Rainfall for the month, ⅛ inch. A haze like Indian summer, caused by burning prairies, was observed for weeks.

December. Rather warm. Thermometer above 60° on the 3d and 28th. No ice gathered in the month.

January. For two weeks the thermometer was only seen above 32° on 2 days. The coldest January since 1867.

February was colder still. Average thermometer for one week (4th to 10th) was 12½°. Papers said it was the coldest spell for 20 years. On the 10th the thermometer was 3° below zero. The temperature for the first 3 weeks averaged 21.2°. The winter was very cold after New Year. It was noted for its sleets and scarcity of snow until February. There was sleet on the ground almost uninterruptedly for 6 weeks in January and February. Numerous accidents occurred in the cities. Water and ground froze to a great depth. Immense gorges and fields of ice formed on the Delaware and Susquehanna rivers.

March 24th, a 6 inch snow fell.

HENRY C. HALLOWELL,
ALLAN FARQUHAR.

APRIL 3d, 1876.

Last snow in 1874-75 was..........................April 24th.
First snow in 1875-76 was ....October 31st.

April 13th, 2 inches of snow; 18th very cold; average of the day, 27⅔. Hot fires kept up all day, and overcoats required whenever out of doors. On the 19th the thermometer sunk to 19°, the lowest on record for April. Ice on ponds would bear a rabbit. The ground remained frozen until afternoon. 29th, first peach blossoms in orchards. Month very cold, with 6 snowy days. Latest season on record; being a month later than 1871.

May 5th. Forests absolutely unchanged in appearance. 7th, strawberries just in bloom, (I have known ripe ones gathered on this day). 9th, thermometer 84°; 10th, 73° at sunrise, which is surpassed by few summer mornings. 21st, thermometer 91°. Coldest spring for many years.

June 11th. First mess of strawberries. 24th to 27th,

thermometer 95° at noon for 4 successive days. The first 20 days in June averaged 67°; the last 10 days, 79°.

July 6th. Very hot at noon; followed by a thunder-storm. Lightning struck Ashton store, indulging in strange freaks, but doing little damage.

August, cool and very wet. Highest thermometer 86°. Nearly 9 inches of rain fell on 16 days, which promoted luxuriant vegetation, but failed to affect wells, which were very low through the whole summer and fall. The coolest summer on record.

September 24th, thermometer 39°; a mild frost.

October 13th, first killing frost. 26th, thermometer 75° at noon.

November 30th was very wintry; average of the day, 17°. Month rainy and much corn was injured. The autumn foliage was more than usually fine.

December 20th, the only first-rate ice-getting weather of the winter. 23d, thermometer 66° at noon. No snow to speak of during the month. The year 1875 was the coldest on record (dating back to 1867); every month, except May and December, being below the average.

January 2d. Thermometer 67° at noon; the average for the day was 57⅔. There has been no day warmer since. The 19th was the warmest morning since September 17th. 28th, thermometer 69° at noon. Lilac buds were swelled. 29th, thermometer 59° at 7 A. M.; 30th, 21°; a difference of 38°. Month's average 39°, the warmest January on record. Hardly any snow.

February 2d. A powerful wind caused destruction to trees and fences. 3d, first *bona fide* snow of the season, 5 inches deep. The winter of 1875-76 was the warmest on record, and remarkable for the almost total absence of snow.

March 17th. A sunny, beautiful morning, followed by a short, but violent storm of hail and snow—a model St. Patrick's Day. 19th, thermometer 13°, the coldest I have known so late. 20th, a wild equinoctial storm of snow and rain. 28th, a rainstorm carried away a portion of the wall of Brooke Grove dam.

The season, which promised to be an early one (myrtles and daffodils being in bloom March 15th), seems now almost stationary. Little or no plowing has been done for 4 weeks, and gardens, with rare exceptions, still remain untouched.

April 2d, 1877.

Last snow in 1875-76 was...................... March 24th.
First snow in 1876-77 was......................October 15th.

Monthly Notes.

April 12th. Thermometer 75°. First day of real spring. Month very dry; there was rain on but 6 days.

May 1st. Thermometer 31° at 7 A. M.; decidedly the lowest I have known in May. It was fortunately too dry to kill all the fruit, but considerable damage was done to peaches in some places. This was the third successive dry May.

June. Considerable Fultz and other weak-strawed wheat was lodged by windy rains in the early part of the month. On the 24th the hot spell commenced. The warmest June on record.

July. A month to be remembered. Among the many sultry days I select 4, viz. On the 2d, thermometer 98° at noon; 8th, thermometer 85° at 9 P. M. (the highest I have known at that hour); 10th and 11th, both 99° at noon. The 10th was the warmest day on record—79° at sunrise, 99° at noon, and 81° at 9 P. M.; an average for the day of 86⅓°. This extraordinarily hot spell closed on the 22d. For 29 successive days the noon temperature never once fell below 86°. These 29 days averaged 73° at sunrise, 92° at noon, and 78° at 9 P. M., making the average temperature for this period just 81°, which is 1¾° warmer than I ever knew it for the same length of time. In the country the comparatively cool nights made it quite endurable, but in cities (notably Philadelphia) even they brought no relief; the thermometer being 90° or 92° at sunrise on several days, and sleep before midnight was out of the question. There was a heavy rain on the 30th. The last week being quite cool, brought the average for July below that of 1868.

August was very dry, only 1½ inches of rain. The next warmest summer I have known, and the very driest. Only 8½ inches of rain fell in the 3 months, being 4½ inches below the average for 3 years preceding.

September. The drought broke on the 7th, and very soon we had no cause to complain on *that* score. From the 14th to 24th there were 3 floods, making 8½ inches, or as much as fell during the whole summer. Farmers were alarmed about wheat-seeding, forgetting the promise that seed-time and harvest shall not cease.

October 15th. Snow fell the night before, and the ground was white all day; a sight I never before knew in this month. This was the coldest day until November 24th. Month very cold and dry.

November 1st. Thermometer 75° at noon; on the 2d 74°, the highest on record for November, and warmer than any day in the preceding October. This was the warmest November on record (since 1867); the lowest thermometer being 28°. Wheat got an excellent start.

December 8th. A moderate day, the thermometer being 33° at 9 P. M.; but at 3 o'clock next morning a northwest gale struck us which continued all day, uncapping hay-stacks, and scattering fodder-shocks over the fields where farmers were so improvident as to leave them out. Thermometer 5° at sunrise, and only reached 9° at noon. The 18th was the commencement of 6 weeks' sleighing. 29th, rain froze on trees and shrubbery; this, illumined by a full moon, made the night of the 30th a glimpse into fairyland. The coldest month for at least 10 years, the average being 9° below the normal for December. So closed the great Centennial year.

January 1st. The deepest snow for probably 20 years. 1 foot deep on a level, but a high wind next day piled drifts 5 to 6 feet high, rendering roads in places impassable and everywhere risky. For the rest of that week upsets were the order of the day (or rather night). On the 5th the thermometer ranged from 13° on the Manor to —10° in the Patuxent valley. There was a full 6 weeks of sleighing, the first time for many years. This brightened up the neighborhood wonderfully, and some of its effects (if report is to be relied on) will be permanent.

February was a beautiful month; the warmest February for at least 10 years, with little wind and but 5 days of falling weather.

March 9th. Thermometer 59° at 7 A. M.; on the 10th 17°, a variation of 42° in 24 hours, at the same time of day. 18th, thermometer 11°; 19th, snowing all day (nearly); 20th, thermometer 13°, and snowing till noon. 24th, thermometer 70° at noon. Verily, no one can say our climate is monotonous.

APRIL 1st, 1878.

Without an attempt to treat of *all* interesting facts connected with the weather for the past year, I shall follow its course and select the most striking features that have been noted down.

May. The first 10 days were very cold, being 2° below the average for April. With the 16th, however, commenced a week of hot summer weather, averaging 75½°, or more than 26° warmer than the first 10 days. On the 20th the thermometer was 93°, which was exceeded by but 2 days during the summer.

June 21st and 26th, violent storms, accompanied by destructive lightning; that on the 21st lodging uncut wheat; that on the 26th scattering shocks about. Great fears were entertained that the noble crop would not be housed in safety, but little was seriously injured. A very large crop raised despite the dry May and wet June.

August 21st. A gust, accompanied with hail, reduced the temperature from 88° to 64° in three-quarters of an hour. There was only 11° variation in the noon temperature for the whole month of August—78° to 89°.

September 1st. A slight earthquake at 11 P. M. Not a drop of rain in the last 2 weeks. July, August, and September, taken together, were the driest on record.

October 4th. There began a series of heavy rains. At 3 P. M. the storm culminated in a kind of waterspout. Nearly 4½ inches fell within 12 hours. Newly-seeded wheat fields were disastrously washed; Brooke Grove and other dams carried away. On the 8th another deluge, 2½ inches fell in 6 hours, making 7 inches within 4 days, nearly as much as the total for 3 months preceding. About 6 inches more rain fell in the month than the average for 4 preceding Octobers.

November 4th. The first destructive frost. 22d to 24th the flood-king still *reigned*. 4 inches fell on the 24th alone. The effects on the Potomac river were terrible; the canal much damaged. The warmest and wettest November on record. The same can be said of the whole fall of 1877.

December. The heavens were very interesting. On the 8th was a partial occultation of Venus by the moon. Either coquetting with the dark border, or lingering perched on the end of the horn, the planet presented a beautiful sight. On the 13th could be seen all the visible planets in the southwestern sky, including the moon. 29th, a bouquet of 8 wild flowers was gathered in the open air. Decidedly the warmest winter month on record. Not a flake of snow seen, and the lowest thermometer 21°.

January. The ground whitened for the first time. 6th to 8th, the only cold snap, which enabled most persons to fill their ice-houses. The 31st was such a day as comes once in 20 years. Wild blasts from the east dashed sleet and snow everywhere; the tightest buildings were not proof against it. There were but 3 inches of snow on a level, but it piled in drifts 5 and 6 feet high, while fields generally were almost bare. Lanes running north and south were rendered impassable for days.

February. Thaws and rains made the roads like old times, through the first half of the month,—a very warm February. Thunder and frogs heard on the 21st; flocks of robins seen on the 25th. As much appearance of spring as is ordinarily seen a month later.

March contained many lovely days and little disagreeable weather. On the 11th farmers (that is, *poor* farmers) sowed oats, and wheat looked *too* forward to make the best crop. Upon 10 out of the past 13 St. Patrick's Days has it rained, or snowed, or hailed, or sleeted, or done something characteristic of the day. Some rain has fallen upon 11 out of the past 15 Sundays. 24th, barometer fell to 28.88 inches. There was a rainstorm followed by a northwester. Thermometer 20° next morning. Peaches were injured and wheat blades scorched.

A wonderful winter; only 6 days on which snow fell. Average temperature for November, December, January, February, and March was 40.4°, all except January being the warmest on record. This is more than 5° higher than the average for 10 previous years; so look out for a grand crop of weeds, insects, etc.

APRIL 7th, 1879.

Discarding the system used on former occasions, your statistician will treat of nature's phenomena in a new way, assured that full description will prove more acceptable than bare mention of facts and figures.

Therefore, instead of following through the past year, jotting down notes in each successive month, I shall divide my work into chapters, not confining myself to the exact order of occurrence.

General Temperature.

Last spring was 5° warmer than the preceding year. Summer, owing to a very cold June, and in spite of a hot July, was rather cool on the whole. Fall, normal; and winter 6½° colder than last year, though not one of the very coldest. The year 1878 was the warmest for the past 12 years; averaging 54°.

Rain and Snow.

Snow fell on 20 days last winter. First snow December 8th. Last snow (we hope) April 5th. Deepest was on

March 2d, 8 inches. June, July, and October, all had an unusually heavy rainfall, while in September, February, and March it was very light. 52 inches fell during the year 1878, being an average of 1 inch per week.

Early Season of 1878.

Last spring was one of the earliest seasons ever known. The 7 months ending with April had all, except January, been remarkably warm. The lowest temperature in April was 41°. Wheat heads were seen April 27th, and by May 8th the fields were fully out. April 30th the following is noted: "Cherry and lilac leaves full-sized; oats hide the ground; plenty of clover in bloom; Colorado and other bugs in profusion." By May 9th the forests were nearly as in June. Fireflies, May 18th. There was a severely cold spell from the 11th to 13th, when the thermometer fell to 37°, and sweet potatoes, beans, tomatoes, and probably wheatfields, were damaged by a white frost.

The Great Hailstorm.

On Sunday, the 28th of April, a vast, copper-colored cloud passed over this section from southwest to northeast, accompanied by violent thunder and heavy rain. In the centre of its path, a strip extending from the District line nearly to Ellicott City, and from 1 to 1½ miles wide, was visited by the most destructive hailstorm ever experienced in this vicinity. Where heaviest, the hailstones lay to the depth of 2 or 3 inches in the fields (enough for sleighing), while they were piled in drifts 2 feet deep on the banks of streams. Although followed by hot weather, a pile was found a week later in E. P. Thomas's woods estimated to contain 5 bushels. Had an army of African locusts passed over it, this region could hardly have presented a more desolate appearance than it did on the morning after the storm. Rich wheatfields just coming into head were mangled to pieces, their fine promise utterly destroyed. Not content with tearing off every vestige of blossom from fruit trees, the remorseless destroyer so bruised and battered the trees themselves that in all its track there hardly remained a peach tree worth preserving. Rank clover was pared off so close to the ground as hardly to afford pasture; while as for the forests, 6 weeks later they looked almost as barren and drear as we see them now. Fortunately no person was hurt, nor live stock killed, but the damage to crops, etc., in this section was estimated at $10,000. The storm lasted a little over half an hour.

Celestial Phenomena.

On the 6th of May there was a transit of Mercury over the sun's disk. September 5th, an occultation of a bright star in Sagittarius. This phenomenon is well worth watching, as showing how even the brightest stars are but mere points of light. Slowly as the moon travels, yet, even with a good telescope, the instant a star is touched by the moon's edge its light totally disappears.

Special Rains.

There was rain upon 19 out of the 25 Sundays ending with June 9th. On June 17th and 18th, 3⅗ inches fell. Wheat was laid flat, but, fit emblem of truth, rose again. July 19th, thermometer 96° at noon, followed by a storm during which 3 inches fell in 3 hours. 3½ inches fell on the 23d of October.

Hot Weather.

A hot spell lasting 26 days ended July 21st.

Low Barometer.

On October 23d, during the storm spoken of above, the barometer sunk to 28.54 inches; and on December 10th, when a warm morning was followed by a heavy rain, turning into a savage snowstorm by night, it was 28.46 inches, the lowest I ever saw it.

Cold Weather.

About noon on Thursday, January 2d, commenced a spell of such weather as we trust not often to experience. After a mild forenoon a powerful northwestern gale sprung up, which hardly paused for 3 days. At 12 M. the thermometer was 37°; at 4 P. M., 21°; at 9 P. M., 6°. Next morning (Friday, January 3d) it was —3°, and blowing harder than ever. Saturday and Sunday both, 3° at 7 A. M., after which it slowly moderated. Potatoes froze in cellars always thought secure, while conservatories and pits could not save the flowers in many places.

The Recent Thaw.

On the 11th of March, thermometer reached 70°, and the frost left the ground a few days later; snow that had lain for 3 months disappeared, and the effect on turnpikes is known too well to be recorded here.

April 5th, 1880.

My daily record of current events having been recently discontinued, this report will necessarily be less complete than some that have preceded it. Following no special system, since none has been proved the best; wearying you with no long columns of bare statistics, since for general minds these carry little interest, while persons wishing such dry facts can obtain them better by applying to the writer, than by hearing them discharged bombshell fashion into the ears of a public assembly; with a desire less to cover the whole ground than to confine this report within the limits of your patient attention, I shall now touch briefly upon nature's most striking events since our last assembling together.

Since early fall a warm southern current has generally prevailed. October was the warmest on record, being 8° above the average; December was very warm, while both the following winter months surpassed all precedent; January being more than 8°, and February 6°, warmer than our average. The winter demands comparison with those of past years. The warmest known before (speaking with the usual conceit of young persons who imagine their diminutive span of life includes all things worth knowing) was that of 1875-76, averaging 26.6°. The average for past 12 winters, $32\frac{1}{2}°$. This past winter averaged $39\frac{1}{4}°$, being $6\frac{3}{4}°$ above the normal, $9\frac{1}{4}°$ above last year, and nearly $2\frac{3}{4}°$ higher than the warmest before known. There was, naturally, quite a scare about ice; but we had a spell in early February that saved us—except those who preferred waiting to get 5 inches of clear ice rather than gather such snowy indifferent stuff as most of us were content with and thankful for. March was colder than January, yet warmer than the average.

There were 11 days on which snow fell, beginning November 20th and ending March 13th. The deepest was but 6 inches, February 2d and 3d.

More than $7\frac{3}{4}$ inches of rain fell between the 16th and

20th of May, while but $\frac{1}{5}$ inch fell on the other 26 days of May. The same irregularity was shown in July; $\frac{3}{4}$ inch falling upon the first 24 days, and nearly 6 inches upon the 25th and 26th. During this flood, bridges on Hawlings river were carried away, and it was actually dangerous to cross certain places where there is usually no stream at all, the water rushed by so furiously. During 32 days ending August 26th there fell $15\frac{2}{3}$ inches of rain, an average of almost $\frac{1}{2}$ inch per day for a month. Then the flood-gates were closed, and with that fondness for going to extremes for which our weather (as well as perhaps some other things in Sandy Spring) is so noted, a dry spell set in that lasted considerably more than 3 months. During this period of over 100 days ending with the 4th of December, but 4 inches of rain fell—less by an inch than during 24 hours of July. It was difficult to get wheat ground in proper condition, and to the drought we owe the present scarcity of timothy.

Several events in October and November were so peculiar as to deserve mention. October 1st the thermometer was 78°; October 2d, 81°; 3d, 85°, which was 5° higher than the highest recorded in October before. This year there were 5 days above 80°. The average of the first 18 days was nearly 69°, being more than 16° above the October normal, being warmer than any September on record, and warmer than June in 1878. Average noon temperature for this period $77\frac{2}{3}$°. November vibrated between Labrador and Florida. Average of the first week 37°, which was lower than that of any month this winter. 2d week averaged 63°, hardly a figure for September to be ashamed of. Then a second Polar wave struck us, and the average for the 3d week was $35\frac{1}{2}$°.

The barometer stood highest on October 26th, during

the heart of the dry spell, 30.11 inches. Lowest, February 3d, just *after* our deepest snow, 28.86 inches.

There was an occultation of Venus on October 13th at 10 P. M.; also a fine one of Mars at the close of St. Patrick's Day, which for an amazing wonder was actually clear.

Now I will ask you to stand with me upon the hill near where the Emory road joins the Washington turnpike. Time, September 3d; hour, 6 P. M. It has been showery through the day, but now the sun has burst out low on the horizon, casting a brilliant rainbow against the leaden eastern sky. Your eyes are suddenly called to the southeast, where you see a whirling copper-colored funnel driving to the northward. It grows darker and rises from the ground for a short space; then a white column-like smoke is seen among the tree-tops beneath; they join again, and the air above is filled with tossing shingles, boughs, and no one knows what besides. The colors change, sometimes black and gloomy, then lit up as by an internal (or infernal) fire. A loud, rushing, roaring sound, as of a great loaded freight train crossing a bridge. The spectacle dies away in the northeast, and you realize your first experience of a cyclone. Although more awful in its progress and effects than the hailstorm, this calamity occasioned comparatively little damage. Like it, no persons were injured, though who can tell what might have befallen a human being exposed to the full fury of the whirlwind! Tracing out its path from A. J. Cashell's place, through the lands of G. W. C. Beall, Jos. T. Moore, Jas. H. Stone, Wm. H. Farquhar, and others, to where the savage wind-demon spent his wrath upon Cyrus Bowen's little grove, what a scene of enormous destructive energy meets our eyes! The track of the storm varied in width from 25 to 100 or more yards; not all visited alike, but as if dipping down upon some spots with especial severity, then leaving others comparatively uninjured. Giant trees were uprooted, twisted off, or torn asunder, lying in every direction; branches carried rods or miles—no one knows; potatoes dug up; even the very gravestones wrenched from their places and thrown flat upon the ground. "In the hereafter angels may roll the stones from our graves away," but we trust for the sake of those who come after us that it will not often be done in *that* way.

Allan Farquhar.

April 4th, 1881.

With no carefully prepared record to draw from; with only frail memory, aided and refreshed by files of the rough drafts of old weather-charts for the signal service; you need hardly expect a full report. Such as it is, however, it shall be confined strictly within the domain of fact.

Half of the rain in last April fell on the 29th. Not a drop from that day to the 22d of May. Rain fell on but 4 May days, and the total was less than $\frac{7}{8}$ of an inch; the least ever known in this month. The hay crop was cut short, young clover killed out, plowing sod resembled quarrying, while gardens in some localities painfully near home proved failures. Very hot with it all, being $3\frac{1}{2}$° above the warmest previous May (that of 1872).

June 12th was rather the warmest morning in the whole summer; 76° at sunrise. Reached 93° at noon, and soon after 2 P. M. a violent local storm set in, inflicting considerable damage to trees and buildings at Fair Hill, Willow Grove, etc., besides lessening the wheat crop by suddenly killing off fields that had been green the day before. Two days later fell the first soaking rain since April. It postponed wheat harvest until in some fields wire alone could hold the dead-ripe sheaves together.

July 5th the weather was *muggy*. No clear sunshine, but not especially ominous. Yet between 7 and 10 P. M., a space of 2½ hours, 5 inches were poured out; it did not rain in drops, but the bottom seemed to have dropped out of some immense tank suspended in the air. By half-past 10 the stars were shining tranquilly. The effect of this deluge was observable the whole season; it was largely answerable for the greatest corn crop produced in recent years. July gave us nearly 8½ inches of rain, the most recorded for this month. The weather not oppressive except on the fatal 13th, when the heat struck down one of the foremost men in talent and originality of thought that this county ever knew.

But for the kindness of the Montgomery County Agricultural Society we should have suffered grievously with drought in September, as three-fourths of the rain that fell in the month fell on the week of the Fair. The total rainfall for August, September and October was considerably less than that for July alone.

This long, cold, hard winter cast its first shadow before on October 1st, when a frost nipped some exposed fields of corn. On the night of the 6th of November a storm centre, only second in violence to the cyclone of the year before, passed through the neighborhood from the same direction as have all our most disastrous storms lately, viz. S. S. W. Its greatest power was shown at Rockland, where many of the trees adorning that beautiful home were torn up or mauled about as if in the hands of a malignant demon. The roof of the Bank was lifted up, and a dwelling near by had its walls cracked and chimney blown off. The storm was very severe at Bloomfield, taking especial delight in slaying down the grove of pines near the house. The yard locusts were doubtless saved, as some at Rockland had been, by being so slender as to bend before the gale.

Winter began in earnest on the 18th of November. Thermometer on the 19th, 18°; 22d, 12°; 23d, 13°; 24th, 12°, etc. A number were filling their ice houses on Thanksgiving Day. But all other cold spells were forgotten in the snap which was included between December 29th and January 1st. The thermometers behaved out of all reason. Mine, more sober and dignified than the rest, only recorded —7°,—7°, and —10° for the three mornings; but —20° and —25° were common; while in some the mercury huddled way down in the bulb till they thought it was lost. One observer, not being satisfied with only 16° below zero, took his thermometer to a point 100 yards distant from the house and at a level about 25 feet lower, when it fell to —24°.

There were very nearly 8 weeks of unbroken good sleighing, from December 20th to about the middle of February, when the rain and warm weather carried away the snow so fast that things were generally liquefied. The poor dam at Brooke Grove went out again, this time past recall. Just before the thaw the barometer rose to 30.13 inches, the highest for the year. Lowest, March 30th, 28.61 inches.

Severe sleets on the 9th and 21st of January deserve mention, as some trees that had stood the cyclone and two hurricanes were broken by this new enemy. This was the coldest winter on record in this locality; the average temperature for 6 months ending March 31st, 1881, was about 8° colder than for the 6 months ending March 31st, 1880.

What aspect does kind nature wear at this, her favorite season? We have had just one day of spring thus far; March 16th, when it actually was 63°. Wheat fields are about as forward as sometimes on the 1st of March. What encouragement can there be for early gardening and planting when on a clear day in April I found snow on a tree in our orchard at 5 o'clock in the afternoon, which had lain there all day, even with the sun shining; when it has snowed upon 6 days of the past week, and when the noon temperature thus far in April has averaged more than 25° below the noon average for April last year?

There were 24 snowy days this winter (besides I don't know how many in April). First snow, November 13th; last snow (judging from the present outlook) about the 17th of June!

Blessed is the nation that has no history! And we can well hope for less material to fill our Meteorological Reports in future. Striking events in that line may be interesting, but, as a rule, are not profitable.

April 3d, 1882.

There has surely been enough weather in the past two years to satisfy the most ardent craver of excitement. Extremes have been the order of the day; bitter, protracted cold; fierce, still more protracted, unseasonable heat; washing storms followed by months of almost unbroken drought—all combine to form ample material for a lively narrative; but I long since gave up my fondness for meteorological gymnastics, and would ask no more racy and varied report for 1883 than the following:

"April, normal; May, normal; June, normal," and so around to March again.

April 5th, 1881. "Ground frozen too hard to plow sod; a tramp frozen to death near Laurel," etc. The first week in April averaged 32.9°; just fair winter weather. Plowed garden on the 25th. Then the pendulum flies back, and by May 12th the thermometer runs up to 92° at noon, and only sinks to 83° by 9 P. M., which is higher than any night during the whole summer of 1880 at the same hour; and has not been surpassed since, not even by the 7th of September. Next day 94° at noon. The 2d week in May averaged 75.4°, being very nearly equal to the average temperature of the hottest summer known. May 18th, first soaking rain since March. No flies worried us until the 17th of June; but they made up for it at the other end of summer. The great comet was first seen on the 25th. On the 27th two inches of rain fell in a half-hour, washing cornfields and levelling acres of wheat. This storm was especially severe at Norwood. June was the only month between March and December which had a rainfall up to the average. July 6th, thermometer 95°, which for two months we fondly hoped would be the warmest for the year. On the 7th a heavy thunderstorm, the lightning killed two large oaks on our place, one of which could ill be spared. Only 4 days in August on which any rain fell.

On the 20th of August began a spell of weather that rivalled the well-remembered four weeks of '76, and is without a parallel at this season of the year. From that time until October 5th, a period of 46 days, a tropical heat blazed at the parched and thirsty earth, the coldest day rising to 73°, and on but 7 out of the 46 days failing to reach 80° at noon. The climax was reached on the ever-memorable 7th of September, which was without exception the hottest day I ever saw. No work was attempted, all we did was to *exist*, and rejoice that our suffering President had been removed from the stifling, sickening atmosphere of the Potomac flats to the cool, healthy breezes of the seaside. Our thermometer was 98°; only 7° higher than I ever saw it in September before; but other instruments showed 100°, and one as high as 103°. Next day it fell to 94°, and we reached for our overcoats and arctics. There was no soaking rain between the 10th of July and 10th of September—just the critical two months for corn; no wonder then that the crop was cut very short. The drought was not finally broken until October 24th, so for the third successive year farmers drove their drills through clouds of dust and among clods like the debris of brickyards.

When the long 7 weeks of torrid summer ended on the 4th of October, did autumn tranquilly descend upon the earth like gathering shades of the twilight, and by a gradually lessening temperature prepare us for the changing season? Not much, it didn't! After reaching 87° on the 2d, decidedly above any record for October, and more befitting July than the month when chestnuts fall and gums turn crimson, the thermometer subsided for a day or two into its usual rut of about 82° or 83°. Then with scarce as much warning as is granted us by a summer thunder-gust, a fall of 50° gave us ice half an inch thick, a killing frost, and all the accompaniments of a winter morning—a change in less than 40 hours from Brazil to Greenland. As if satisfied with this display of power, in two days more 46° out of the 50° variation were recovered.

September, October, November and December were each and all warmer than any for 15 years. The rainfall for 5 months ending with November was but 14 inches, while the three winter months ensuing show a record of nearly 17 inches, being more than double the average for winter.

Only one night this winter did the thermometer sink below 16°, namely, January 24th; still there was a chance for all to get ice of a fair quality. There were 11 snowy days, but only one deep snow, that of February 4th, when 13 inches fell in one day. There was a solid 3 inches already on the ground when this deep snow fell, but instead of bringing us good sleighing, it simply ushered in spring, for the thermometer rose to 40° or higher every day for two weeks thereafter.

Still, after all these changes and extremes, our outlook now is not all discouraging. Wheat never made a healthier show on the first of April; stock have come out of the winter in decidedly better condition than last year, while farmers have been able to commence their spring work at least two weeks earlier than in 1881.

Average Temperature.

	1868	1869	1870	1871	1872	1873	1874	1875	1876	1877	1878	1879	1880	1881	1882	Av. for 15 yrs.
Jan......	28.1°	36.5°	38.3°	31.2°	29.5°	28.4°	36.7°	26.4°	39.0°	28.4°	31.4°	29.0°	40.1°	26.7°	31.6°	32.1°
Feb......	26.7	36.8	33	34.4	31	31.3	34.3	25.5	35.2	37.2	37.4	29.6	38.8	30.6	38.2	33.3
March ..	41.9	37.5	36.9	46.7	33.1	37.4	41.2	37.2	37.2	38.9	47.5	41.2	39.9	37.9	42.5	39.8
April....	47.3	50.6	51.7	56.7	52.9	50.1	44.2	46.4	49.2	51.3	56.7	49.9	53.6	48.5	49.9	50.6
May	59.7	59.6	63.1	63.5	64.9	60.5	60.7	61.4	62.2	60	60.4	62.9	68.3	66.1	57	62
June....	70.2	71.3	73.3	72.5	73	72.1	73.8	70.9	73.9	72.3	67	71	72.3	68.5	71.3	71.6
July	79.2	74.7	77.2	73.4	78.5	76.7	74.6	75.5	78.1	76.3	77.8½	76.2	74.8	75.5	73.5	76.1
August..	72.8	73.3	74.1	75.3	76	72.7	69.7	70.9	73.3	74	73	72.2	72.8	73.8	71.2	73
Sept.....	64.7	65.6	65.7	60.6	66.3	65.3	67.3	62.6	63.5	65.3	66.6	61.9	65.7	74.5	66.6	65.5
Oct	51.2	47.6	55.4	55.4	52.9	51.8	52.9	52.3	49.4	56.8	54.9	60.5	52.9	60.8	58.7	54.2
Nov ..	42.3	38	43.5	40.9	38.6	37.5	41.8	39.4	44.5	44.8	43.6	43.3	38.6	45.9	41.2	41.6
Dec......	29.4	35.7	33	29.7	27.2	37.9	35	35.6	25.1	40.7	31.3	38.8	27.6	40.8	31.8	33.3
Year...	51.1	52.3	53.8	53.4	52	51.8	52.7	50.3	52.5½	53.8	54	53	53.8	54.1	52.8	52.8

Maximum Temperature in each Month.

	1868	1869	1870	1871	1872	1873	1874	1875	1876	1877	1878	1879	1880	1881	1882	Av. for 15 yrs.
Jan......	4th 49°	30th 58°	17th 66°	15th 61°	12th 53°	16th 57°	23d 69°	22d 47°	28th 69°	20th 52°	26th 54°	28th 63°	20th 62°	13th 42°	16th 58°	57.3°
Feb......	*52	13 65	18 52	25 63	24 57	4 57	23 76	25 55	11 63	22 63	21 64	26 53	27 66	12 58	15 59	60.2
March...	17 78	28 67	21 64	17 74	29 63	15 69	19 71	15 65	6 68	2 70	11 72	11 70	5 74	16 63	27 66	68.9
April....	30 81	27 83	15 84	8 88	26 89	9 85	15 67	1 73	28 76	24 80	23 83	26 82	15 85	26 84	2 80	81.3
May.....	30 83	31 89	*87	*91	10 92	28 86	31 88	23 91	*89	20 93	30 85	31 89	*93	13 94	9 83	88.9
June....	*92	20 94	*95	*93	*92	19 93	29 99	*95	27 95	26 93	*89	*93	*93	27 90	25 94	93.3
July	*99	11 96	18 97	11 96	3 97	3 95	10 95	6 96	*99	27 97	19 96	16 97	13 94	6 95	*92	96.1
August..	30 91	21 97	4 93	16 95	13 92	3 92	20 94	6 86	7 92	*89	5 89	3 90	25 91	*94	7 88	91.5
Sept	*87	*87	2 85	*82	9 91	1 88	12 89	*86	1 89	1 85	1 86	1 84	4 89	7 98	2 85	87.4
Oct.. ...	1 72	2 73	1 78	15 80	6 79	17 73	29 74	26 75	6 73	20 76	9 77	3 85	*78	2 87	18 75	77
Nov.....	10 74	*63	9 67	1 68	25 61	16 61	6 68	13 63	1 75	2 65	25 65	12 77	6 66	9 71	1 75	67.9
Dec......	20 48	12 55	4 57	*51	2 55	12 71	3 62	23 66	14 59	20 65	10 58	4 62	5 53	14 69	6 48	58.6

* Same maximum on more than one day in the month.

Minimum Temperature in each Month.

	1868	1869	1870	1871	1872	1873	1874	1875	1876	1877	1878	1879	1880	1881	1882	Av. for 15 yrs.
Jan.....	18th 8°	26th 19°	9th 13°	*10°	31st 4°	30 —12°	17th 7°	10 —2°	*16°	5 —1°	8 — 3°	3d —3°	14th 9°	1 —10°	24th 4°	3.9°
Feb	8 —2	28 15	21 8	6 8	1 5	24 0	9 12	10 —3	5 10	14 17	4 17	15 9	5 11	2 — 1	4 20	8.4
March..	3 6	5 10	17 19	*29	5 3	4 2	24 19	*13	19 13	18 11	25 20	1 19	25 20	6 23	25 21	15.5
April...	13 21	4 28	*33	*37	*30	26 35	*25	19 19	*30	*30	*41	3 26	12 27	5 22	12 24	28.5
May	9 41	3 39	12 43	11 43	*42	*44	*39	3 33	1 31	3 39	13 37	3 37	1 37	1 41	3 34	39
June.....	*55	*49	12 56	*55	5 53	*50	2 51	13 52	1 49	23 51	6 48	*49	3 48	*53	2 50	51.3
July	*63	6 55	4 60	*53	20 63	12 59	31 59	13 60	27 57	14 61	23 60	1 57	30 58	*61	*57	58.9
August.	13 55	8 49	*55	20 55	31 55	25 54	*50	*56	22 51	5 59	27 56	10 54	16 58	19 56	30 54	54.5
Sept	18 40	*40	*46	22 37	*47	*42	*49	24 39	28 41	23 44	*45	26 37	30 46	18 57	29 45	43.7
Oct......	18 27	*25	19 35	*31	30 32	30 24	15 29	14 30	*29	*39	29 28	26 26	19 28	6 32	*42	30.5
Nov	28 25	*23	20 21	29 23	*14	21 17	30 21	30 15	30 28	30 20	5 28	22 13	*12	25 20	*23	20.2
Dec.....	*11	*19	30 4	21 —3	22 2	22 19	15 15	18 12	*3	*21	25 11	27 11	*—7	*21	*6	9.7

* Same minimum on more than one day in the month.

Average Temperature of Seasons.

	1868	1869	1870	1871	1872	1873	1874	1875	1876	1877	1878	1879	1880	1881	1882	Av. for 15 yrs.
Winter*	28.6°	34.2°	35.7°	32.9°	30.1°	29°	36.3°	29°	36.6°	30.2°	36.5°	30°	39.2½°	28.3°	36.9°	32.9°
Spring ..	49.6	49.2	50.6	55.6	50.3	49.3	48.7	48.3	49.5	50.1	54.9	51.3	53.9	50.8½	49.8	50.8
Summer	74.1	73.1	74.9	73.8	75.8	73.8	72.7	72.4	75.1	74.2	72.6	73.1	73.3	72.6	72	73.6
Fall......	52.7	50.4	54.9	52.3	52.6	51.5	54	51.4	52.5	55.6	55	55.2	52.4	60.4	55.5	53.8

* Ending with February of the year named.

Days on which Snow fell.

1867–8	1868–9	1869–70	1870–1	1871–2	1872–3	1873–4	1874–5	1875–6	1876–7	1877–8	1878–9	1879–80	1880–1	1881–2	Av. for 15 Wint's
35	22	29	18	25	23	23	19	10	22	6	20	11	24	13	20

Rainfall.

	Rainy Days.					1873		1874		1875		1876		1877	
	1868	1869	1870	1871	1872	days	in.	days	in.	days	in.	days	in.	days	in.
January...	12	9	9	10	8	9	3.23	8	2.58	9	2.51	8	1.61	7	4.25
February..	8	9	11	10	7	11	5.03	7	2.78	7	2.34	9	3.97	5	1.58
March......	10	13	10	9	14	8	3.01	8	1.68	10	3.66	11	6.28	14	3.85
April	13	10	12	8	6	12	3.68	15	6.84	8	2.96	6	2.02	12	3.71
May	13	16	14	9	6	14	6.45	8	2.40	6	1.46	8	2.90	8	1.25
June	10	19	12	7	7	5	1.71	8	2.02	10	2.72	7	2.79	9	5.10
July	11	11	10	14	8	9	2.07	8	3.52	9	3.67	9	4.11	9	2.93
August	11	5	7	7	10	14	11.49	8	3.44	16	8.83	7	1.56	8	2.42
September.	16	7	8	5	6	8	4.92	8	6.96	8	3.13	12	10.53	8	3.09
October.....	12	9	6	9	9	7	6.03	1	.13	6	1.88	9	1.67	9	8.32
November.	7	11	6	9	8	10	3.83	6	2.83	7	5.26	11	3.94	10	9.76
December.	7	14	5	6	9	8	1.13	9	1.89	13	3.70	7	1.34	5	2.36
Total	130	133	110	103	98	115	52.58	94	37.07	109	42.12	104	42.72	104	48.62
Av. pr. mo.	10.8	11.1	9.2	8.6	8.2	9.6	4.38	7.8	3.09	9.1	3.51	8.7	3.56	8.7	4.05

	1878		1879		1880		1881		1882		Av.R. days for 15yr.	Av. inch. for 10yr.
	days	in.	days	in.	days	in.	days	in.	days	in.		
January...	9	4.09	10	2.55	11	2.00	10	2.20	15	5.97	9.6	3.10
February..	7	2.41	8	1.92	10	2.12	8	3.73	8	4.65	8.3	3.05
March......	10	3.39	10	1.53	13	4.98	11	5.46	11	4.06	10.8	3.79
April	8	3.21	8	3.01	9	3.21	11	1.61	6	1.90	9.6	3.21½
May	10	4.60	8	7.97	4	.85	8	1.71	14	4.73	9.7	3.43
June	10	5.98	11	3.11	10	4.33	11	7.33	7	3.35	9.5	3.84
July	9	7.75	8	6.69	7	8.41	8	2.81	9	4.04	9.3	4.60
August	13	5.19	13	9.71	13	2.65	4	2.11	14	7.07	10.	5.45
September.	9	2.04	7	2.01	6	2.71	5	3.31	10	6.78	8.2	4.55
October.....	7	5.90	5	.99	8	2.35	8	3.62	7	.73	7.5	3.16
November.	6	3.32	8	1.16	12	3.21	7	2.22	7	.87	8.3	3.64
December.	9	4.23	10	4.56	13	4.10	11	6.01	5	1.80	8.7	3.11
Total	107	52.11	106	45.21	116	40.92	102	42.12	113	45.95	109.6	44.94
Av. pr. mo.	8.9	4.34	8.8	3.77	9.7	3.41	8.5	3.51	9.4	3.83	9.1	3.74½

APRIL 2d, 1883.

The year just closed deserves our profound thankfulness. Complaint might be made of the wet spring and the cold winter, the backwardness of the present season or the potato-rot last fall, the low price of hay or the defeat of the Republican party; but the grand fact remains that this has been the most productive year our farmers ever knew. It is rare indeed that a great wheat and corn crop both occur the same year; yet the year 1882 saw the largest of either ever gathered in the State of Maryland.

On April 12th last year the thermometer was 24°, and the promise for peaches was disastrously blighted; another of the many illustrations proving the truth of that familiar adage, "The early worm gets caught." A singular snow occurred on the 23d of April. There was very little here, but near Washington, and Fairfax county, Va., six or seven inches fell and sleighs travelled freely.

May was the coldest and about the wettest on record. Average temperature for the month 5° below the normal. On the 3d the thermometer sunk to 34°, being the coldest ever known in May except May 1st, 1876. There was an abrupt stride from winter to summer on the 9th, when it rose to 83°, and the heat told on both men and horses, but this was the only hot day during the month. On several days coal fires were kept going all day. The first wheat head was seen on the 21st, and fields were only fairly out by the 30th. There was rain on 12 out of 13 consecutive days, ending May 16th, and the sun was visible but once between the 4th and 15th. Instead of enjoying a fine view of the conjunction of Venus and Jupiter in the early part of the month, these planets could not once be seen for 15 successive evenings. There was much trouble in getting cornfields in fit order to plant.

On the 9th of June we had our first saucer of strawberries—just one month later than in 1878.

July was very temperate; not a single oppressive day, and the average noon temperature for the month was under 83°, which was very favorable for our enormous harvest. The other extreme was reached, however, on the 4th, which was the coldest July day in history; the thermometer was 58° at noon, being the lowest at that time of day until the last of September. Take the summer all through it was the coldest on record, being nearly 2° below the average for 15 years.

Although the year 1882 had no especial floods, and indeed the rainfall was but very slightly above the normal, still the showers were so generally distributed that it seemed a very rainy year. There were 113 rainy days, being 4 more than the average. Owing to a succession of copious rains through August and September, and to the warm October, fall pastures carried more stock and to a later period than usual. Besides the corn, there was a great growth of potatoes, but unfortunately these latter rotted to the extent of thousands of bushels.

Only 1.6 inches of rain fell during the two months of October and November; the ground became very hard for fall plowing. The coldest in October was 42°, and we continued to use Lima beans and sweet corn until the first week of November. No corn-husking was done in October except what farmers afterwards regretted. First frost on November 3d; the first snow, November 26th. On the 28th a 4-inch snow caught whole fields of corn unhoused.

The great astronomical event of the year, the transit of Venus on the 6th of December, was observed here in spite of thin clouds which prevailed all day; most of us preferring to take our chances of even a cloudy transit of Venus this time rather than to wait until the next one.

There were 18 rainy and snowy days in January, the most in any month for 14 years.

February 2d, 1883.	Thermometer	at 7 A. M.,	15°
" 4th, "	"	" " " "	16
" 6th, "	"	" " " "	19

The past winter has been long and cold; all the five months, except February, being below the average. Coal fires have been needed almost all the time, and there was abundant opportunity for hauling ice. Yet the lowest thermometer was 3° on the 23d and 24th of January. The far Northwest experienced one of the coldest winters ever known; still it was of some benefit as showing that cattle and sheep can stand even this severe weather with very little loss. The breaking up of winter was, in some localities, far worse than the continuance; rapid melting of snow under warm and copious rainfall raising the Ohio and other rivers to a disastrous height.

This has been decidedly the coldest March for 11 years, averaging 34½°, or near 5½° below the normal. Right good sleighing on the 23d and 24th. The month went out like a roaring lion, and sweet April was ushered in under "Grim Winter's cold white wind-swept mantle."

This record would fall sadly short of its true purpose were no allusion to be made to two of the most beautiful and wonderful sights ever beheld in the heavens. On Sunday night, the 16th of April, I was awakened a little before midnight, and glancing out the north window saw the whole sky illumined with a strange light. We often see reddish streaks in the north with a white band, and occasionally a little wavering and changing; but here for the first time was the Aurora Borealis in all its grandeur. To those who shared the rapture of witnessing this awful manifestation of unseen power, any description would be needless, save to recall the impression; while to those who failed to see it, human language can no more portray that ever-changing yet ever-beautiful panorama than the dripping of a rainspout can mimic the thunders of Niagara. Imagine yourselves under an illimitable dome whose ceiling is the loveliest, most delicate drapery; imagine this drapery of every conceivable shade of exquisite blending colors, no two pieces alike, and the same piece never appearing the same for two seconds together; imagine flashes of white and rosy light starting out of utter darkness, too swiftly for the eye to follow; and through all this glorious pageant imagine the tranquil radiance of the same familiar unchanging stars that have watched this earth since man first gazed in wonder at "their eternal ray"—these were the sole motionless dwellers in a transfigured sky.

In the southeast, just over the horizon, at 5 o'clock on a morning in early October, a strange visitor could be seen, shining bright against the background of the moonless heavens. The giant comet had swung past his perihelion, and was now pursuing his erratic journey into the distant depths of ether, not to return for thousands of years. May his next appearance, with his glowing ball of a head and curved scimitar of a tail, show him not only a brighter and better world than he now leaves, but our Narrow Gauge Railroad and an enlargement of this Lyceum!

ALLAN FARQUHAR.

INDEX

www.ingramcontent.com/pod-product-compliance
Lightning Source LLC
LaVergne TN
LVHW020526100826
845148LV00010B/1357

* 9 7 8 0 7 8 8 4 1 4 0 9 1 *